Clinical Pastoral Care for Hospitalized Children and Their Families

John B. Hesch

Footprints

One night a man had a dream. He dreamed he was walking along the beach with the Lord. Across the sky flashed scenes from his life. For each scene, he noticed two sets of footprints in the sand: one belonging to him, and the other to the Lord.

When the last scene of his life flashed before him, he looked back at the footprints in the sand. He noticed that many times along the path of his life there was only one set of footprints. He also noticed that it happened at the very lowest and saddest times in his life.

This really bothered him and he questioned the Lord about it.

"Lord, you said that once I decided to follow you, you'd walk with me all the way. But I have noticed that during the most troublesome times in my life, there is only one set of footprints. I don't understand why when I needed you the most you would leave me."

The Lord replied, "My son, My precious child, I love you and would never leave you. During your times of trial and suffering, when you see only one set of footprints, it was then that I carried you."

Author unknown

THIS BOOK BELONGS TO

Library of Congress Cataloging-in-Publication Data

Hesch, John B.
    Clinical pastoral care for hospitalized children.

    Includes bibliographies and index.
    1. Church work with sick children.   2. Chaplains,
Hospital.   I. Title.   [DNLM: 1.   Child, Hospitalized—
psychology.   2. Hospital Departments.   3. Pastoral
Care.   4. Religion and Medicine.   WX 187 H571c]
BV4335.H39   1987   259'.4   87-2322
ISBN 0-8091-2871-3 (pbk.)

Published by Paulist Press
997 Macarthur Boulevard
Mahwah, New Jersey 07430

Printed and bound in the
United States of America

Contents

Preface v

1. Child Development and the Clinical Context 1

2. The Chaplain's Role with Patients and Their Families..... 25

3. The Chaplain as a Member of the Health Care Team 45

4. The Pastoral Visit..................................... 72

5. Coping with Stress: Defense Mechanisms................ 95

6. Prayer as a Form of Pastoral Care 117

7. Terminal Illness and Death 145

8. Theological Reflections 176

   Index 192

To Mike Stine

Preface

This book is written in order to provide assistance to ministers, ministerial students, and chaplains who work with hospitalized children and their families. It does not pretend to be a comprehensive guidebook to clinical pastoral care, nor is it to be taken as a substitute for actual hospital ministry carried out under a qualified supervisor. The attempt here is to build upon basic knowledge and experience in the field of clinical pastoral care and to help readers apply what they already know to the very special area of working with children.

The work between a chaplain and a hospitalized child is very far from being a private affair. There is, first, a sphere of interaction between chaplain and child. Second, the chaplain must interact with the child's parents and family. Third, the chaplain must expect to function as a member of the health care team in order for pastoral care to become an integrated part of the healing experience. This book supports an integration of these spheres and encourages good communication among patients, families, chaplains, and other members of the health care team.

The terms "chaplain" and "minister" are used here more or less interchangeably. Both may be applied to those who minister to the sick in a health care facility. A chaplain is usually one who has an official, even salaried connection with the health care institution; the minister may be working on a voluntary basis either as the chaplain's associate, or simply visiting members of his own congregation who happen to be hospitalized.

In the style of presentation which has been adopted here, clinical vignettes are followed by reflection on them. In each case the vignette reflects an actual clinical experience. The non-essential aspects of the characters' identity have been altered to protect their privacy; all names used are fictitious.

The author gratefully acknowledges the invaluable help of John G. Corazzini, Ph.D., Director of University Counseling Services, Virginia Commonwealth University, and Emily Luscher Parr, M.D., Fellow, American Academy of Pediatrics, both of whom read the entire manuscript and offered many helpful corrections and suggestions. Additional thanks go to Grace Kelly Marino, R.N., Carole Kahwajy, Barbara Sue Dawson, and Robert Matthew Marino, who offered proofreading services, valuable suggestions, and a great deal of moral support. A final word of thanks is due to the anonymous people, especially the children, whose stories are told here.

General Resources

Dorland's Illustrated Medical Dictionary, 26th ed. Philadelphia: W. B. Saunders, 1981.

Kaplan, Harold I., M.D., and Benjamin J. Sadock, M.D. *Modern Synopsis of Comprehensive Textbook of Psychiatry/III,* 3rd ed. Baltimore: Williams & Wilkins, 1981.

Stedman's Medical Dictionary (illustrated), 24th ed. Baltimore: Williams & Wilkins, 1982.

1.

Child Development
and the Clinical Context

Introduction

An understanding of the experiences, needs, and problems of children who are in the hospital presupposes an understanding of children in their normal circumstances. Theoretical knowledge is in no wise a substitute for extensive practical experience working with children. Only with the latter can the chaplain hope truly to understand children, to empathize with them, to communicate effectively with them, and to help meet their spiritual needs. Nevertheless, a basic familiarity with developmental psychology and its theories can be a tremendous advantage for the chaplain who seeks to organize and understand his various practical experiences. Reflection upon clinical experience and its analysis by means of a coherent theory which is received by fellow professionals leads to deeper insight, which in turn enables the chaplain both to minister more effectively to the children in his care and to communicate more clearly with professional colleagues.

There are many different theories of child development which are in use in current professional and educational literature. Most of these theories are known by the names of the thinkers who developed them and by a brief description of their central theme or structure. For example, one will find reference to the psychosexual stages of development of Sigmund Freud, the eight stages of ego development of Erik H. Erikson, the genetic epistemology of Jean Piaget, the stages of moral growth of Lawrence Kohlberg, the social learning theory of Albert Bandura, the educational theory of Maria Montessori, etc. Presuppositions, concepts, and terminology can vary

1

greatly from one theory to the next. This is not surprising when one remembers that the various theories were created in different contexts, by individuals with different educational backgrounds, to meet different needs or to solve different problems.

The developmental theory of Erik H. Erikson has been selected for presentation here. The reasons for this selection are the following: (a) Erikson's theory has occupied an important place in psychological literature for at least two decades; virtually all child care professionals will have at least passing familiarity with it. Sharing some of this knowledge will help the chaplain to communicate more easily with other members of the health care team. (b) Erikson's theory was developed in conjunction with his own clinical work, making it appropriate for use in a hospital setting. (c) At the same time, Erikson's focus is not on pathology, but on the normal development of the healthy personality. This will be helpful to the chaplain because most of the patients and families he encounters in his work will enjoy a basic mental health rather than suffer from psychopathology. In addition, it is not the chaplain's role to offer psychotherapy; he requires, then, a theory which does not have pathology or therapy as its overriding focus. (d) Unlike many other developmental theories, Erikson's does not stop with the end of childhood. Rather, it spans the entire life of the individual. This will be helpful to the chaplain who must deal not only with child patients, but with older siblings, parents, grandparents, and other adult relatives. (e) As will be illustrated below, the author has found Erikson's theory particularly helpful in his own clinical pastoral work with children.

All of this is not to say that Erikson's theory is the best among the many options; such a judgment would be impossible and improper to make. Rather, it is to say that this author has found Erikson's theory of development to be particularly helpful in his own pastoral care of hospitalized children and their families.

Erik H. Erikson

Born in Frankfurt, Germany in 1902, Erikson was raised by his mother and his stepfather, who was a pediatrician. After graduation from *gymnasium* (high school) he attended art school briefly, but was uninterested in the conservative discipline of the academic life. He became a wandering artist, and while living in Vienna became interested in the psychoanalytic movement there. Eventually he was accepted as a student, and after working under Anna Freud, the youngest daughter of the famous psychoanalyst Sigmund, he was graduated from the Vienna Psychoanalytic Institute in 1933. With the rise of Naziism, Erikson, who came from a Jewish home, emigrated to the United States of America and set up a private psychoanalytic practice in the Boston area. For a time he was enrolled as a candidate for a Ph.D. in psychology at Harvard, but abandoned formal study without having earned any degrees.

In 1950 Erikson published a major work, *Childhood and Society,* which presented his theory of ego development. A second edition, revised and enlarged, appeared in 1963.[1] This was followed in 1968 by *Identity: Youth and Crisis,* which focused on the developmental crises of adolescence.[2] Both have become modern classics, and other important works were published as well. Erikson has continued to be a leading figure in the fields of psychoanalysis and human development.[3]

The Ego and Its Stages of Development

Erikson's theory of psychological development involves eight stages which span the entire life of the individual. At each of these stages, the ego is confronted with a developmental crisis, the successful resolution of which leads to further healthy growth; the failure successfully to resolve the crisis leads to immaturity and possible pathology. (It should be noted that the resolution of each crisis or the failure to do so is not total; one should think of a continuum between success and failure.) An understanding of these crises and their effects helps the chaplain to evaluate the needs of those placed in his care and to offer pastoral care competently. In order to understand the stages of development, we need to understand what it is that is undergoing development.

Erikson regards the human person as dynamic rather than static, "as a process rather than as a thing, for we are concerned with the homeostatic quality of the living organism rather than with pathological items which might be demonstrable by section or dissection."[4] It is also important to note Erikson's focus on the healthy

---

[1]New York: W. W. Norton.

[2]New York: W. W. Norton.

[3]A great deal of autobiographical material is found in Erikson's *Life History and the Historical Movement* (New York: W. W. Norton, 1975).

[4]Erikson, *Childhood and Society,* p. 34.

and developing organism rather than only upon one which is considered aberrant.

For the human organism there are three inherent principles of organization, and, in keeping with the dynamic view of this organism, the three principles are described as processes: the somatic process, the ego process, and the societal process. These three processes are all aspects of one grand process, i.e., human life. The somatic process concerns that which is purely physiological. The societal process concerns the impact that other individuals and the larger society have upon the developing personality. The ego process concerns the organism's psychological development.

The theory of development which will be considered here concerns the ego process. The ego is "a concept denoting man's capacity to unify his experience and his action in an adaptive manner."[5] The ego organizes experience in such a way as to ensure the individual a sense of coherent individuation and identity. It enables the person to withstand shocks or unpredictable events which occur in the somatic and social processes. Thus it may be said to integrate endowment (somatic process) with opportunity (social process). It is important to emphasize that the ego is a concept and not a thing; nor is it the person or the mind.

> The ego, then, is an "inner institution" evolved to safeguard that order within individuals on which all outer order depends. It is not "the individual," not his individuality, although it is indispensable to both.[6]

The ego is a postulated process which is essential for the establishment of a sense of individuality and identity within the human person.

The epigenetic development of the fetus *in utero* provides an analog for ego development in the child and the consequent formation of his sense of identity. As the fetus grows, tissues differentiate into various organs. As each organ begins to form, there is a critical period when it either forms properly or does not. If something goes amiss during the critical period and the organ is not formed properly, the subsequent health and even survival of the organism is placed in jeopardy. There is a fixed sequence for the development of each part,

---

[5]Ibid., p. 15. Erikson consistently uses the masculine pronouns, presumably to refer to both sexes. For the sake of clarity and accuracy, whether quoting directly or paraphrasing from Erikson, his usage will be followed.

[6]Ibid., p. 94.

and each development takes a specific and determined period of time. Proper rate and sequence of growth are essential, and later stages build upon the previous ones.

Analogous to the growth of the fetus *in utero* is the development of the ego. This development occurs in stages of fixed sequence and duration. This development, this ego process, takes place within the context of the other two processes, the somatic and societal. It is dependent upon somatic readiness and societal stimulation.

> Personality, therefore, can be said to develop according to steps predetermined in the human organism's readiness to be driven toward, to be aware of, and to interact with a widening radius of significant individuals and institutions.[7]

Having established that ego or personality development occurs in stages, it would be well to state what is understood by "stage," or, its frequent synonym, "crisis." We have noted that the ego organizes experience in such a way as to enable the person to withstand shocks or unpredictable events which occur in the somatic and societal processes; it integrates the two processes and establishes an awareness of individual identity. Human growth is presented from the point of view of conflicts which the healthy, or vital, personality endures and survives, "re-emerging from each crisis with an increased sense of inner unity, with an increase of good judgment, and an increase of the capacity 'to do well' according to his own standards and to the standards of those who are significant to him."[8] Thus each stage concerns a period during which a new type of crisis is faced and dealt with in a manner that enhances the person's ability to function in his world.

But why is each stage of growth also a crisis?

> Crisis is used here in a developmental sense to connote not a threat of catastrophe but a turning point, a crucial period of increased vulnerability and heightened potential, and therefore, the ontogenetic source of generational strength and maladjustment.[9]

Remembering the analogy of the developing fetus, we can see that each developmental crisis is a time in which the acquisition of a new capacity is required. This is a crisis because the success or lack of it

---

[7]Erikson, *Identity*, p. 93.
[8]Ibid., pp. 91–92.
[9]Ibid., p. 96.

regarding the new acquisition impacts on the person's subsequent ability to function well. Viewed positively, we might view each stage as an opportunity for the individual to grow in new ways. With the new acquisition, a radical change in perspective occurs. "Each new stage becomes a crisis because incipient growth and awareness in a new part function go together with a shift in instinctual energy and yet also cause a specific vulnerability in that part."[10]

We have said that the developmental crises occur in a specific sequence and at a given rate. The personality acquisitions which occur at each crisis become part of the integrated personality, and thus each is systematically related to all the others. They all depend on the proper development in the proper sequence of each one. Yet, lest this sequence be viewed too rigidly, it is well to remember that each acquisition exists in some form before "its" decisive and critical time normally arrives.

Stage One:
Basic Trust versus Basic Mistrust

This stage occurs during the first year of post-partum life. An infant is characterized by immaturity of homeostasis. He is unable alone to meet even his most basic needs, such as nourishment. This immaturity of homeostasis is balanced in two ways, one originating outside the infant and one originating within him; thus we may call this balancing a mutual regulation to ensure homeostasis. The first technique occurs outside the infant: techniques of provision, or ways of "giving," provide the infant with basic needs such as nourishment, warmth, and physical safety. The second technique of achieving homeostasis occurs within the baby himself: he becomes increasingly able to receive and he develops new ways of "getting" what he needs. He becomes proficient at sucking and swallowing, at finding the maternal nipple or its substitute, at grasping and at biting.

The task of ego development which accompanies this first crisis evolves from the two techniques of ensuring homeostasis, and thus has two parts. First, the baby must learn to rely on sameness and continuity of outward providers.

> The infant's first social achievement, then, is his willingness to let the mother out of sight without undue anxiety or rage, because she

---

[10]Ibid., p. 95.

has become an inner certainty as well as an outer predictability. Such consistency, continuity, and sameness of experience provide a rudimentary sense of ego identity. . . .[11]

Second, the baby must trust himself and the capacity of his own organs (such as his mouth) to cope with urges. As forms of comfort become more familiar the infant becomes increasingly aware of himself as distinct from his caretakers.

It is clear that the core issue relating to this twofold task is one of basic trust. Thus this first critical stage is one which is characterized by the polarity of Basic Trust versus Basic Mistrust. This, then, is the first task of the ego: the firm establishment of enduring patterns for the solution of the nuclear conflict of basic trust versus basic mistrust in mere existence. The establishment of a sense of basic trust is critical, for this sense is the most fundamental prerequisite of mental vitality.

Stage Two:
Autonomy versus Doubt and Shame

This stage occurs during approximately the second and the beginning of the third years. The crisis for the developing infant is the challenge to achieve a sense of free will and self-control, or autonomy. At this time his first emancipation is played out, namely, emancipation from his mother.

"Muscular maturation sets the stage for experimentation with two simultaneous sets of social modalities: holding on and letting go."[12] The infant experiences a sudden and often violent wish to have a choice: to appropriate demandingly, or to eliminate stubbornly. These two tendencies are in conflict, which is dramatically demonstrated by the child who at one moment clings desperately to his toys and the next moment exuberantly tosses them out of the window. Although the desires to hold and to let go are expressed in many ways, the anal zone becomes a focal point at this stage. "The anal zone lends itself more than any other to the expression of stubborn insistence on conflicting impulses. . . ."[13] The outcome of this developmental crisis is dependent upon the experiences which surround the child's

---

[11]Erikson, *Childhood and Society,* p. 247.
[12]Ibid., p. 251.
[13]Erikson, *Identity,* p. 108.

learning to control his bowels. If the child, who is unable to control his bowels, is made to feel ashamed by this, the shame is a blow to his sense of autonomy: he has failed in his attempt at the exercise of free will. Doubt is the sibling of shame: the elimination which the child had thought was good is called bad, and the child is filled with doubt.

The development of a healthy sense of autonomy, then, is the task which corresponds to this second stage.

> A sense of self-control without loss of self-esteem is the ontogenetic source of all sense of *free will*. From an unavoidable sense of loss of self-control and of parental overcontrol comes a lasting propensity for *doubt* and *shame*.[14]

Thus this stage is characterized by the polarity of Autonomy versus Doubt and Shame.

Stage Three:
Initiative versus Guilt

This stage, which Erikson calls the "Ambulatory Stage," occurs from about the end of the third year to about the sixth year, or the beginning of school age. In the previous stage the child became firmly convinced that he was a person in his own right; now he seeks to find out what kind of person he can become. There are three developments which support this stage and which work to bring about its crisis: the child has greater freedom of movement (i.e., he becomes ambulatory) and therefore establishes a wider, and to him an unlimited, radius of goals; he has mastered speech sufficiently to talk about and ask about innumerable things; he becomes aware of and fantasizes about his own power, and this frightens him.

The successful resolution of the previous developmental crises creates in the child a new sense of hope and responsibility, which are qualities of initiative.

> [The] child suddenly seems to "grow together" both in his person and in his body. He appears "more himself," more loving, relaxed and brighter in his judgment, more activated and activating. He is in free possession of a surplus of energy which permits him to for-

---

[14]Ibid., pp. 109–10.

get failures quickly and to approach what seems desirable (even if it also seems uncertain and even dangerous) with undiminished and more accurate direction. Initiative adds to autonomy the quality of undertaking, planning and "attacking" a task for the sake of being active and on the move, where before self-will, more often than not, inspired acts of defiance or, at any rate, protested independence.[15]

To the basic social modalities of taking and releasing the child in this stage adds *making*. This may be described as "being out to win," i.e., taking pleasure in attack and conquest. The child is highly competitive and can become extremely jealous of others and their real or imagined successes.

This is also the time that the child becomes aware of sexual and genital differences. He is very curious about these differences and excited by sexual discovery. Such an awareness and excitement is called infantile genitality.

The danger in this stage is that the child will experience guilt over the contemplated goals and initiated acts as he enjoys and experiments with his newfound power. Goals or acts which are aggressive or coercive may be particularly guilt-inducing. While the child craves power he also fears it because of what it might accomplish: thus he fantasizes himself a powerful tiger but in his dreams he runs for dear life.

This conflict regarding power creates in the child's psyche a permanent division:

> Here the most fateful split and transformation in the emotional powerhouse occurs, a split between potential human glory and potential total destruction. For here the child becomes forever divided in himself. The instinct fragments which before had enhanced the growth of his infantile body and mind now become divided into an infantile set which perpetuates the exuberance of growth potentials, and a parental set which supports and increases self-observation, self-guidance, and self-punishment.[16]

Thus the child begins to learn a sense of moral responsibility and self-restraint.

Finally, this stage is a period of time when the child is more ready than ever to learn quickly and avidly. He copies role models of

---

[15]Erikson, *Childhood and Society,* p. 255.
[16]Ibid., p. 256.

the same sex in his effort to adopt socially acceptable and therefore less conflict-producing personal goals.

Stage Four:
Industry versus Inferiority

This stage takes place during the school age years, i.e., from about six until the beginning of adolescence. During this time the child gradually becomes aware of a need to be able to contribute productively to society. The fantasies of play are no longer sufficiently satisfying to him; he must learn to make tangible contributions. His exuberant imagination is tamed and harnessed to the laws of impersonal things.

> [The] normally advanced child forgets, or rather sublimates, the necessity to "make" people by direct attack or to become papa and mama in a hurry; he now learns to win recognition by producing things. . . . He develops a sense of industry—i.e., he adjusts himself to the inorganic laws of the tool world.[17]

It is during this time that the fundamentals of productive technology are developed.

In a modern industrial society, this learning takes place to a tremendous extent in organized schools. Because the skills learned there, especially basic literacy, are so far removed from specific adult roles in the society, the school setting becomes a world all by itself for the child, with its own goals and limitations, its achievements and disappointments. In order to learn, the child needs a structured school environment which places firm expectations upon his behavior and accomplishments:

> [Children] at this age do like to be mildly but firmly coerced into the adventure of finding out that one can learn to accomplish things which one would never have thought of by oneself, things which owe their attractiveness to the very fact that they are not the product of play and fantasy but the product of reality, practicality, and logic; things which thus provide a token sense of participation in the real world of adults.[18]

---

[17]Ibid., p. 259.
[18]Erikson, *Identity*, p. 127.

The danger at this stage is that the child will develop a sense of inadequacy or inferiority rather than a sense of competency. If he despairs of his abilities or his status among peers he may be discouraged from identification with them. "To lose the hope of such industrial association may pull him back to the more isolated, less tool-conscious familiar rivalry. . . ."[19] The child will come to consider himself doomed to mediocrity or inadequacy. It is precisely for this reason that in the educational setting emphasis should be placed upon what the child *can* do rather than upon his failures or inabilities. It is also important to avoid over-emphasizing the importance of performing concrete tasks to the point that the child comes to believe that "I am what I make." Such an attitude limits identity.

In contrast to other stages, this fourth stage of development does not spring from an internal crisis:

> This stage differs from the earlier ones in that it is not a swing from an inner upheaval to a new mastery. Freud calls it the latency stage because violent drives are normally dormant. But it is only a lull before the storm of puberty, when all the earlier drives re-emerge in a new combination, to be brought under the dominance of genitality.[20]

It is a calmer and very productive time for the growing child.

Stage Five:
Identity versus Role Confusion

With the advent of puberty, childhood proper comes to an end and youth begins. This is the period of adolescence. Rapid physical growth and the physical and especially genital changes brought on by sexual maturation call into question the child's previously established sense of continuity. The youngster's task is to integrate these changes and his wider societal relationships with his ego identity.

> The integration now taking place in the form of ego identity is, as pointed out, more than the sum of the childhood identifications. It is the accrued experience of the ego's ability to integrate all identifications with the vicissitudes of the libido, with the aptitudes developed out of endowment, and with the opportunities offered in

---

[19]Erikson, *Childhood and Society*, p. 260.
[20]Ibid.

social roles. The sense of ego identity, then, is the accrued confidence that the inner sameness and continuity prepared in the past are matched by the sameness and continuity of one's meaning for others, as evidenced in the tangible promise of a "career."[21]

Youths need above all at this time a moratorium period for the reintegration of the identity elements from the previous four developmental stages. The childhood milieu has been replaced by a larger and more vaguely defined milieu: "larger society." A brief review of these earlier identity elements will highlight the problems of the adolescent. First, regarding *trust,* the youth looks for people and ideas to have faith in, but also to whom he may prove himself to be trustworthy. Thus he tries to develop in himself the virtue of fidelity. Because he fears a foolish, all too trusting commitment to a person or cause, he expresses his need for faith in loud and cynical mistrust. Second, regarding *autonomy* and *free will,* the youth wishes to choose freely an avenue of duty and service within society, yet is afraid of ridicule and self-doubt. He would rather appear foolish to his elders than to his peers or to himself. Third, *initiative* and *imagination* become important as the youth begins to find objects for his trust. He tends to place his trust in those peers or elders who will give imaginative scope to his aspirations. Fourth, *industry* becomes a key concern as the youth struggles to select an occupation and career.

Social values guide identity formation, and the youth is particularly responsive to the ideology of a society.

It is an ideological mind—and indeed, it is the ideological outlook of a society that speaks most clearly to the adolescent who is eager to be affirmed by his peers, and is ready to be confirmed by rituals, creeds, and programs which at the same time define what is evil, uncanny, and inimical.[22]

The danger in this stage is that of role confusion. The inability clearly to define his role in society is very threatening to the youth, and the inability to settle on occupational identity is usually most disturbing of all. Such inability can precipitate severe psychological pathology.

The youth develops several kinds of defenses against the threat of identity confusion. Clannishness is one such defense: "in-groups" are formed based upon arbitrary and insignificant modes of speech,

---

[21]Ibid., pp. 261–62.
[22]Ibid., p. 263.

dress, gesture, etc., and those who are unable to conform are rigidly and cruelly excluded. The definition of personal identity through interaction with others is common:

> To keep themselves together [youths] temporarily overidentify, to the point of apparent complete loss of identity, with the heroes or cliques and crowds. This initiates the stage of "falling in love," which is by no means entirely, or even primarily, a sexual matter—except where the mores demand it. To a considerable extent adolescent love is an attempt to arrive at a definition of one's identity by projecting one's diffused ego image on another and by seeing it thus reflected and gradually clarified. This is why so much of young love is conversation.[23]

It is an interesting note that when youths seek to resolve their identity crisis in a country or society which is losing or has lost its group identity, the youths become particularly vulnerable to cruel totalitarian doctrines.[24]

Stages Six, Seven, and Eight: Beyond Identity

Stage Six occurs during early adulthood and involves the crisis of Intimacy versus Isolation. The developmental task for the young adult is to learn to risk the vulnerability required to have an intimate loving relationship with another. True psycho-social intimacy is much more than mere *sexual* intimacy: it is both the counterpointing and the fusing of the identities of two individuals. The exploitative, self-seeking sexuality which can characterize the adolescent becomes tempered by an ethical sense and by love for the partner. Failure to attain true intimacy with another results in isolation. This inability to take a risk with one's identity by sharing true intimacy with another is often accompanied by fears regarding the outcomes of intimacy, e.g., children.

The crisis of Generativity versus Stagnation occurs during early middle and middle adulthood and is the seventh developmental stage. Generativity is primarily the individual's concern for establishing and guiding the next generation. It includes the concepts of productivity and creativity, that is, living up to one's full potential,

---

[23]Ibid., p. 262.
[24]On this theory see Erikson, *Identity,* pp. 74–90.

but does not stop there. For generativity leads to an expansion of ego-interests and a libidinal investment in what is generated. Those who fail at this task end up with a sense of stagnation, boredom, and interpersonal impoverishment. They tend to treat themselves indulgently as if they were children.

The eighth and final developmental stage concerns the crisis of Integrity versus Despair and takes place during late adulthood. While no clear definition of integrity can be given, certain of its attributes can be named. It is the ego's accrued assurance of its proclivity for order and meaning; it is the acceptance of the course of one's life, of the persons and institutions which have been significant; it is acceptance of the fact that this life is the only one, that the individual has "had his chance"; it is a sense of camaraderie with people in other times and places who have contributed creatively to the development of society; it is the individual's readiness to defend the dignity of his own life style. When integrity is not achieved the result is despair. The individual is disgusted with life; he looks back longingly on "wrong choices" he has made; he feels that life is all too short and tends to deny that death is its final boundary; he may express contempt for the world; all of this points to a feeling of disgust with himself.

Putting Erikson's Theory to Use:
Age Related Crises in the Hospital

STAGE ONE:
BASIC TRUST VERSUS BASIC MISTRUST

Anna, a six month old girl, was hospitalized on the nursery unit for observation and possible treatment after being in an automobile accident in which her mother, a single parent, was also injured. Her mother was placed in another hospital. Anna's injuries were slight, and it was unlikely that she was in any pain, but, not surprisingly, she cried almost constantly when awake and would not be comforted by any of the unit personnel who were responsible for her care.

For a child in Stage One, continuity in care-taking is important for the development in the child of a sense of basic trust. Separation from his mother (or primary care-taker) often results in extreme anxiety and rage. As the child develops, he gradually learns to accept such separations, knowing that they will be temporary, and trusting that his basic needs will still be met.

Anna was separated suddenly and violently from her mother, a separation which endured longer than any other of her young life. Possessing no language skills and limited thinking ability, it was impossible for Anna to be told that the separation would be temporary, and it was impossible for her to understand its cause. Filled with fear and anger, she could only scream.

Anna's experience is often called Separation Anxiety, and much has been written about it.[25] While fear of separation from parents is common to most young children in the hospital, it is the most important, if not *the* anxiety of hospitalized infants.

STAGE TWO:
AUTONOMY VERSUS DOUBT AND SHAME

Regina, a precocious and intelligent two year old girl, was hospitalized for the treatment of bone defects in both ankles and feet. She had been placed in traction. Each lower leg and foot was wrapped with cloth bandages. At the sole of each foot, a hook was placed in the wrappings; a cord was fixed to each hook. The cords were connected to a fixed bar three feet above the mattress of Regina's crib. Thus, she sat or lay with her feet and legs hoisted up in the air.

Chaplain Carlton encountered Regina in the children's playroom, where her crib had been placed for the afternoon. Never having met Regina, Chaplain Carlton smiled brightly, cupped the child's face in her hands, and said, "Hi, sweetheart!" Regina, obviously angered, said emphatically, "Stop that!" Surprised to hear such a command issue from such a little person, the chaplain asked, "You don't want me to touch you?" The firm reply was a resounding "NO!" "All right, then," said the chaplain. "If you don't want me to touch you, I won't." Regina immediately broke into a huge grin, and asked the chaplain to play with her. Their subsequent relationship was warm and friendly, with Regina eventually asking Chaplain Carlton for goodbye hugs when their visits ended.

Regina was a little person who had lost control of her life and her body. Against her will, she had both legs tied up day and night

---

[25]See, e.g., J. Robertson, *Young Children in Hospitals* (London: Tavistock Publications, 1958) pp. 20–23.

in an awkward, uncomfortable, and incapacitating position. Her repeated pleas to be released had always met with kind but firm refusals. Trapped as she was, she struggled for some sense of autonomy, for some control over her own circumstances.

Chaplain Carlton helped Regina by listening carefully to her desire to regain some of her lost control. By saying, "If you don't want me to touch you, I won't," she was allowing Regina to exercise some control over her situation. She was empowering Regina and fostering her attempts to achieve greater autonomy. The child's delight at finally having some authority over herself is thus understandable, even predictable.

A less skilled and empathetic chaplain might have frustrated herself or the patient. If the chaplain had interpreted the child's assertions as rudeness or antisocial behavior, and responded with a reprimand, she would have contributed to the child's sense of shame and self-doubt. On the other hand, the chaplain might have interpreted the child's actions as rejection and concluded that her professional skills were inadequate, that she was not fitted for work with children, or that she had made an error in trying to be friendly. In this case, none of these conclusions on the chaplain's part would have been warranted.

STAGE THREE:
INITIATIVE VERSUS GUILT

Richard, an intelligent four year old, was hospitalized for severe dehydration. He was the second of four brothers. The family had driven out of state to visit relatives. Shortly after their arrival there, Richard began to vomit violently. Suspecting that he was reacting to an irritant in the relatives' home, his parents put the children back in the car and began the long drive home. By the time they arrived, Richard was so sick that he had to be hospitalized. An intravenous solution was set up with the needle in Richard's arm. His gown was pinned down to the bed to prevent his moving about excessively and pulling out the needle. Because there was a shortage of full-size beds on the unit, he was placed in a crib, which was a tremendous embarrassment and source of shame for him. When his mother came in to see him, he looked up at her and asked, "If I promise to be a real, real good boy, will you let me come home to live with you again?"

Pre-school children are self-centered little people, and their thinking and reasoning displays a definite and pervasive egocentricity. They tend to relate all the world to themselves, to think in terms of their own needs, and to believe that others share their own beliefs and knowledge.

The thinking of pre-school children takes on a magical character.[26] They make implausible or even impossible connections, believing erroneously that there are causal links between events when there are none.

These two features of their thinking, its egocentricity and its magical character, make pre-school children susceptible to feelings of guilt. They often believe that they cause things to happen which in fact were completely beyond their control. Their fantasies of power lead them to believe they are the cause of many important events. When the event is perceived as bad, the child reacts by feeling guilty.

Richard felt responsible for his own illness and hospitalization. Certain features of the experience reinforced his tendency to blame himself and feel guilty. The family had taken off on a vacation, which had to be aborted because of his illness. No one was happy about the family having to return home. The drive was long and inconvenient. Richard had made messes when he vomited.

Some of the things Richard experienced in the hospital took on a punitive tone for him. Putting in the intravenous needle hurt. He was then pinned down to the mattress. His imprisonment was made complete by placing him in a crib, a place for babies which was humiliating for him.

As the chaplain works with pre-school children in the hospital, he needs to remember their egocentric and magical way of thinking and their susceptibility to feelings of guilt for real or imagined offenses. In the case of illness, the child needs repeated reassurance that no one is to blame: the illness is not the child's fault; it is not his mother's fault; it is not his father's fault; it is not his brother's fault; etc. Children with religious upbringing may imagine that God himself is punishing them by means of the illness. Such a belief in divine punishment may have been created or reinforced by well-meaning family members or clergy. The child may have been taught that God is One Who Punishes. He may have been told that his illness is "God's will." The child may then catalogue his recent behavior, re-

---

[26]See S. Fraiberg, *The Magic Years: Understanding and Handling the Problems of Early Childhood* (New York: Charles Scribners, 1959).

calling infractions of domestic or school discipline, and conclude that he is being punished by God for one or more specific acts.

Stating directly and clearly that no one is to blame for the illness and that the child is not being punished is often sufficient. Many pre-school children can discuss and understand these concepts readily. They may even dismiss the idea of blame or punishment quickly and cavalierly.

Dramatic play and storytelling can also help the pre-schooler to understand that he is not being punished with illness. The chaplain can tell the child the following story or a similar one, with appropriate variations for the particular circumstance.

Once upon a time there was a little girl named Laura who lived with her mother, her father, and her little sister. Laura liked to play with her friends, watch Sesame Street, and color with her crayons. One day, Laura's tummy started to hurt. It hurt and hurt. Laura cried. Her mother gave her medicine, but it still hurt. Laura was very sick.

Finally, Laura's mother called the doctor. He said that Laura had to go to the hospital so that he could take care of her. Laura went to the hospital. They stuck a needle into her arm. It hurt, and it made Laura cry.

After the nurse put the needle in, Laura remembered that she had had a fight with her sister, Stacy, the day before. Laura had been really mad. She had hit Stacy. Laura's mother made her go to her room for punishment. Laura thought getting a tummy ache and going to the hospital was more punishment. She thought she got sick because she was bad and hit her sister.

Poor Laura! She didn't know that getting sick is not punishment. She didn't know that the doctor and nurses wanted to make her well, not punish her. She didn't know that the people in the hospital love children and want to make them feel good and make them well so they can go home and play!

Such a story can be helpful as the chaplain seeks to put across to the child the message that sickness is not punishment and that the child need not feel guilty about being in the hospital. In listening to the story, the child's role is essentially passive. Dramatic play can help the child actively to express his own feelings and beliefs, and at the same time provide the chaplain with an appropriate forum for putting across his own message.

If a comment made by the child, his family, or a member of the health care team indicates that the child is interpreting his illness as punishment from God, the chaplain can explore this with the child and seek to correct his erroneous interpretation of his illness. The following is one possible technique.

The chaplain presents the child with two puppets, a child puppet, and a Jesus puppet. He explains that the child puppet is sick in the hospital, and the chaplain assumes that role. He invites the child to use the Jesus puppet. He says, "Let's pretend now that Jesus comes to visit the little boy. What does he say? What does he do?"

The child's portrayal of Jesus will reflect his own beliefs of Jesus vis-à-vis his own situation. Thus, he might portray Jesus as comforting the sick child, healing him, or, possibly, chastising or punishing him. In the former cases, the chaplain can reinforce the child's beliefs by saying, "Yes, Jesus loves children. He wants them to be well and go home again." But if the child sees Jesus as one who punishes, the chaplain may seek to correct this belief by exchanging roles in the dramatic play. Portraying Jesus with the puppet, he could embrace the sick child puppet, say comforting words, and reassure the sick child puppet of his love.

Such techniques may seem deceptively simple. However, they can be powerful tools for discovering what a child is thinking and for helping him to assess his situation more realistically and appropriately. Before deciding to employ such methods, the chaplain should attempt to assess the family's religious beliefs and values with great care and sensitivity. Obviously, the use of a Jesus puppet is not appropriate for a child whose religious background is other than Christian. Furthermore, families of certain religious backgrounds would be deeply offended were any puppet or picture used to portray God. The chaplain must remember that his role is to support the patient and family in their religious faith, rather than to challenge or deny their beliefs.

Ronny, an eight year old boy, was hospitalized with an acute attack of appendicitis. Emergency surgery was performed at night and his recovery progressed nicely. On the second day after surgery, when things calmed down in their home, Ronny's parents noticed that his five year old brother, Pete, seemed to be depressed. He stayed alone in his room, had little appetite, and was listless, unhappy, and uncommunicative. Believing that Pete was jealous over all of the attention that Ronny was getting, the parents tried to make him feel special by giving him small gifts and taking him out for pizza. Instead of feeling better, Pete seemed worse for all of their attention. He wanted to give his new toys to Ronny. Finally, in a fit of tears, Pete "confessed" that the previous week during an argument with Ronny, he had said, "I hate you and I hope you drop dead!" Pete now believed that his hostile feelings had caused Ronny's illness. He was consumed with guilt and anxiety.

Pete's feelings about his brother's sudden illness are not atypical among pre-school children. With his magical and egocentric style of thinking, he assumed that his own emotions of anger had been powerful enough to cause his brother's appendicitis attack. Had the illness never occurred, Pete would probably have forgotten all about the incident. When the illness did strike, however, Pete recalled his earlier feelings of hostility and concluded that he was to blame. Not only did he feel guilty and unworthy of his parents' love and attentions, but he feared punishment, shame, and retribution which might occur when his dreadful act was "discovered."

Pete needed badly to be "let off the hook" on which he had placed himself. His parents reassured him that hostile feelings are normal, and that feelings do not cause bad things to happen to other people. They enlisted the aid of their minister, who reinforced these ideas for Pete. He assured Pete that he did not cause Ronny's illness, that Ronny would have developed appendicitis regardless, and that no one was angry at him for having been angry at his brother. Pete was also assured that Ronny was recovering nicely and would come home in a few days, and that soon everything would be back to normal.

STAGE FOUR:
INDUSTRY VERSUS INFERIORITY

Martin, a ten year old boy, was hospitalized after being struck by an automobile and sustaining a fracture of the femur. He was placed in traction, his leg being hoisted up in the air over his hospital bed. He was unable to move from the bed or to roll over onto his stomach or onto either side. When Chaplain Taylor visited Martin on his fourth day in the hospital, he was depressed and unhappy. In their conversation, Martin commented that he was "stupid" and that his friends might make fun of him for having been hit by a car.

Martin's feelings of inadequacy stemmed from several factors. It was indeed his own careless behavior that caused the accident: he had run into a busy street at full tilt without looking at the traffic.

Once he was settled in the hospital bed and was no longer in pain, he desired, naturally, to engage in his normal activities. Due to being in traction, he was quite unable to do the things that he loved most. He could not play ball, ride his bicycle, climb trees, play games with other children, or even go outdoors. He was unable to attend school or be with his friends. Neither was he able to attend to his basic bodily needs without the help of his parents or nurses: he could not even go to the bathroom or dress himself.

It seemed to Martin that all of the skills and independence which he had acquired throughout his life had suddenly been taken away. He felt that he had suddenly lost competence to do the most basic things in life. He interpreted this experience of loss as meaning that he was an inadequate person, stupid and subject to the ridicule of peers.

Chaplain Taylor helped Martin to express his feelings of lost competence and power. He acknowledged the pain that this was causing Martin. He then began to help Martin to focus on the things that he was still able to do. He pointed out that from his bedside he could control the television in the room and summon the nurse when he needed help. He could choose when to eliminate, when to take a nap, and how to spend much of his time. He could do much of his schoolwork as well as engage in creative pursuits such as assembling model cars and airplanes, painting, sculpting with clay, making greeting cards for friends, etc. He could use his bedside telephone to call his friends or family when he wanted to.

Over a period of days, the health care team opened up to Martin a whole vista of activity. He learned to engage in various pursuits and to care for himself more and more. Soon his sense of industry and competence returned, and the remainder of his hospital stay was uneventful.

STAGE FIVE:
IDENTITY VERSUS ROLE CONFUSION

Tony, a fourteen year old boy from the midwest, entered the hospital to be evaluated as a candidate for a kidney transplant. Both of his diseased kidneys had been removed some months previously, and since that time he had been kept alive by means of dialysis. At the time of his admission, the donor candidate was a thirty-five year old female cousin. Chaplain Johnson met Tony when the decision was made to go ahead with the transplant. They discussed many issues, but the chaplain noticed that Tony often called attention to his own physique, asking the chaplain if he had sufficient hair on his legs for a fourteen year old, a "normal" voice, etc. Tony also emphasized the female character of the donated kidney, announcing that he had named it "Betty." The chaplain responded to Tony's concerns about his masculinity by assuring him that receiving a kidney from a woman would in no way make him effeminate or compromise his masculinity. Sensing the emergence of a critical issue, the chaplain noted Tony's anxiety in his chart notes and, just to be sure, communicated his concern personally to the attending physician. One of the interns on the unit became aware of Tony's concern, and, in an effort to reassure him through teasing, remarked, "Well, you might need a bra after surgery!" Unfortunately, Tony's anxiety about his masculinity only increased, and an interdisciplinary health care team meeting was called to discuss the problem

Chaplain Johnson had become an important person to Tony and family because he shared their particular church affiliation. He was able to achieve good rapport with Tony quickly, and it was in this context that Tony's revelations of his anxieties took place.

Because of Tony's age and stage of development, he was particularly vulnerable to crises of identity. In this case, what seemed most in doubt to Tony was his *sexual* identity, his feeling that he was a masculine person. It seems quite understandable that having the organ of a female implanted in his body could cause Tony to feel less masculine. Tony may have erroneously connected kidney function with genital function (an easy mistake for a child to make since urine flows through the penis), and this may have exacerbated his distress. For Tony, the intern's teasing remark served only to give credence to his belief that receiving a woman's kidney would make him effeminate.

Chaplain Johnson acted responsibly when he reported the situation to other members of the medical team. He sensed correctly that this was an issue of fundamental importance for Tony and his self-conceptualization, and that a psychiatric consult was indicated. He wisely avoided any attempts to handle the situation alone or to practice amateur psychiatry.

The opinions and recommendations of the consulting psychiatrist and clinical social workers became key in the interdisciplinary meeting of the health care team. A number of team members had not heard of Tony's concern about his masculinity, and they listened as the chaplain related his experience of this. The mental health consultants acknowledged that Tony's anxieties were of critical importance. One physician questioned whether the surgery should be delayed or called off entirely. It was finally concluded that postponing the transplant even for a short time would have a devastating effect on Tony and his family, and that this factor outweighed others. Plans were made to reassure Tony in positive ways that his male identity would remain intact after the transplant.

The surgery took place successfully as scheduled. Tony's last remark to his mother before entering the operating room was that he had a lot of hair on his legs.

Conclusion

A working knowledge of the experiences, needs, and problems of children in their normal circumstances is necessary for the hospital chaplain who seeks to minister to them in a clinical setting. From among many theories of child development, that of Erik H. Erikson was selected for presentation and use here. Erikson's theory proposes eight stages of ego development which span the entire life of the individual. The first five stages, which span the time from infancy to adolescence, were used to analyze and discuss age-related crises in actual clinical experience.

The temptation to employ simplistically a theory such as Erikson's is to be avoided. While it is convenient and helpful to think of a child's development as occurring in distinct stages, each with its own conflict, developmental task, or issue, it is unrealistic to expect children to compartmentalize rigidly their personal development. Any thinking person, for example, may react to illness or injury by believing that he is responsible or at fault, even when the contrary is clearly true. Or again, any person who becomes incapacitated may experience a painful identity crisis. Rather than predicting in an absolute way how people think and react at different life stages, Erikson's theory suggests predispositions or tendencies which are specific to certain ages and levels of personal development. An awareness of this helps the chaplain to know what to look for and helps him to know how a patient is *likely* to be reacting to a stressful situation. Finally, an adequate grounding in theory can help the chaplain to organize and understand the raw data of his clinical experience.

RECOMMENDED READING

American Academy of Pediatrics. Committee on Hospital Care. *Hospital Care of Children and Youth.* Evanston, Ill.: American Academy of Pediatrics, 1978.

Erikson, Erik H. *Childhood and Society,* 2nd ed., rev. and enl. New York: W. W. Norton, 1963.

—. *Identity: Youth and Crisis.* New York: W. W. Norton, 1968.

Fraiberg, S. *The Magic Years: Understanding and Handling the Problems of Early Childhood.* New York: Charles Scribners, 1959.

Robertson, James. *Young Children in Hospitals,* 2nd ed. London: Tavistock, 1970.

Thomas, R. Murray. *Comparing Theories of Child Development.* Belmont, Cal.: Wadsworth, 1979.

Wright, J. Eugene, Jr. *Erikson: Identity and Religion.* New York: Seabury, 1982.

2.

The Chaplain's Role with Patients and Their Families

Introduction

Chaplain Wagner was making her rounds in the intensive care unit of the large city hospital where she was employed as a member of the pastoral care department. She paused at the bedside of a critically ill ten year old boy to pray for a few moments before she went to the waiting room to see his parents. While she was there, the patient's heart stopped beating properly. Alarms went off and the cardiac team quickly gathered around the bed to attempt resuscitation. Chaplain Wagner stood a few feet away and continued to pray quietly as she watched. Suddenly, the attending physician looked up at her and shouted, "Who the hell are you, and what the hell are you doing here?" Frightened and intimidated, Chaplain Wagner quickly and wordlessly left the unit.

Chaplain Wagner had no ready response for the doctor, and this reflected her own lack of a clear idea as to the chaplain's role in a clinical setting. Doubts about identity and role often plague the hospital chaplain.[1] He finds himself in a setting where virtually all other employees have clear roles and duties; often these have been written out in great detail in hospital or medical manuals. It can be disconcerting if his own role and duties lack similar clarity.

At first blush it might sound clear enough to assert that the chaplain's role is to provide pastoral care for patients, families, and,

---

[1] Cf. Samuel M. Natale, S.J., *Pastoral Counseling* (New York: Paulist, 1977), pp. 8–26.

sometimes, hospital staff. Ambiguities abound, however, in such a definition. Is the chaplain, who usually has a denominational preference or affiliation, to minister to all patients, or only to those of the same denomination? Is his primary duty to care for the patient, or the patient's family, or both? What is his relationship to the patient's own minister and church? Is the chaplain the "pastor of the hospital staff"? And perhaps most fundamentally, what is pastoral care?

Many models of pastoral care have been developed over time and are still in use today.[2] Some church traditions have regarded pastoral care as primarily the administration of sacraments and the "cure of souls" by recommending certain remedies for spiritual problems. Others place emphasis on pastoral conversations wherein the minister argues with all of his intellectual power in order to persuade a person to give assent to a particular religious creed or belief. Still others consider it most important for the minister to persuade a person, through an act of will, to accept salvation from Jesus Christ. Some models of pastoral care make heavy use of psychology and clinical jargon from the mental health field; others eschew one or both. In some models the minister's visit will have a fairly rigid structure; in others, there is little or no structure. Finally, each model will have its own (at least implicit) presuppositions in the form of world view, articulated theology, and informally held religious beliefs and values.

Out of respect for the readers' various religious beliefs, values, and affiliations and their various understandings of themselves as ministers, no attempt will be made here to select one model of pastoral care as normative. Instead, various roles that the chaplain or minister may properly and effectively assume in the clinical setting will be discussed. This does not mean that his function there is simply "up for grabs," but that there exists a variety of functions which may legitimately be placed under the rubric of pastoral care.

The Chaplain as Friend

Chaplain Hoover received a midnight call from the neonatal unit, requesting his presence for a father whose baby was dying. The child, whose mother was in another hospital, had been born several hours previously. He suffered from severe congenital heart defects

---

[2]For an excellent summary, see E. Brooks Holifield, *A History of Pastoral Care in America* (Nashville: Abingdon, 1983).

for which there was no possible treatment, and was dying. When Chaplain Hoover arrived on the unit, he was taken to a small room where the child's father was holding him while sitting in a rocking chair. The father was simply rocking the baby and waiting for him to die, which he was told would happen in several hours or less. When the chaplain entered the room, the father said, "Chaplain, I don't want any religious stuff. I don't want you to pray or anything. I don't need to hear any lectures either. I'm just very scared, and I wanted somebody to be with me." Chaplain Hoover sat down, and over the next two hours, as the two men talked, the baby periodically sputtered, gasped, and continued to breathe laboriously. Finally, the infant died. The two men spent a little more time together, talking about the baby's death and what it meant to the father. Finally, each left the unit.

The most unusual thing about the father's request of the chaplain was his forthrightness. It often happens that patients or families need friendly support while at the same time they are uncomfortable or unfamiliar with religious language or activity. Chaplain Hoover might have reacted quite negatively to the father's introductory declarations. Had he been judgmental, he might have said, "Don't turn your back on God. Now is the time that you need him most!" Had he been rigid about his own role, he might have retorted, "Then why in the world did you have them call a *chaplain?*"

Exhibiting a lack of sensitivity and respect for the father's feelings and values, he might have suggested baptizing the child before he died. Or, feeling inadequate to operate outside of a religious framework, he might have attempted to pass off his responsibility by saying, "What you really need is not me, but a social worker."

By listening carefully to the father's stated needs, and by his willingness to view his own role flexibly, the chaplain was able to minister effectively to the distraught father. Sitting down and waiting with the father for the death of the baby was a powerful statement of support and caring. In their conversation, Chaplain Hoover was able to help the father to talk about his feelings and those of his wife, to begin his own grieving process, and to make realistic plans about handling the funeral details, such as notifying relatives of the death, etc. It was appropriate for the chaplain to spend time on these tasks, for these were some of the same things that he would have wanted to do had the father been a religious person of his own persuasion.

Even though religious language was not used in their conversation, Chaplain Hoover was able to understand the encounter as a profoundly spiritual one, full of religious significance for himself, if not for the father. For a couple of hours he joined another human being on a painful and tragic portion of his life's journey. Together, they confronted the ultimate mystery, the ultimate finality: death. In sharing himself this way with another, the chaplain showed his deep love of others. Being a friend to a person in need is a form of ministry just as much as feeding the hungry or proclaiming the Gospel would be. Indeed, the chaplain's presence to the father in his time of fear and sorrow was probably the most powerful proclamation of God's love which was possible under the circumstances. The father left the situation with a good feeling toward the chaplain, and possibly, toward the church, as a result of that ministry. Had the chaplain insisted on an overtly religious encounter, the father's feelings would undoubtedly have been negative: anger, resentment, or even disgust.

Part of being a friend is accepting another person as he is, and not attempting to change him. As people who feel called to proclaim a message, ministers often succumb to the temptation to preach to those who are not ready to hear, or to attempt to manipulate and mold people to fit the minister's own preconceptions about who the "good person" should be. The hospital is an entirely different setting from a church building or a street corner. People in the hospital are people in pain, people in trouble, people with needs which are often urgent and desperate. The best ministry in these circumstances is that which attempts to respond to the needs these people feel, and not necessarily to the needs that the chaplain feels *for* them. Friendship and support, without strings attached or unstated expectations on the chaplain's part, are basic and powerful components of his ministry.

The Chaplain as Surrogate Parent

Chaplain Lockner was making his rounds on the pediatric unit when he stopped in to see Mike, an eight year old boy with spina bifida and hydrocephaly, who had been hospitalized for possible revision of the shunt, or tube, which drained excess fluid from his head down into his abdomen, where it would do no harm. As he entered the room, the chaplain could see that Mike was crying. Before him on the bedside table was his dinner, obviously untouched. When the chaplain asked Mike why he was crying, he sobbed, "I'm hungry and there's nobody here to cut my meat for me!" Chaplain Lockner quickly obliged by cutting up the child's pork chop, and then stayed with him to visit while he ate his dinner. Mike stopped crying, ate a hearty meal, and seemed to feel much better.

Once again we see a chaplain responding to a patient's needs rather than adhering rigidly to his own preconceptions of what constitutes ministry. Children who happen to be in the hospital are still children, and they continue to require the same parenting that they need at home. It is desirable to have one or even both of the child's parents stay in the hospital with him. Some hospitals for children provide a parent bed in every room and encourage parents to stay with the child round the clock. Often, however, other demands which are placed on parents of hospitalized children make it impossible for them to do more than visit briefly once each day or so. There may be other children at home who require as much or more parenting as the child in the hospital. Parents may work at a job from which they can take no time off. Transportation to and from the hospital may be difficult for parents, particularly if their home is far away. Sometimes parents are themselves hospitalized during their child's hospital stay, perhaps because the family was involved together in an accident.

When parents are not able to be adequately present to their hospitalized children, the hospital staff usually seeks to fill the void. This is easier said than done. Health care professionals working in the hospital have many assigned duties and busy schedules. Rare indeed is the technician, doctor, or nurse who will have time to stay with a single child and look after his non-medical needs. Providing consistent care and supervision for a particular child is further complicated by the fact that shifts change every eight or twelve hours, so that in the course of a single day a dozen or more people may be providing care for him. On a hospital unit where some children may be seriously ill or even dying, where medications must be dispensed, dressings changed, vital signs monitored, and treatments and therapies given, cutting up a pork chop understandably (and properly) takes a low place on the list of priorities. In Mike's case, practically any hospital worker who was aware of his dilemma would have stopped to help. The chaplain happened to be the first one to discover this particular need, and was able to take care of it himself.

Chaplain Lockner's action in this case had more significance than merely helping a child to eat, although that in itself was im-

portant. This experience of the chaplain's care and concern helped
Mike to see him as a person who was there to help and who could be
trusted to do good things. Good rapport was established between the
two, and later Mike was able to share with the chaplain some significant concerns. Their relationship moved onto a religious plane
when Mike asked the chaplain why he was born with spina bifida,
and whether God had wanted him to be that way. Chaplain Lockner
avoided the temptation of being an answer man, and their shared
discussion and prayer became an important therapeutic component
of Mike's hospital care. A simple act of human kindness on the chaplain's part opened the way for a serious ministerial encounter with
a patient who had deep spiritual concerns.

*Kelly was a ten year old girl who was hospitalized with a liver
infection. An intravenous drip was set up and she was confined to
bed. Both of her parents worked outside their home, and once the
medical emergency was over, they were no longer able to be present
in the hospital during daytime hours. Chaplain Abbott stopped in to
visit Kelly, whom he found playing with a coloring book while sitting
on the floor of the room. After a minute, Ms. Johnson, her primary
care nurse, came by and scolded Kelly for having gotten out of bed.
Kelly obediently climbed back in bed, but once the nurse left she
jumped back down to the floor. Chaplain Abbott responded by saying,
"All right, then. Since you disobeyed Ms. Johnson, you cannot watch
television for the rest of the afternoon!"*

In this case the chaplain's attempt to discipline a disobedient patient was distinctly inappropriate. First, the command to stay in bed
had come from another staff member, not himself. In seeking to enforce the nurse's behavior requirements of the child, the chaplain
was intruding on that relationship. Second, it is often the case that
each patient has assigned to him a primary care nurse, whose responsibility it is to manage the carrying out of doctors' orders and to
be responsible for direct supervision of that patient. Kelly had a primary care nurse, and if Chaplain Abbott felt that her behavior was
unreasonable and needed correction, he should have spoken with the
nurse, whose prerogative it was to make any decisions about disci-
plining the patient. Third, his comments tended to reinforce Kelly's
feelings of rejection.

Chaplains must remember that they are members of the health
care team, and that it is important not to infringe on the roles of
other members of the team. Chaplain Abbott could have responded
more appropriately to Kelly's misbehavior by saying, "Ms. Johnson

just told you how important it is for you to stay in bed. She is here to help you and she knows a lot about how to make kids get well again. Please do what she asks and get back in bed." In taking this tack, the chaplain not only asked the child to conform to behavioral expectations, but he also explicitly supported the nurse while not infringing on her own authority to discipline her patients. Had Kelly continued to refuse to comply, the chaplain could have left the room, reported the situation to the nurse, and left it to her to decide how to handle it. She might or might not have asked the chaplain to help her with managing the patient's behavior, but it was important that the chaplain respect her relationship with the patient.

The Chaplain as Liaison

Matthew was a nine year old boy hospitalized for surgical repair of hypospadias, a defect in the urethra. Chaplain Seward saw him in his hospital room several hours after his surgery. Matthew's face was red, and though he was not crying, his eyes were teary. Chaplain Seward gently asked Matthew about his surgery and they discussed it for some moments. Seeing that the boy seemed to be in pain, the chaplain asked, "Does it hurt you now?" Matthew answered that he was in a great deal of pain. He went on to explain that the nurse had offered him an injection for it, but, fearful of the needle, Matthew had lied to her and said that he was not in pain. Chaplain Seward explained that the injection would take only seconds and that it would bring great relief. He asked Matthew if he (the chaplain) could help him to tell the nurse that he was, in fact, in pain and needed the injection. The boy assented, the chaplain pushed the nurse call button, and when she came into the room, he explained that Matthew was in pain, but was afraid of the injection. The nurse talked with Matthew a few moments about this, and he agreed to have the injection. One half hour later, he was resting comfortably.

Had Chaplain Seward not intervened, Matthew might have suffered quietly for hours because of his fear of receiving an injection for post-surgical pain. He was able to trust the chaplain with the truth, perhaps because he sensed in him someone who could be trusted to help, perhaps because the chaplain, as a non-medical person, seemed to be a safer one in whom to confide (the chaplain, after all, never gives injections or other painful treatments), or perhaps just because the chaplain happened by at a time when the boy finally became desperate for pain relief. Whatever the reason, the chaplain became aware of a breakdown in communication between patient and nurse, and helped to get an important message through. In so doing he helped to spare the patient a great deal of physical suffering.

The chaplain will often find himself in the position of being able to function as a liaison between the patient and the medical staff. In fulfilling this function, great caution is to be observed. The chaplain must be careful not to place himself in a position between patient and staff. It is important for the patient to communicate with the medical staff directly, and this should be the primary means of communication. There is a great difference between Matthew's situation, where the chaplain stumbled onto a communication problem, and a situation where a chaplain might set himself up as a go-between. In the former case, the chaplain can be of real help; in the latter, he can actually undermine the good health care which the staff seeks to provide. Even in situations like Matthew's, the chaplain's goal is to help the patient communicate directly with the appropriate medical person; thus, Chaplain Seward called the nurse into the patient's room to talk with him, rather than attempting to assume total responsibility for conveying the necessary information.

In communicating concerns of the patient or about the patient to the medical staff, the chaplain must remain aware of the boundaries imposed by confidentiality. There are no easy guidelines here, except that, in this author's opinion, the confidentiality of a patient's communications with the chaplain is always presumed and given the benefit of the doubt. When the patients are children, the boundaries become even less clear; pre-schoolers, for example, have little real concept of the nature of confidentiality (if the reader is skeptical of this claim, he should attempt to get a four year old to keep a secret). With older children and adolescents, the chaplain should attempt to obtain the permission of the patient before passing on something the patient has told him to other staff members; this was done in the case of Matthew. In soliciting this permission, the chaplain can explain to the child that he hopes to help the situation and how improving communication between patient and staff will help.

In a difficult situation, should the chaplain choose to break a confidence, he should be sure that the need is urgent enough to outweigh the bad effects of the breach of confidentiality. These bad effects may include the following: The chaplain's relationship with the patient may be destroyed; trust may be completely compromised. The patient may feel that he has been violated and his privacy has been invaded (and it may well have). The chaplain may create an awkward situation for the medical staff by giving them information which the patient does not wish them to have, and which they might not be able to act upon. The patient may warn others that the chaplain has violated a confidence, further compromising his ability to minister on the unit. The chaplain, in coming to a decision about whether to break confidentiality, must assess the urgency of the need to communicate, the feelings of the patient, the capability of the (child) patient to understand what confidentiality is, and the probability that breaking confidence will actually lead to good results which in the end benefit the patient. The inexperienced chaplain or minister who confronts this kind of dilemma would benefit from consultation with a fellow professional, especially a medical doctor, psychologist, or clinical social worker, before coming to a final decision.

Our discussion thus far has concerned the conveying of information from patient to staff. What is the chaplain's role in communicating medical information from the staff to the patient? In a word, minimal.

Doris was a fifteen year old girl hospitalized for the removal of several teeth and reconstruction of her mandible. Chaplain Simmons visited her two hours before surgery was scheduled to take place. At that time, Doris was frightened and was particularly apprehensive about anesthesia. She told the chaplain that no one had explained to her what kind of anesthetic she would have, whether general or local, whether intravenous or gaseous, etc. She did not know how long the surgery would take, or where she would be taken when it was over. The chaplain suggested that these questions could be best answered by a nurse, and Doris agreed. With the nurse's help, a preoperative orientation was hastily arranged for Doris, and her surgeon was asked to explain to her the medical procedure which was about to take place. Doris entered surgery greatly relieved.

Chaplain Simmons correctly assessed Doris's greatest need at the time of his visit: she needed to know what was going to happen to her. The lack of information precipitated her anxiety. He acted wisely in not attempting to speculate about details of the upcoming procedure, such as how long it would last or whether Doris would be asleep during surgery. Chaplains ordinarily do not have medical training, and this renders them unqualified to pass on medical information to patients. Their comments which take on medical content should be couched in only the broadest of terms. For example, to the anxious parents of a child who is undergoing open heart surgery, he might say, "Heart surgeries often take quite a while. It's really hard just to sit and wait, isn't it?" Or, to a child who is anticipating a tonsillectomy, the chaplain might comment, "After it's over, your throat will probably be sore. Have you ever had sore throats before?" In each case, the chaplain made a comment and then used the opportunity to draw out the parents or the patient and help them to articulate what they were experiencing or feeling. Remarks such as "This type of surgery is eighty percent successful" or "The doctor will probably prescribe a course of antibiotics for you" are not appropriate coming from the chaplain.

Even in cases where the patient or his family must be told that death is going to occur, it is the responsibility of the medical staff to convey this information. The chaplain might be present with the patient or family at the time to support them. Afterward, he may discuss with them what the medical staff has told them, giving support, pastoral care, and helping them to cope with the medical reality. But it is not the role of the chaplain to explain the medical situation.

The Chaplain as a Symbolic Religious Figure

Rose was a fifteen year old girl hospitalized on an adolescent unit. She had cancer which had metastasized (spread throughout her body) and she was within a week or so of death. She and her parents were committed members of an evangelistic church in another state. Rose asked to have a chaplain come to see her. When Chaplain Ryan came by, Rose asked him to lay hands on her in prayer and cure her cancer. Her parents were supportive of this request. All three looked expectantly at the chaplain.

Chaplain Ryan was confronted with role expectations on the part of the patient and her parents which he believed he could not possibly fulfill. The fact that the patient was of an evangelical tradition, while he himself was a minister of a high church tradition, served only to augment the disparity of their respective ideas about the role of the minister. However, even the minister who cares only for members of his own tradition or congregation will often find that patients or their families will have expectations which he cannot possibly fulfill, or which he chooses not to fulfill.

Ministers are symbolic people. However they regard themselves, other people view them in various ways that may or may not be consistent with the minister's own self-concept. Ministers are looked up to as holy people who are especially close to God. Because of this perception of closeness to God, they are often believed to be filled with special wisdom, possessed of certain, sometimes magical powers, and invulnerable to the struggles and pains which afflict all other human beings. To some people, the minister is larger than life and more than human. Furthermore, a person's concept of God usually influences directly his concept of the minister: if God is viewed as ominous and judgmental, so is the minister; if God is viewed as a loving Father whose tenderness is ever present, the minister is likewise viewed as a loving, affirming person.

When role expectations are in conflict, clarification is the remedy. In this case, Chaplain Ryan explained that he was not a faith healer. He went on to say that he did, however, believe in praying for and with the sick, and that he would be happy to pray with Rose and her parents, asking that God cure her if it were his will to do so. He affirmed his belief in the importance and goodness of prayer, and Rose and her family felt comforted and supported when he prayed with them.

Some families might have been put off by such a clarification. They might have dismissed the chaplain as a person lacking in faith and asked instead to be helped by a minister of their own tradition. In dealing with such a request, the chaplain could help the family to get in touch with a minister of their choice, being careful to follow hospital protocol as he did so.

In Rose's case, however, she and her parents received the chaplain's clarification positively. They said that they were happy to have him pray with them. Chaplain Ryan spent ten minutes reading from the Bible and praying with Rose and her parents, as well as with a friendly nurse whom Rose invited to join in. Afterward, Rose and her parents seemed satisfied and pleased with the experience. In the end, Rose did die of her cancer. Her parents were able to accept her death without bitterness or a crisis in faith. Had Chaplain Ryan made a promise he could not keep—to heal Rose—her parents might have felt betrayed or lacking in their own faith when her death occurred.

The fact that the minister is so often viewed as a symbolic religious figure with special significance is not a bad thing. Precisely because of the significance with which people invest their ministers, their presence in times of distress can provide great comfort. The patients and their families feel that someone important cares about their plight and wants to spend time with them, giving help, encouragement, and support of various kinds. Patients are often calmer and more optimistic after a visit from a religious figure. Often, too, the minister's visit helps them to integrate in a positive fashion the experience of illness with their religious beliefs, beliefs which may be for them of fundamental importance and which may form in part their own self-concept and understanding of life. The chaplain should not seek, therefore, to neutralize his own symbolic importance to the patient and family. Rather, he should be careful to make sure that he does not foster unrealistic expectations on their part, which his failure to achieve could precipitate strong negative feelings.

The Chaplain as a Link
to Institutional Churches

Chaplain Baker was summoned to the hospital in the middle of the night at the request of parents whose two year old son had been critically burned in a house fire. As he was sitting with them, hearing about the fire, the doctor came in to tell the parents that their child would not live. When they heard the news, the mother asked Chaplain Baker to baptize her son before he died. After a brief discussion with them about the nature of baptism and their own religious beliefs, the chaplain and parents dressed in gowns, masks, and gloves (to protect the other patients on the burn unit from infection), and went in to the child, where they were joined by the attending physician and two nurses. In a brief ceremony, using sterilized water provided by one of the nurses, Chaplain Baker baptized the dying child. The parents and medical personnel joined in the prayers, and all were deeply moved.

Chaplains and ministers who work in hospitals will be called upon from time to time to perform official church functions for patients and families. This will be especially true when the patient's family are members of a church which has a belief in sacramental rituals which are outward signs of God's saving presence. In this connection, one thinks immediately of the Roman Catholic Church, but the hospital chaplain should be aware that there are many other church traditions or denominations which profess belief in the importance of sacramental rituals. Hospital chaplains are called upon to baptize, to confirm, to bring holy communion, to pray over and anoint the sick, and even to officiate at funeral services after a patient has died. In fulfilling these functions, chaplains serve as links between patients and institutional churches.

Obviously, a particular chaplain cannot be expected to provide such a link with all of the different denominations. Were a Methodist minister, for example, to attempt to confirm a Catholic child, the Roman Catholic Church would not recognize this act as a valid sacrament. In a similar vein, a Baptist minister could hardly be expected to bring holy communion to Episcopalian patients who do not share his belief in the nature of this sacrament.

Baptism is perhaps the most frequent religious ritual which the chaplain is called upon to perform. When a child is in danger of death, or when his condition is definitely terminal, many parents will seek to have him baptized if this has not already been done. The so-called "high church" traditions tend to emphasize the importance of child baptism; thus Roman Catholic or Episcopalian parents generally have an urgent desire to have a child baptized whose life is imperiled by illness or injury. Other church traditions downplay the importance of child baptism or even dismiss it entirely; parents of these traditions may or may not have a desire to have their dying child baptized. The chaplain involved with a family whose child is in danger of death must enter into dialogue with them in an effort to sound out their feelings on the matter of baptism and to assess its importance for them. He must be most careful to listen to the beliefs and desires of the *family,* and not to foist upon them his own ideas about whether a child should be baptized. In their fear and grief, some parents may believe that baptism has magical significance: grasping at straws to save their dying child, they may believe that baptism is a cure for physical illness. When this occurs, the chaplain should be careful not to encourage such magical thinking or to foster unrealistic expectations on the part of the parents (see above, The Chaplain as a Symbolic Religious Figure). But the chaplain should be ready to respond to the feelings which they express, be they feelings of fear, or perhaps even of guilt and failure.

It is fortunate in the case of baptism that the question of who is to be the minister of the sacrament is usually easily solved. Most church traditions which view baptism as an efficacious sacrament also consider its administration by almost any person to be valid, as long as the minister of the sacrament is sincere in his act and wishes to baptize the child out of respect for his parents' religious beliefs. If necessary, the chaplain can assure the child's parents that he is baptizing the child into their own church, and not the chaplain's. Thus the fact that a child of Presbyterian parents is baptized by an Episcopalian priest does not automatically make the child an Episcopalian.

In this age of increasing inter-communion among the denominations, the chaplain is confronted with a number of questions as he seeks to decide whether to bring holy communion to certain patients. Has the patient been receiving communion in his own church? What beliefs does the patient have about communion? What beliefs does the chaplain have? Are these two belief systems compatible or in conflict? What are the regulations of the chaplain's own church regarding the administration of holy communion? Does the patient really desire to receive communion, or does the chaplain (or parents, or other family members) desire that the patient receive communion? The hospital chaplain must be careful to respect not only the religious beliefs of the patient, but those of his own church tradition as well. The Roman Catholic priest, for example, knows that his own church is skeptical of inter-communion and sees it as a rare exception rather than as a common practice. Finally, the chaplain must be careful not to administer communion in the form of food or drink unless the patient is able to consume them; pre-operative patients, for example, generally have a period of time when they are allowed absolutely nothing to eat or drink. When patients are not allowed to consume anything, a warning sign is placed in the room or on its door reading "NPO," the initials standing for *non per os,* Latin for "nothing by mouth." Whenever there is any doubt about whether a patient may eat or drink, the chaplain should check with his nurse before administering communion.

The desirability of the chaplain performing other religious rituals with patients must be evaluated carefully in each individual case. The chaplain must seek to keep a balance among various factors: the patient's religious beliefs, those of the chaplain, the realities of the medical situation, the needs and desires of the patient and his family, and the limits which may be imposed by the clinical setting and the treatment which the patient is undergoing. Because chaplains in hospitals usually minister to patients of various religious persuasions, flexibility on the chaplain's part is essential. In those cases where the particular chaplain is unable to fulfill the religious needs of the patient, he may best be of aid by helping him to be in contact with a minister of his own tradition who can fulfill those needs.

Tommy was an eight year old Roman Catholic boy admitted to the hospital in the terminal stages of acute leukemia. Tommy and his parents wanted him to receive his first communion, a significant religious milestone for Roman Catholics, before he died. Sister Jean,

*a Catholic nun on the pastoral care staff of the hospital, was asked
to assist Tommy and his family. Sister Jean met with Tommy once
a day for a few days to give him the instruction that Catholic children
are required to have before receiving this sacrament. She was even
able to obtain a child's workbook such as Tommy would have used
had he been in Sunday school. When Sister Jean and his parents felt
that Tommy was adequately prepared for first communion, a small
sacramental celebration was held in his hospital room. Thereafter,
Tommy received communion frequently, until he died about two
weeks later.*

In this case, the patient had a specific religious need that a chaplain of his own faith was able to satisfy. Had his death been even
more imminent, Sister Jean probably would have dispensed with any
attempts at formal instruction and given Tommy his first communion immediately. As it was, her consultation with his physician and
parents indicated that he had at least several days, and perhaps even
several weeks, to live; given this time, she concluded that a brief period of instruction would be helpful for the child. Tommy was confined to his hospital room and thus cut off from his own religious
community. Nevertheless, Sister Jean was able to provide a number
of links between Tommy and his church: a short course of formal instruction similar to that which his friends were receiving in Sunday
school; a child's workbook such as he would have used at home; and,
when the time was right, the actual celebration of his first communion. These links were important to Tommy and his family and
helped foster for them a sense of connectedness with their church.
This fulfilled a need which they felt with especial keenness when
they were facing the crisis of impending death.

*Betty was a twelve year old girl suffering from cystic fibrosis, a
childhood disease whose course is long and ultimately fatal. During
the several weeks that she stayed in this hospital, Betty and her family came to know Chaplain Dunn. They were not affiliated with any
particular church, and told the chaplain that they professed no formal religious creed. They did say that they believed in a "good and
powerful God who created the world and watches over all of us." They
often asked Chaplain Dunn to pray with them during his visits to the
hospital room. When Betty died, they told him that they wanted to
have a religious funeral service. Since they had no contacts with any
other clergy, they asked Chaplain Dunn to officiate. He readily com-*

plied, and, together with Betty's parents, planned services for the funeral home chapel and the graveside.

It is not uncommon for a hospital chaplain to become particularly close to a patient's family during a prolonged hospitalization. When death occurs, it becomes natural for the family to desire the chaplain's participation in their rituals of mourning, and the chaplain may well share this desire. Even families who have a religious affiliation and a minister or pastor of their own may invite the hospital chaplain to participate in or even officiate at funeral services for the deceased patient. While the chaplain will need to be realistic about his work load and his ability to be part of funeral services, it is important to remember that pastoral care of a patient's family does not cease immediately when the patient dies. In addition, chaplains will want to take care of their own emotional needs. Mourning for a child by participating in funeral services may be an important activity for the chaplain as he seeks to deal with his own pain at the time of loss.

The Chaplain as an Ethical Consultant

Frances was a six month old girl hospitalized in Intensive Care for treatment of a severe viral infection. She soon ceased to breathe on her own and was placed on a respirator. As the infection continued unabated, her kidneys, her liver, and finally her brain stopped functioning. At the end of a week she was still on the respirator and an electroencephalogram showed no brain activity. At this point the attending physician suggested to her mother, a single parent, that heroic measures to save Frances' life be stopped, because there was no longer any hope of recovery. He wanted to give a "no code" order so that when her heart stopped beating, no measures would be taken to resuscitate her. Her mother trusted the doctor, but had questions about whether the no code order would be morally acceptable. Chaplain Gray was called in to assist the mother in making this decision. Chaplain Gray happened to share the same religious affiliation as the mother, and therefore could speak with some authority about the moral teaching of their church. She reassured Frances' mother that the doctor's suggestion was not only morally acceptable, but, given the circumstances, the preferred course of action. She assured her that her decision to follow the doctor's recommendation was not wrong. The mother was at peace with her decision to allow the no code order, and shortly thereafter Frances died.

Chaplains or ministers are often looked to by patients or families who are presented with a moral dilemma in the hospital. Frequently they are regarded as people who can assist the family in "knowing what God would want us to do in this situation." At other times, families regard chaplains not as interpreters of the divine will, but simply as trained moralists who are able to give wise counsel about the appropriate way of handling a medical problem, especially at a time when their own emotions prevent their objective assessment of the situation. When the chaplain and the patient's family share the same or at least similar religious traditions, giving advice which does not offend the family's religious sensibilities is easier.

The field of ethics and moral decision making is a specialized one, and the area of medical ethics is more specialized still. To further complicate matters, various religious traditions arrive at different answers to the same medico-moral dilemmas. No attempt can be made here even to survey the important medical ethics literature; the interested reader should embark on his own course of study within his own religious tradition. A general principle of medical ethics, however, is held and promoted by this author: Good medicine is good ethics. Concretely, this means that generally the chaplain or minister can support in good conscience the consensus of medical experts who are working on a case, and that, further, their good will and good intentions toward the patient are to be presumed. The non-specialist in the field of medical ethics should be extremely cautious about suggesting to families that the health care team's consensus about the management of a certain case could be immoral.

Ellen was a four year old girl hospitalized for the surgical removal of a brain tumor. When the time came for her parents to sign the consent forms, her mother told the neurosurgeon that she was a member of a religious sect that believed blood transfusions to be morally wrong. Therefore, the mother said, she could not sign consent forms which allowed a transfusion to take place. The surgeon, on his part, believed that a transfusion would be necessary to save Ellen's life, and he felt that he could not operate unless he felt free to give her one. Ellen's father was in favor of giving the doctor permission for the transfusion, but did not know how to deal with his wife's objections. Chaplain Eastman was asked to see the parents and attempt to help them out of their dilemma. In the meantime, the medical staff began making plans to request a court order for the transfusion if parental consent could not be obtained.

Chaplain Eastman found himself in the awkward position of being asked to give ethical advice to a mother who had not asked for it. He disagreed strongly with the mother's belief about blood transfusions, yet he felt that it was not proper for him to enter into debate with her or to challenge the validity of her faith. He saw himself as one who was there to offer help and support, rather than as a moral arbiter who decides what is best for others to believe and to do.

When Chaplain Eastman introduced himself to Ellen's parents, he told them that he knew of the problem about the blood transfusion. He explained that he had not come to argue with the mother or to put pressure on her. Rather, he said, he wanted to offer his personal support to both parents and to ask them if he could in any way be of help. Ellen's mother was relieved that the chaplain had not come to do battle. She asked him to stay and talk with her. She went on to explain that she had worked out a compromise herself, one which she hoped would be satisfactory to all: she would allow her husband to sign all of the consent forms, and while she herself would not sign them, neither would she offer any opposition.

Chaplain Eastman sensed in Ellen's mother a conflict between wanting to uphold the religious ideals which she professed and wanting to do everything conceivable to save the life of her child. She had found a way to "let herself off the hook," a way which proved to be satisfactory to all concerned. Chaplain Eastman supported her efforts to find a solution, and in this way avoided taking on any antagonistic or adversarial roles. Ellen's mother declined the chaplain's offer to pray with her, but did say that she needed his continued presence and personal support, which he readily gave. She was grateful to him for not attempting to challenge her religious beliefs.

When a patient or family come to the chaplain with a medical ethics dilemma, they are almost always facing a crisis. When people are in a crisis situation, it is not the time to challenge their religious beliefs or to catechize them according to doctrines that the chaplain accepts. In such times, they need support and nurture more than confrontation and challenge. If the chaplain shares their church affiliation, or at least is aware of their church's moral teachings which are relevant to the care of the patient, he should seek to clarify for them what their own tradition says; it is improper for him, however, to challenge what that tradition says and argue with the patient's family. Pastoral care in a hospital setting includes neither proselytizing nor academic debate.

Conclusion

The chaplain's effectiveness in the clinical setting will be weakened to the extent that he is unclear about his proper role there. While it would be difficult, if not altogether impossible, to define pastoral care in such a way that all church denominations would accept, the minister working in the hospital legitimately takes on certain roles as he provides pastoral care to patients and their families. These roles include friend, surrogate parent, liaison, symbolic religious figure, link to institutional churches, and ethical consultant. Some chaplains will feel comfortable in any of these roles; others will select some and eschew others. The religious background of the patient's family, their needs, the religious background of the chaplain, and his position as a member of the health care team are the basic factors which will determine the shape of pastoral care in the hospital. It is to the last factor, the chaplain's position as a member of the health care team, that we now turn.

RECOMMENDED READING

Ashley, Benedict M., O.P. and Kevin D. O'Rourke, O.P. *Health Care Ethics: A Theological Analysis.* St. Louis: The Catholic Hospital Association, 1978.

Clinebell, Howard. *Basic Types of Pastoral Care & Counseling.* Nashville: Abingdon, 1984.

Curran, Charles E. *Issues in Sexual and Medical Ethics.* Notre Dame: University of Notre Dame, 1978.

Hardgrove, Carol B. *Parents and Children in the Hospital: The Family's Role in Pediatrics.* Boston: Little, Brown, 1972.

Holifield, E. Brooks. *A History of Pastoral Care in America.* Nashville: Abingdon, 1983.

Kennedy, Eugene. *On Becoming a Counselor: A Basic Guide for Non-Professional Counselors.* New York: Seabury, 1977.

Lee, Ronald R. *Clergy and Clients: The Practice of Pastoral Psychotherapy.* New York: Seabury, 1980.

Natale, Samuel M., S.J. *Pastoral Counselling: Reflections and Concerns.* New York: Paulist, 1977.

3.

The Chaplain as a Member
of the Health Care Team

Introduction

Chaplains Zellig and Hart sat down together over lunch in the hospital cafeteria. Chaplain Hart was new on the job, and began to express great frustration and dissatisfaction with his working situation. He complained that the staff was not cooperative: they were reluctant to discuss patients with him; his visits in patients' rooms were often interrupted. He experienced some of the nurses as aloof and uninterested in his contributions. He did not feel that his presence was valued. In contrast, Chaplain Zellig responded by expressing her happiness with hospital work. She felt that she was regarded as a valued member of the health care team. She told of how doctors and nurses often asked her to consult on a case. Staff members often responded to her chart notes about patients. Frequently she was invited to attend rounds and interdisciplinary conferences about problem cases. She experienced the staff as friendly and supportive of her work in the hospital.

Hearing the stories of the two chaplains, one could be led to conclude that they worked in two different hospitals, or at least in two different wings of the same institution. However, the difference in the chaplains' respective experiences was the result not of two separate clinical settings, but of their own very different operating styles. Chaplain Zellig was able successfully to become a valued member of the health care team; Chaplain Hart was not. His lack of success was caused by his own approach to the job.

In this chapter we will take a look at the role of the chaplain as a member of the health care team. Although this book as a whole has been prepared for any minister who visits children in the hospital, this chapter pertains only to those whose presence in the hospital is frequent and regular. It is written especially for those who are actually members of pastoral care departments of hospitals.

It is difficult to imagine how the minister of a church who visits the hospital only occasionally can become a member of the health care team in the sense described below. This is not to say that the occasional presence of ministers from the broader community is not necessary and valuable, for indeed it is. But the minister who works in the community and visits the hospital on an infrequent basis will have a more modest role *vis-à-vis* the health care team than is described here.

A Member of the Team

The chaplain who desires truly to be a member of the health care team must be prepared to make commitments to that team. He must plan to devote time to being with other members of the team, not only for the proximate purpose of providing care to patients and their families, but also to establish relationships—relationships on which may be built mutual trust and positive regard. It is not absolutely necessary for a chaplain to be on friendly terms with other members of the team, but if he is not, his work will be hindered. Professional efficiency aside, it is also more pleasant to work with people with whom one enjoys some degree of friendship and mutual acceptance. All of this requires a commitment of time and energy.

Being a member of a team means sharing with other members. In the clinical setting, health care team members must learn to share resources such as space and funding. They must share available time so that each person will have the contact he needs with patients. They must share information, for it is rare for just one member of the team to have all of the relevant facts about a case. Further, sharing almost always means compromise. Members of any effective team have learned to compromise, to be willing to put aside personal preferences in favor of the needs and desires of others and for the greater good of the patient. For example, when pre-operative time with a patient is limited, various team members will have to find a way to divide that time up, so that each may perform his job; it may well be that no one gets the full amount of time with the patient that he would like to have, and such compromises must be made with a willing spirit.

An important part of being on a team is supporting the other team members. Attitudes of encouragement, trust, positive regard, and respect help make any team function smoothly and efficiently. The chaplain who is able to convey such positive attitudes toward other team members will find them returned toward himself.

The health care team is a professional team. Each of the members has received specialized training to enable him to perform certain specific functions. The chaplain, too, should have received specialized training in areas such as theology, ethics, and clinical pastoral care. In the hospital he becomes a significant and even symbolic person for patient, family, and staff. Precisely because his training is in non-medical areas, he brings to the health care setting unique insights and abilities. The chaplain who is able to employ these in ways which are supportive to other members of the team will be well received and even sought after. His presence as a contributing member of the team will be valued highly.

Getting Acquainted

As the chaplain begins his work in a hospital, he will want to become acquainted with as many other staff members as possible. It is especially important for him to spend time on the units where he will be working. As he makes his rounds, he should make it a point to introduce himself to other staff members and to remember their names. When time permits, he will want to become involved in informal discussions; these will help lay the foundation of friendship which will greatly facilitate his work as time goes by.

The chaplain will be valued more highly by the staff if he shows an active interest in patients and their families. Merely performing the functions which his position requires will not elicit anyone's admiration! But the chaplain who inquires about patients' conditions, their treatments, progress, and prognosis demonstrates a real concern for the welfare of other human beings which reaches beyond the requirements of the job.

In a similar way, the chaplain will strengthen his relationships with other team members if he shows concern about their work as well as his own. When he asks others how their work is going and responds supportively to their answers, he begins to create a professional alliance which not only facilitates his work, but helps the patients as well. Such acts of support and interest help other staff members to take the chaplain seriously and to feel willing to share with him important information about patients. He, in turn, can share his own insights, and this exchange of information benefits the patients.

As he begins his work in a hospital, the chaplain should make it a point when entering a unit always to check in with the head nurse. He should introduce himself and state his intentions: "Good morning. I'm Chaplain Jones from the Pastoral Care Department, and I'd like to see Jimmy Smith in 212." Or, "I'm making rounds this morning, and I'd like to check in on some of the patients on this unit." Such an introduction accomplishes a number of things. First, it allows the head nurse, who is responsible for the unit, to know who is coming and going and being with the patients. For some unit heads more than others, this kind of knowledge is important for their sense of having adequate control over the units for which they are responsible. Second, it provides the chaplain with an opportunity to ensure that his time with patients will be quality time. If he wants to have time with a certain patient, it is wise to inquire whether any procedures are scheduled; otherwise, he might be interrupted while the patient is taken to have x-rays, physical therapy, etc. Third, the chaplain may take the opportunity to inquire of the nurse whether she knows of any patients or families who are in special need of pastoral care. Fourth, it gives the nurse an opportunity to bring up any areas on her own agenda. For example, she might have follow-up comments about the chaplain's visit with a patient the previous day.

As the chaplain continues his work on a unit, he will want to broaden his contacts to include other staff members in similar exchanges. For example, a primary care nurse is often assigned to each patient; it can be helpful for the chaplain to speak with primary care nurses before he visits their patients. Or, he may find that the child life workers or "playladies" on a particular unit know a lot about the patients, and he may find conversations with them to be fruitful. The broader a chaplain's contacts among the staff, and the more lines of communications which he establishes, the more efficient and satisfying his work will be.

Building Trust

While making his rounds on a surgical unit, Chaplain Xavier stopped in to see a ten year old boy who had undergone abdominal surgery two days before. He found the boy to be alert but uncommunicative. Chaplain Xavier tried for ten minutes to engage the boy in conversation, but never succeeded. Before leaving the unit, he decided to check in with the boy's primary care nurse and to tell her of his frustrating experience. She seemed surprised at first to hear the story, and then exclaimed, "I thought it might have been just me! He won't talk to me, either." As other members of the staff were consulted, it became apparent that the patient was quite withdrawn. Ultimately, a psychiatric consult was requested, and the boy began to receive emotional help.

Difficulties such as Chaplain Xavier's provide unique opportunities for the chaplain to build up trust with other team members. Had the chaplain been defensive about his lack of success with the patient and been embarrassed to mention it, it is possible that the psychiatric consultation would never have taken place. Be that as it may, his willingness to share his frustration with another member of the staff was instrumental in creating an alliance between himself and the primary care nurse. His own gesture of trust toward the nurse invited her to take a similar risk and to share her own apprehensions about working with this patient. Their mutual support made it easier for them to consult other team members, with good results in the end. Chaplain Xavier's experience with this particular case is not at all unusual in the clinical setting. Trust begets trust, and creative alliances among health care team members tend to draw in other members—a snowball effect takes place. Conversely, the chaplain who attempts to hide his own doubts and insecurities by always appearing to be completely in control and all-knowing will find it difficult to elicit trust from other team members. They might see such a person as intimidating, pretentious, or even out of touch with reality; however a completely self-assured front is interpreted by others, it will not encourage an open sharing of information.

Chaplain Lang was visiting Mr. Gant, the father of an eight year old girl hospitalized for diagnostic testing. In their conversation, the chaplain asked Mr. Gant if she could be of help to him during the hospital stay. He replied in great anger, "Yes, you sure can! My daughter's nurse is terrible! She never comes when we call. She handles my daughter roughly. I don't think she is the kind of person who should be allowed to be around children. I know you're just the chaplain, but is there something you can do?" Chaplain Lang's response was non-judgmental vis-à-vis the nurse, but she did acknowledge Mr. Gant's feelings of anger and encourage him to talk more about what elements of the situation were so frustrating. After sharing this with him, she assured him that she would look into the matter. Approaching the nurse in question, Chaplain Lang introduced herself and explained that she had just visited with Mr. Gant. She said, "He is very angry and upset today. He seems to feel that his daughter is not getting the kind of care she needs. I'm really not sure what would satisfy him. Have you had any problems with him?" The nurse replied that indeed she had; Mr. Gant had been angry and rude whenever she entered the patient's room; she herself was getting angry. Chaplain Lang answered, "Sounds like you're having a hard time with him. I wonder if Mr. Meyer [the hospital's patient representative] might be a help to us." When the nurse responded positively to this suggestion, Chaplain Lang asked her if she would be willing to place the call to Mr. Meyer. She agreed to do so. "In the meantime," the chaplain continued, "can I be of help to you in any way?" "Not really," the nurse answered, "but I am glad that we talked about it." Checking back in with Mr. Gant, Chaplain Lang assured him that the hospital's patient representative would be by to discuss the problem.

Chaplain Lang's experience with Mr. Gant was a crisis in the making. Depending upon how she responded, she could have built up a relationship of trust with the nurse and other team members, or helped to create an atmosphere of mistrust and defensiveness. It was important that Chaplain Lang respond sympathetically to Mr. Gant's complaints, but at the same time not subvert his daughter's medical care by casting any aspersions on medical personnel. Had she replied, for example, "I've heard that about that nurse! She really shouldn't be around kids," Mr. Gant's confidence in the health care team's ability to help would have been further undermined; his daughter's confidence also would have been compromised, and this would have been equally as serious. When the patient loses confidence in the health care team's ability to help, harm results because the patient-caretaker alliance is damaged. Furthermore, Mr. Gant might have used the chaplain's comments further to support his own argument, making resolution more difficult. Instead, the chaplain actually supported both the father and the other members of the health care team by dealing with his anger in a sympathetic and constructive manner.

Similarly, it was important for Chaplain Lang to state the problem to the nurse using non-judgmental language. Statements such as "Mr. Gant says you aren't nice to his daughter," or "I am concerned that this patient is not receiving adequate care," would have been counter-productive, as well as unfair to the nurse. Instead, the chaplain attempted to support her own alliance with the nurse and to treat the situation as a management problem rather than as a personal issue.

In this case, all concerned were fortunate that the hospital had a patient representative, Mr. Meyer, whose job it was to help resolve conflict between patients, their families, and staff members. Being a skilled and loyal member of the health care team, the medical staff had learned to have confidence in his support of them; they had come to view him as a safe person who was truly able to help in conflict situations. As the chaplain's role does not include serving as referee between patients and staff, it was appropriate for Chaplain Lang to suggest consultation with the patient representative. Furthermore, by suggesting that the nurse actually make contact with Mr. Meyer, the chaplain was able to avoid any appearance of interfering or of telling tales. This left the primary care nurse in control of managing the case, which was proper.

This episode helped to build trust between Chaplain Lang and the nursing staff. She was viewed by them as someone who could be counted on to be empathetic, non-judgmental, and overtly supportive of them. This building up of trust greatly facilitated the chaplain's work on the unit. A different approach to this crisis, however, could have radically undercut the chaplain's relationship with other staff members, and hence, her effectiveness on the unit.

Nurses: The Chaplain's Best Friends

We have stated how important it is for the chaplain to develop relationships with other members of the health care team. This is particularly important in the case of nurses. The chaplain will find his relationships with nurses to be especially valuable because of all the team members, it is the nurses who are closest to the patients. They tend to spend more time with patients than other team members and to have a broader and more complete understanding of the patients than others. Because she spends her time on the unit with patients, the nurse's information about them is usually "up to the minute." In addition, on pediatric units the nurses often have extensive and valuable contact with the patients' parents and other family members.

As he arrives on a unit and checks in, the chaplain will want to ask the nurses for information. They are helpful in explaining the

nature of the patient's disease or injury, the treatments and procedures used, as well as their schedule. Nurses can help the chaplain
to understand in human terms what the patient or family has been
experiencing in the hospital. They can tell him what mood the patient is in, whether he is groggy from drugs, in pain, disoriented,
bored, angry, etc. They can help the chaplain find quality time to
spend with the patient by alerting him to scheduled procedures or to
the patient's vacillating alertness. They can inform the chaplain of
the patient's prognosis, i.e., the likely outcome of his disease; it is
important for the chaplain to know before he enters a child's room
whether or not he is expected to recover, and what time frame is realistic. The nurses often know when family members will visit the
patient, and what their concerns are. The chaplain who is beginning
his work on a unit may find that the nurses are hesitant to share
important information with him. Some may believe that he does not
need to know, or does not care to, or that medical information is none
of his business. But the chaplain who approaches the staff in a
friendly and supportive way and who displays a genuine interest in
the patients will find a bond of trust developing between himself and
the staff, and as that happens they will communicate more openly
with him. The chaplain should not be shy about asking nurses for
information which he believes will help him in his work.

Nurses can also function as valuable liaisons between the chaplain and other members of the health care team, particularly physicians whose presence on the unit may be restricted to just a few
minutes a day. For example, in the case of Doris, the fifteen year old
girl who faced surgery but desperately needed to be informed about
the details, it was her nurse who contacted the surgeon and arranged
for the appropriate explanations. Similarly, when Chaplain Xavier
believed that a psychiatric consultation was indicated for a patient,
it was the primary care nurse who made the official request. Whenever the chaplain feels that he must communicate some information
about a patient to another member of the team, nurses can be helpful
in establishing the necessary contacts.

Charting Information On Patients

In the hospital setting, records for each patient are kept in a special binder at the nurses' station. The binder of notes for each patient
is called his chart, and notes written there are called chart notes. In
most hospitals, the charts are divided into sections such as History,

Doctors' Orders, Progress Notes, Nurses' Notes, etc. Many hospitals include a special section for use by chaplains. The chaplain who works in a hospital where this is not done may wish to request that a special chaplain's section be added to the hospital charts. The information recorded in the charts is for professional use only. Therefore, the chaplain should neither hand a chart to a patient nor read his chart and tell him what is written in it. Patients with questions about the contents of their charts should be referred instead to their nurse. The chaplain should remember that it is not his function to communicate medical information to the patient.

As the chaplain visits patients, he will find from time to time that he has important information to convey to other members of the medical staff. Even though he does so verbally, there will be times when such information should be put in writing. For example, some hospitals have a policy that every time a patient receives Holy Communion, this should be noted in his chart, since he has consumed food. Or, the chaplain may want to make sure that all members of the health care team are aware of a certain piece of information, and writing it in the chart helps to ensure this.

Chaplains may or may not be given access to patients' charts in the hospital where they work. If they are denied this access, they may ask nurses to record in the charts for them the information which they wish to convey. If the chaplain is given access to the chart, but there is no special section for him, he may write his notes in the Progress Notes section. In addition, reading through a patient's chart can be a great help to the chaplain who wishes better to understand him. Again, information in the chart is for professional use only.

Whenever a chaplain makes a chart note, certain elements should be included: the date, time, and approximate length of his visit, the purpose of the visit, any information which he wishes to convey to the staff (particularly the administration of sacraments to the patient), recommendations or requests that the chaplain has, his plans for continued contact with the patient, his signature, and his position in the hospital (so that other staff members who wish to consult him may locate him easily). Chart notes should be brief and as objective as possible. Many members of the health care team who read charts are busy people, and they do not have time to read a lot of useless material. The chaplain will convey his information more effectively if he states his point briefly and clearly than if he writes an essay about the patient.

Chaplain Evans was summoned to the hospital in the middle of the night at the request of the parents of a dying infant. When he arrived, they asked him immediately to baptize their baby. Since death was imminent, he did so right away, and afterward spent time with the parents in a nearby conference room.

Below are two sample chart notes that Chaplain Evans could have written about his visit. The first example is too long and is filled with irrelevant information; the second is too brief and uninformative; the third conveys the information more appropriately.

Sunday, September 9, 2:00 a.m.

I was awakened from a sound sleep by the unit clerk on the intensive care unit. She told me that the patient's blood pressure was going down and that things looked pretty bad. The doctors were there but there seemed to be little hope that the patient would survive. She had talked with the parents, and they wanted a priest to come and to baptize the baby. So the unit clerk called me. I came over to the hospital. The patient's parents wanted to have him baptized, which I did. The nurses were very nice and provided the sterile water for me to use. Afterward, I talked for about a half hour with the parents. They are quite distraught, but I think they are doing about as well as could be expected under the circumstances. They told me that they attend St. Luke's Catholic Church, where she is a member of the Ladies' Guild. I told them that I would call their pastor, Fr. Murphy, to tell him that their child was in the hospital. If the child does not survive, he will probably handle the funeral. I had a good visit with the parents, and I am glad that I was called.

Fr. John Evans
Pastoral Care Department

Sunday, September 9, 2:00 a.m.
Patient baptized.

Fr. John Evans
Pastoral Care Department

Sunday, September 9, 2:00 a.m.

Summoned to the hospital at the request of the patient's parents, who wanted him to be baptized before he died. After the baptism, I spent about thirty minutes with them. They are members of St. Luke's Catholic Church, which will provide for funeral arrange-

ments. I will visit the parents daily while the patient is hospitalized, and will offer follow-up pastoral care.

Fr. John Evans
Pastoral Care Department

In writing chart notes, the chaplain aims at achieving not only
brevity, but objectivity as well. In reporting significant events, he
should avoid unnecessary interpretation and simply state the facts
as objectively as possible.

*Chaplain Davis was visiting Larry, an eight year old hospital-
ized with a broken leg, which was in traction. As she talked with the
child, his mother entered the room. Almost immediately, Larry began to cry loudly and threw the objects in his bed around the room.
His mother quickly left the room. After she had gone, Larry told the
chaplain that he was angry with his mother, but would not say why.
When Chaplain Davis attempted to find Larry's mother, he learned
that she had left the hospital.*

Below are two possible versions of Chaplain Davis' chart note
about this incident. The first is inappropriate because of attempts at
interpretation of the episode and lack of objectivity. The second conveys the necessary information more appropriately.

Tuesday, October 1, 11:00 a.m.

During my visit with the patient, his mother entered the room. Apparently she had been at home or at work. When Larry saw her,
he began to cry hysterically. He was filled with blind anger, and
violently threw the objects in his bed around the room. His mother
was frightened and horrified and ran out of the room. Larry told
me he was angry at her, but he belligerently refused to tell me
why—I think because it embarrasses him. There is obviously a
family problem here. When I finished with Larry, I found out his
mother had left the hospital, so I was not able to talk with her. I
think a psychiatrist should be consulted. I plan to call the patient's
mother and ask her what is going on.

Chaplain Ellen Davis
Department of Pastoral Care

Tuesday, October 1, 11:00 a.m.

During my visit with the patient, his mother entered the room. Almost immediately, Larry began to cry loudly. He threw the objects
in his bed around the room. His mother said nothing, but quickly
left the room. I stayed with Larry, who stopped crying and throw-
ing things and told me that he was angry with his mother. He

would not tell any more about it or why he was angry. When I attempted to follow up with his mother, I discovered that she had already left the hospital. I suggest that a psychiatric consultation be requested. I plan to contact the patient's mother in order to offer pastoral care. I will continue to visit the patient daily during his hospitalization.

Chaplain Ellen Davis
Department of Pastoral Care

Finally, the chaplain should attempt in his charting to respect the confidentiality expected of him by the patient and at the same time to convey information which the medical staff might need to know. The chaplain must make a judgment about the level of confidentiality required. Consulting the patient about conveying certain information can be most liberating: in the author's experience, older children often gave him more freedom to communicate material than he would have presumed to have. When in doubt, the chaplain should err on the side of prudence, not revealing material which the patient might wish to be kept confidential.

Albert was a seventeen year old hospitalized with a history of headaches. At the time that Chaplain Forbes first met him, the staff had concluded that the headaches had no organic cause and were beginning to treat the case as a psychiatric one. During their conversation, Albert spoke at length about his poor self-image. He saw himself as a weak, effeminate person who did not merit respect from others. He was particularly concerned about a history of homosexual encounters with an older friend. He asked the chaplain not only about the morality of such acts, but whether they meant that he was homosexual. He stressed that no one else knew about this, and that if his parents found out they might disown him. He was particularly fearful of his father finding out, since Albert viewed him as uncompromisingly tough and masculine. Chaplain Forbes listened sympathetically, gave Albert moral advice, and encouraged him to share his experiences and his doubts about his sexual orientation with his psychiatrist, explaining that it was a psychiatrist's job to help people with this kind of doubts (i.e., doubts about identity).

In the two sample chart notes below, the first goes too far in giving information, thereby violating the patient's explicit wish for confidentiality. The second alerts the staff to the significance of the chaplain's conversation with Albert, but does not violate confidentiality.

Wednesday, November 12, 2:30 p.m.

I spent an hour with the patient today. He told me that he has doubts about his sexual orientation. He has had a series of homosexual experiences with an older friend, and this has led him to believe that he might be a homosexual. His self-esteem is low, and he does not feel he deserves anyone's respect. I encouraged him to share all of this with his psychiatrist. At the patient's request, I will continue to see him about three times a week during his hospitalization.

Chaplain Harry Forbes
Pastoral Care Department

Wednesday, November 12, 2:30 p.m.

I spent an hour with the patient today discussing issues surrounding his self-image and sense of masculinity. I encouraged him to share his concerns openly with his psychiatrist. At the patient's request, I will continue to see him about three times a week during his hospitalization.

Chaplain Harry Forbes
Pastoral Care Department

The chaplain who is able to write chart notes properly and insightfully will find that this facilitates his ministry to patients and their families, as well as fostering good relationships with other members of the health care team.

Pulling with the Team

It has been the author's position that the minister may function as a valuable member of the health care team. The following two episodes are narrated in support of this position. In each case, we see a hospital chaplain functioning usefully as a member of the health care team. The narratives not only report actual clinical experience, but are suggestive of how chaplains may work creatively in similar situations. Because the stories speak for themselves, little comment is necessary. In each case we find a chaplain assessing religious beliefs and needs, providing pastoral care as a representative of an institutional church, acting as liaison between the medical staff and the patient's family, and giving friendly support.

Chaplain Tyson received a call from the hospital at 4:30 in the morning. A five year old girl had been shot accidentally in the head.

It was the hospital's policy automatically to call in a chaplain in such emergencies. When he arrived on the emergency unit, he was met by the unit coordinator, who asked him to assess the religious needs of the patient's mother, to provide necessary pastoral care, and to be a personal support to her. The patient's mother, Mrs. Haskins, was a single parent. She had come to the hospital with her sister, and the two women were in a conference room on the unit.

Chaplain Tyson entered the conference room and found Mrs. Haskins and her sister there. Mrs. Haskins seemed to be in a state of shock: she stared vacantly at the wall, took little notice of things around her, and spoke very slowly and almost inaudibly. After introducing himself, Chaplain Tyson asked her what had happened. Slowly but steadily, she explained that a burglar had broken into her apartment. When Mrs. Haskins discovered him, he fled, shooting wildly with a pistol as he went. One bullet went through a plaster wall and struck her sleeping daughter in the back of the head. The bullet entered deeply into the child's brain.

While she was telling her story, the attending physician entered the conference room. Sitting down, he said, "I'm afraid your daughter is not going to live." As Mrs. Haskins recoiled in horror, the chaplain took her hand and held it tightly in his own. The doctor went on to explain that the bullet had severed a major artery in the brain and had badly damaged the brain stem. He added that the child was unconscious and was not experiencing any pain.

After a few moments, the doctor went on to explain that the little girl's kidneys were needed for possible transplantation into other children. He asked Mrs. Haskins if she would like to donate her daughter's kidneys. Mrs. Haskins seemed confused, and looked questioningly at the chaplain. He explained, "There are other children who need kidney transplants. Your daughter's kidneys are healthy, and the doctors might be able to put them into other children. If they could do this, it would help those other children. This is a choice that you can make. No one will take your daughter's kidneys unless you give them permission to do that." After a moment of consideration, Mrs. Haskins expressed her wish to donate her daughter's kidneys. The doctor had the forms brought in for her to sign, and explained that it would take about an hour before they would be ready to take the child to the operating room to remove her kidneys.

After the doctor left the room, Chaplain Tyson asked Mrs. Haskins if she belonged to a church. When she indicated that she was Roman Catholic, he asked whether he wanted him to call a priest, or whether her daughter should have any sacraments. Mrs. Haskins nodded and asked the chaplain to baptize her daughter, as this had never been done. He told her that he would speak to the staff to make the arrangements for baptism, and would return shortly.

The chaplain spoke with the unit coordinator and explained that Mrs. Haskins wanted to have her daughter baptized. He asked if Mrs. Haskins could be present for this. The coordinator answered affirmatively and went into the treatment room to prepare things. When all was ready, the coordinator and Chaplain Tyson went to the conference room and accompanied Mrs. Haskins into the treatment room where her daughter lay (Mrs. Haskins' sister had meanwhile left the unit to contact relatives). On the way, the coordinator explained to her that many tubes had been put in her daughter and that there was a lot of blood. She reiterated that the child was in no pain.

In the treatment room the little girl lay on her back, naked, on top of the treatment table. On her stomach was a tangle of tubes which led to various places in her body. Several bags of whole blood and clear fluids hung on intravenous poles around the table. A nurse stood beside the table, holding a bag of blood in each hand. As she squeezed the bags rhythmically, blood was forced through the tubes into the little girl's body. A respiratory technician held a clear plastic mask over her face and ventilated her lungs by squeezing a plastic ball which was connected to the mask. The bullet had entered the back of her skull, and from the wound exited a steady flow of blood. This formed a pool around her head, and padding had been arranged to form a sort of dam to keep the blood from running onto the floor. Even so, there were large spots of blood on the floor, and much of the equipment in the room was smeared with it. The child's face was unharmed by the wound, and looked quite normal; she was a pretty girl. Other medical staff circulated around the room, quietly doing their jobs. The atmosphere was urgent but calm.

As they approached the treatment table, Mrs. Haskins hung back, as if afraid to approach. The chaplain and unit coordinator each took her hand, and the coordinator assured her that it was all right to approach the table and to touch her daughter. Gingerly she caressed the child's face, beginning to cry and moan softly. After a few moments, Chaplain Tyson asked if she were ready to have her child baptized. She nodded, and he baptized her in a brief and simple ceremony. At the end, he invited all present to join in the Lord's Prayer, which they did.

For the next forty-five minutes, Mrs. Haskins and the chaplain stood by the table, waiting for the child to be taken up to the operating room. During this time Mrs. Haskins did a great deal of grieving work. She cried and rocked back and forth as she called her daughter's name. She caressed and kissed the child repeatedly and at times bent over to hold her. Chaplain Tyson stayed by her during this time. When Mrs. Haskins seemed weak-kneed, he put his arm around her to help hold her up. He found her tissues so that she could wipe her tears and blow her nose. From time to time blood would overflow the padding and begin to stream onto the floor, making a puddle. When this happened, he would rearrange the padding and place absorbent pads on the floor to soak up the puddles. He helped Mrs. Haskins with her grieving by encouraging her to hold her daughter's hand, to caress her, etc.

When at last it was time to take the child away for the removal of her kidneys, the doctor nodded to the chaplain. He said to Mrs. Haskins, "They are going to take her up to the operating room now. It is time to say goodbye and to leave." Mrs. Haskins held the child tightly once more, nodded to the chaplain, and the two walked out of the treatment room. A policeman waited in the hallway to take Mrs. Haskins to the station for questioning. Chaplain Tyson told her he would call her on the telephone later in the day to talk about the funeral arrangements. Mrs. Haskins left with the policeman.

Later in the day, Chaplain Tyson reached Mrs. Haskins by telephone. She explained that her own priest would handle all funeral arrangements. The chaplain made plans to see her at the funeral parlor when she would be receiving visitors. During that visit, they spoke briefly about their experience of the little girl's death. Since there were others there to be with Mrs. Haskins, the chaplain did not visit for a long time, but left his business card, encouraging her to contact him at the hospital at a later date if she felt the need to talk. Mrs. Haskins never did visit the hospital again, but did call the chaplain to ask whether her daughter's kidneys were actually used in transplants. He did not have that information, but agreed to find out and to call her back to let her know.

Oscar was an eight year old boy hospitalized for the treatment of juvenile diabetes. Oscar had been taking daily insulin injections for a year. A blood sugar imbalance had precipitated his return to the hospital for several days of testing and monitoring. When Chaplain Rivers was making her rounds she met Oscar and his mother, Mrs. Noland. As Mrs. Noland was explaining her son's illness, she stopped suddenly to ask the chaplain what her church affiliation was. She appeared to be delighted when the chaplain said that she was a Presbyterian minister, and said that she, too, was Presbyterian, but also belonged to a prayer group.

Mrs. Noland went on to recount for the chaplain a religious interpretation of her son's illness. She stated that the real cause of diabetes was that Oscar was possessed by a demon. She said that her prayer group had prayed for him and that he had been healed of the disease and had no more need for insulin. Chaplain Rivers asked if Oscar had discontinued his insulin treatment just prior to the present hospitalization. When Mrs. Noland responded in the affirmative, the chaplain pointed out that it did not appear that Oscar was in fact cured. Mrs. Noland replied, "Why yes, I know that. But you know, there is a Bible verse somewhere about a person vomiting out Satan. Well, just the other day Oscar vomited, and said he felt better. I think that when he vomits, he expels the diabetes demon."

In dismay, Chaplain Rivers pointed out that there was no basis for such a belief in their common church tradition. This statement did not appear to concern Mrs. Noland in the least. Indeed, she went on to say that just as Jesus died for the sins of others, little Oscar was able to vomit for others: when someone else, for example his little sister, became ill, Oscar could vomit and thereby expel the demon of illness from his sister. Mrs. Noland then turned to Oscar, patted him proudly on the head, and said, "Oscar has vomited several times in the last couple of days. Just think of how much good he might have done!"

When Chaplain Rivers asked Mrs. Noland whether she had discussed any of this with the doctors, she said, "No. His doctor is not a Christian, and I don't think he would understand." The chaplain suggested that this was very important information for the doctors to have, and asked Mrs. Noland how she would feel about the chaplain telling the doctors. Mrs. Noland's reply was ambiguous and rather non-committal. Chaplain Rivers once more attempted to persuade her that their church would not support such religious beliefs and that they were, in fact, harmful to Oscar. Mrs. Noland, however, seemed to be blissfully unperturbed, and all the more firm in her convictions.

After leaving the patient's room, Chaplain Rivers immediately contacted Oscar's attending physician and reported the substance of her conversation with Mrs. Noland. An emergency psychiatric consultation was called and steps were taken to prevent Oscar from continuing to vomit in an attempt to cure himself or others of illness.

Chaplain Rivers correctly concluded after her conversation with Mrs. Noland that she had encountered a medical emergency in progress. Willful vomiting can be dangerous for any person, but is especially so for a diabetic. Furthermore, it was quite likely that Mrs. Noland's refusal to give Oscar his insulin treatments had caused his hospitalization; further neglect in this area could result in the child's death. Faced with this urgent situation, the chaplain acted appropriately in contacting the attending physician, whom she happened to know. She was unwilling to trust this report to a note in Oscar's chart, as this might have gone unseen for hours, or might even have been overlooked completely. The chaplain was not deluded by Mrs. Noland's religious language into believing that the issues involved were solely religious ones; she recognized quickly that a psychiatric consultation was indicated, and that she alone did not have the resources required to deal with the situation.

Conflict Among Team Members

Jennifer was a sixteen year old girl hospitalized on an adolescent unit for the treatment of anorexia nervosa. Anorexia is an emotional disorder in which the patient is obsessed with maintaining a low body weight. Anorexics often have a distorted image of their bodies: though they may be extremely thin due to severe dieting, they look at themselves in the mirror and see signs of obesity. They employ a variety of techniques in their never-ending quest for thinness: strictly controlled food intake; periods of fasting; vigorous calisthenics and other types of exercise to burn off calories; laxatives to push food through their systems quickly; voluntary vomiting following eating (this practice is called bulimia, and may be a distinct disorder). Most victims of anorexia are female, and a great number are stricken with the disease during adolescence. Anorexia becomes potentially fatal as the victims literally starve themselves to death.

On the adolescent unit, Jennifer was being treated according to the medical model. Before psychiatric treatment, the staff felt that they must first treat her malnourishment and bring about some gain in weight. The focus of treatment, therefore, was on increasing her caloric intake.

When Chaplain Vaughn, who was assigned to work on the adolescent unit, first encountered Jennifer there, two things impressed her immediately: Jennifer's skeletal appearance, and her deep depression. Even through several layers of clothing, Jennifer's bones looked sharp and pointed. The skin of her face appeared to be tightly drawn over the bones, with little or no flesh between. Jennifer seemed to have no energy at all. She did not establish eye contact with the chaplain, and spoke very slowly in tones that were practically inaudible. Her facial features remained blank, and there was not the slightest flicker of emotion in her voice.

After introducing herself, Chaplain Vaughn invited Jennifer to tell her about her stay in the hospital. Jennifer spoke without speed or volume, but steadily. She stated forthrightly that she was hospitalized for anorexia. She said that the doctors wanted her to eat more and gain weight, but that she did not want to. The nurses brought her meals three times a day and remained in the room to watch her eat. She had thirty minutes to finish her meal. When she refused to eat all or even some of her food, she was force-fed with the approximate caloric equivalent of what she refused to consume. A tube was run through her nose, down her throat, and into her stomach; a liquid nutrient was then poured down the tube. Because Jennifer spoke at an extremely slow rate, and because the chaplain frequently had to ask her to repeat inaudible phrases, it took most of an hour to convey this information. The chaplain left, promising to return another day to continue their conversation.

During the second visit, Jennifer opened a notebook and showed Chaplain Vaughn a series of drawings that she had made. Each depicted in some way her experience in the hospital. In one picture Jennifer was held behind a set of bars, as if in a jail cell. In another, a nurse was thrusting a can of liquid nutrient toward her. Other sketches portrayed Jennifer struggling with the staff, hiding in her room, or crying. Throughout the visit, Chaplain Vaughn listened and responded sympathetically, but also reminded Jennifer that the staff was trying to help her and that she could not go home until she was able to cooperate with them. After the visit, she mentioned Jennifer's art work to the head nurse, who was surprised because the medical staff did not know about it. After one or two more similar visits, Chaplain Vaughn was absent from the hospital for a period of one month. When she returned, Jennifer had been moved to a closed psychiatric unit in the hospital. She did not pursue the case, because visits to patients on the psychiatric unit were arranged only on a prescription basis, i.e., the psychiatrist in charge of the case approved of individual visits to patients if he believed them to be of therapeutic value.

Jennifer had been moved to the psychiatric unit because she continued to resist the efforts of the staff and she showed no progress. A minor crisis had precipitated the transfer: Jennifer had been found in her room exercising so violently that she had injured herself. On the psychiatric unit she remained resistant and uncommunicative.

Anticipating her absence from the hospital, Chaplain Vaughn had told Jennifer that she would be gone for a month and would return to work by a certain date; she said that if Jennifer were still hospitalized, she would try to see her after her return. Because of Jennifer's placement on the psychiatric unit, Chaplain Vaughn had decided to terminate her involvement in the case. However, several days after her return from vacation, Jennifer asked the staff if she could have a visit from the chaplain. The staff was pleased because this was the first time that Jennifer had shown any initiative toward developing a relationship with any member of the staff. They felt that this initiative was to be encouraged and supported. The staff was interested in having the chaplain involved for a second reason as well: Jennifer's family had become affiliated with an evangelical church since her hospitalization. They brought her gifts of bibles, and religious tracts, posters, and jewelry. They put these around her hospital room, and attempted to require her to read from the Bible and to wear religious jewelry. Members of the medical staff were at the same time reluctant to interfere with the family's religious life and concerned about the pressure the family was putting on Jennifer. They felt that the chaplain could help to evaluate the significance of this religious activity for Jennifer.

One of the two head nurses on the psychiatric unit contacted Chaplain Vaughn and asked her to visit Jennifer on a weekly basis. The chaplain and nurse met for a conference, and together they agreed that the chaplain would work in three areas with Jennifer: she would help the girl to understand and cope with the religious demands of her parents and give the staff some indication of how important this religion was to her; she would support Jennifer's cooperation with the staff and their treatment plan; she would function as a neutral friend for Jennifer, i.e., a person who did not have to enforce therapeutic behaviors such as proper eating and refraining from excessive exercises. At the same time, the nurse told the chaplain that there were no areas which she was prohibited from discussing.

Chaplain Vaughn began visiting Jennifer in her room on the psychiatric unit. Jennifer was obviously glad to see her, and even smiled when she first came in. As they spoke, Jennifer expressed deep sadness over her plight. She showed the chaplain more drawings which depicted her circumstances in terms of captivity and struggle with the staff. During their second visit, Jennifer began to express her sadness more congruently. As she told the chaplain that she was costing her family a lot of money and was a bad person, she cried. Between sobs, she said that she felt she should grow up in the hospital instead of at home, because she had hurt her family. After this visit, Chaplain Vaughn indicated briefly in her chart notes that Jennifer had expressed a great deal of sadness during their time together.

Several days later, a psychiatric intern stopped the hospital's director of pastoral care in the hospital lobby and said angrily, "You have a chaplain who is coming on the psychiatric unit and getting inappropriate with a patient. You had better do something about it!" The director refused to discuss the situation in such a public place, but said that he would look into it immediately. After a series of telephone conversations, a meeting was set up among the director, Chaplain Vaughn, and the second head nurse on the psychiatric unit, who was also the unit coordinator.

The unit coordinator explained that some staff members had felt that Jennifer had appeared to be agitated after her first visit with the chaplain. Therefore, without the chaplain's knowledge, they visually monitored her second visit with Jennifer. At rounds the next day, the monitor reported to the psychiatric staff that when Jennifer had cried, the chaplain had briefly placed her hand upon Jennifer's shoulder in a gesture of comfort. It was said by some that this gesture was inappropriate and probably agitated the patient. They further suggested that the chaplain's visits were harming the patient by diffusing the therapeutic focus. The staff did not agree in their assessment of the situation or on its proper management. It was after this meeting that the intern, who was not assigned to the case, had spoken with the director of pastoral care in the lobby.

The unit coordinator went on to state that she did not agree with those who said that the chaplain's visits were harmful or created a problem. She noted that over a period of several months in the hospital, Jennifer had failed to make any significant progress. In her view, the staff was frustrated by this lack of progress and were in conflict with one another over the proper course of action to take. She stated her belief that the primary therapist was angry that Jennifer had volunteered information to the chaplain that she had refused to him in their therapy sessions. She opined that the staff was jealous because Jennifer wanted a relationship with the chaplain, but not *with them, and that they were seeking a scapegoat upon whom to place blame for her lack of progress. She believed that the chaplain, who was present on the unit only weekly, was an easy scapegoat.*

Chaplain Vaughn was angry for several reasons. She felt that she had gone out of her way to cooperate smoothly with the staff, and that they had failed to return the courtesy by communicating directly with her. She felt that it was unfair to receive such radically inconsistent feedback from different staff members about her involvement in the case. She felt that having a staff member monitor her visit without her knowledge was a breach of professional ethics. She also felt defensive about her own involvement with Jennifer; she felt that she had been accused of some kind of improper conduct and that she had to defend her actions.

Chaplain Vaughn told the coordinator that she would be willing to terminate her involvement with Jennifer immediately. The coordinator responded by stating that in spite of it all, the staff strongly desired her continued involvement on a weekly basis. The chaplain replied that she would be willing to do so, but would drop the case immediately if any more inconsistent feedback was received; she said that she was unwilling to engage in conflict with other staff members and that if this occurred she would prefer to drop the case entirely. The coordinator pointed out that this demand for consistency was unrealistic, given the human factors involved. She suggested that Chaplain Vaughn communicate only with her. Chaplain Vaughn agreed to schedule all future contacts with Jennifer through the coordinator and to speak with her before and after each visit. She agreed to continue on a week-by-week trial basis.

After this meeting, several formal administrative complaints were made by the director of pastoral care and some members of the psychiatric staff. None was made by Chaplain Vaughn or about her. Chaplain Vaughn was able to continue her weekly visits with Jennifer until she was discharged some months later.

In commenting upon this conflict situation, we will prescind from any judgments of the psychiatric staff and focus our attention on Chaplain Vaughn and her actions. What is striking about her experience is the contrast between the great care she took to communicate with the head nurse who asked her to see Jennifer on the psychiatric unit and her failure to communicate at all with other important members of the health care team. She failed to speak with the psychiatrist in charge of the case, with the psychiatric intern assigned to it, and with the admitting pediatrician. Her neglect of communication with these people, whose involvement in the management of therapy was central and vital, reveals some assumptions on her part, assumptions which turned out to have been erroneous. Chaplain Vaughn assumed that the head nurse who first contacted her was a spokesperson for the entire health care team. She assumed that the various members of the team were in agreement about the desirability of her involvement with Jennifer. She assumed that the nurse could give her sufficiently clear and complete instructions about the role that she should take as a member of the team. She assumed, for that matter, that her colleagues all regarded her as a team member!

Having been invited to continue her participation in Jennifer's treatment, Chaplain Vaughn should have been more aggressive about making contact with other members of the health care team, especially with the psychiatrist in charge. In addition, she should have asked to attend rounds on the psychiatric unit when Jennifer's case was being discussed. This would have facilitated communication between herself and other staff members who felt concern over her involvement in the case. In addition, as has been discussed above, time spent getting to know other members of the team is of considerable importance for building trust; the lack of a trusting relationship was certainly a major, if not the major, precipitating factor in this incident of conflict. In addition, if the unit coordinator's claim that staff members had feelings of jealousy toward Chaplain Vaughn were true, or if they were indeed divided among themselves as to the proper course of treatment, the chaplain probably could have discerned these problems by attending rounds; had she known that these factors were present, her own style of ministry to Jennifer or her way of relating to the staff might have changed.

When Chaplain Vaughn met with the director of pastoral care and the unit coordinator, her feelings of being threatened by the accusations of colleagues caused her to negotiate in a rigid and unrealistic manner. Feeling threatened and hurt by inconsistent feedback, she demanded that such inconsistency cease. Later, when she felt more secure personally, she realized that any team is made up of members who see things differently, at least to some extent. It is not reasonable to expect that all members of the health care team will always agree on all specifics of treatment and management. A more reasonable expectation is that disagreements can be discussed in a professional manner which respects the dignity and worth of each team member, and with a view to arriving at a solution that will benefit the patient. But even this will not always be possible: members of the health care team, no matter how professional and competent, are still human beings whose feelings can be hurt and who can be locked into a too-narrow perspective; humans do not always have the very best motivations for their decisions, and they are not always kind toward each other. The chaplain who wishes to function as a member of the team must be ready to live with such imperfections, to compromise, and to try to achieve whatever level of communication seems to be realistically possible in a given set of circumstances.

It happened that the agreement which Chaplain Vaughn reached with the unit coordinator was followed by a cessation of overt conflict with other members of the health care team. Even so, the communication problem was not really solved; it was merely relocated. Under this new agreement, the chaplain continued to communicate with just one member of the team. The assumptions which were operative under her initial agreement to be involved in the case on the psychiatric unit remained. The subsequent cessation of overt conflict was more likely a result of the tumult stirred up by angry outbursts and formal administrative complaints than of any real resolution of conflict or improvement in communications. Chaplain Vaughn continued not to communicate directly with the physicians in charge of the case; neither did she attend rounds or otherwise establish relationships with other team members.

A chaplain who was more secure in her own role and her own importance as a member of the health care team might have seen more readily her value in helping the patient. Chaplain Vaughn had indeed established friendly and trusting rapport with Jennifer, something that other team members had not been able to do. The therapeutic potential of this relationship was high, particularly since Jennifer had failed for so long to make progress. A more assertive chaplain might have insisted upon being included to a greater degree in the treatment plan.

In a similar vein, Chaplain Vaughn should have protested the monitoring of her visit with the patient; had she been more secure in her role, she might have done so. Rather than ignoring the visit, she should have approached the monitor to express her displeasure. As it was, this breach of professionalism was left unaddressed, and

Chaplain Vaughn's standing among her colleagues was lessened. This further compromised her ability to function well on the unit.

It has not been our purpose here to discuss exhaustively the resolution of conflict; entire books have been written on the subject. This single example of conflict is instructive in that it demonstrates the importance of clear communication among members of the health care team and that it serves as a reminder that professional health care workers are also human beings with many human faults, faults which will at times get in the way of helping patients. Any chaplain who works in a hospital can expect to encounter conflict situations, and must accept them as a matter of course (which is not to say, of course, that many conflicts may not be prevented or resolved easily after they do occur). In responding to conflicts among staff, chaplains all too often err on the side of being too unassertive and giving up too much because they feel like second class members of the health care team. When chaplains are more secure in their sense of value as members of the team, their responses to conflict situations are more appropriate and better benefit the patient.

Minister to the Staff

Chaplain Owens had stopped by the room of a hospitalized infant to see the parents, but found them to be absent from the room. As he was leaving, Miss Edge, a phlebotomist (one who draws blood samples) entered the room to obtain a blood sample from the baby. As they introduced themselves, Miss Edge commented, "I'm glad to see you working in this hospital. I think that faith is so important." She went on to tell the chaplain how much she hated to cause children pain as she stuck them with needles. She said that before every such procedure, "I get down on my knees right beside the bed, no matter who else is in the room, and I pray to God that I will be able to do my work well and cause the child as little pain as possible." The two spent some time discussing her feelings of guilt over causing pain in children, and Chaplain Owens supported her feelings that her health care work was blessed by God, and that it was a great thing to help take care of other people. He encouraged her in her desire to be a spiritual person, and before they parted they prayed together for a few moments, each mentioning in prayer several patients who were particularly sick.

As chaplains spend more and more time in the hospital setting getting to know staff members, they will find that more and more of them wish to relate to the chaplain as minister. Ministering to other members of the staff can become an immensely important part of the chaplain's work. Not only does this help to meet a real need, but it does wonders for building up relationships of trust with other health care workers.

Miss Edge's struggle with her feelings of guilt over the pain she caused her patients is not uncommon among health care workers, particularly among nurses who often are responsible for carrying out some of the most painful treatments, such as changing bandages on burn victims. They will sometimes look to the chaplain for help in coping with these and other work related stresses.

Chaplains are also consulted from time to time concerning ethical dilemmas. There has been a great deal of press coverage concerning "when to pull the plug," and this is certainly a common problem, but there are scores of other difficult decisions which must be made in the hospital, e.g., whether chemotherapy should be administered, whether drugs may be withheld, whether imperfectly formed babies may be left to starve to death, etc. Physicians who know and trust a chaplain will want to consult him as an ethical expert as they face some of these difficult decisions.

The chaplain who is available to other staff members will also find that they approach him for help in dealing with problems not related to their work. They may come to discuss marriage problems, problems with children or parents, etc. Others will approach the chaplain for what amounts to spiritual direction. Such areas fall easily within the purview of the hospital chaplain.

The chaplain may also contribute meaningfully to the spiritual life of the hospital community by providing religious services on a regular basis. In ideal situations, these are interfaith services where staff, patients, and families may all come together to worship. In some hospitals, it is even possible to transmit services from the chapel to televisions in the patients' rooms. There may also be times when special services are helpful. These times include not only religious holidays such as Christmas, Easter, or Yom Kippur, but religious services may be held around special or significant events in the life of the hospital community, such as the death of a patient, the anticipation of a dangerous surgical procedure, or the completion of a new wing. It will be appropriate to open some of these special services to the hospital community at large, and to provide others for special groups within that community.

Conclusion

Chaplains who are able to become members of the health care team in a hospital will find their work greatly facilitated. Essential to functioning as a member of the team is a commitment to spend time in the hospital, both with patients and with staff members, a willingness to work with others and to compromise, a positive regard toward other team members, specialized professional training, an effort to build relationships of trust with other health care workers, and a striving to communicate well and often with them. The chaplain will find it particularly important to establish good contacts among the nursing staff. Chaplains who work on becoming accepted members of the health care team will find their ability to minister to patients and their families greatly enhanced, and will also be able to minister effectively to other members of the team.

RECOMMENDED READING

Anderson, Peggy. *Children's Hospital.* New York: Harper & Row, 1985.

Ashley, Benedict M., O.P., and Kevin D. O'Rourke, O.P. *Health Care Ethics: A Theological Analysis.* St. Louis: The Catholic Hospital Association, 1978.

Curran, Charles E. *Issues in Sexual and Medical Ethics.* Notre Dame: University of Notre Dame, 1978.

Plank, Emma N. *Working with Children in Hospitals: A Guide for the Professional Team,* 2nd ed., rev. and enl. Chicago: Case Western University, 1971.

Robinson, Geoffrey C. *The Hospital Care of Children: A Review of Contemporary Issues.* New York: Oxford University, 1980.

4.

The Pastoral Visit

Introduction

Anticipating their visits to sick children in the hospital, many ministers are concerned with questions such as "What should I say?" or "How should I act?" Although each pastoral visit will remain a unique experience and thus no strict pattern of interaction or set of rules is applicable, the author has found that certain techniques and patterns are useful in most circumstances. The ideas presented here may not be employed in a mechanical, cookbook fashion; they will, however, serve as guideposts along the way. Each minister must develop his or her own style of ministry and relating to other people. Such development is the product of time and experience. Only when the minister succeeds in making his ministry an expression of his own faith and personal experience will he be truly effective in his work. Furthermore, just as the shape of his faith and experience will change over time, so will the form of his ministerial presence.

Establishing Contact with Patients

The minister who is anxious to "say the right things" to a hospitalized child may be unaware that at times skillful work is required just to make any communication with the child possible. Hospitalized children are generally surrounded by family members and health care workers, and often other sick children as well. The minister certainly does not want to ignore such people; indeed, it is just as much his function to minister to the patient's family as to the patient himself. Still, the minister may experience his efforts to obtain quality time with the patient as a struggle.

Before entering the patient's room, the minister should make a preliminary decision as to whether he wishes to speak with the patient at all. At first blush this might sound strange, but it must be remembered that some patients will be infants, some will be sleeping or even comatose, and others may even be entirely absent from the room, undergoing a medical procedure in another part of the hospital. This is where a check-in with the nurse can be most helpful. Nurses can inform the chaplain of important facts such as the patient's age, medical condition, readiness for a pastoral visit, etc. They often have valuable information about the patient's family as well. (See "Nurses: The Chaplain's Best Friends," above.) If the minister has decided that he wishes to speak with the patient, and on entering the room sees that he is present and alert, he will find it helpful to greet the child before he greets others in the room. This puts out several messages: The chaplain has a friendly attitude toward the patient. The chaplain has come to see the patient and talk with him, rather than coming merely to talk about him to others. The chaplain considers the patient to be at least as important as others who are present. This is the patient's room (or section, or bed) and he has a right to know who is coming into his space.

The minister who is visiting his own parishioners will presumably be known to them and therefore will not need to introduce himself or explain his presence. The situation for the hospital chaplain is quite different. Not only is he generally a stranger to the patient on his first visit, but he may not assume that the child has any experience of church life, or even knows what a chaplain or a minister is. Many hospitals list patients according to their stated religious affiliation, but this may reflect the family's heritage or memories more than it reflects the patient's experience of organized religion. For example, a Catholic priest may visit a child whose religious affiliation is listed as Roman Catholic, only to discover that the child is unbaptized and has never set foot in a church of any kind, and that his parents have not practiced their faith since before they were married. With adults, even the unchurched almost always know what a chaplain or minister is; the same may not be assumed with children.

One of the chaplain's very first tasks in an initial visit, therefore, is to make sure that the patient knows who he is and what he does. It is common for children, especially those in the pre-school and primary years, to assume that a visiting chaplain is a doctor, nurse, or technician. Therefore the chaplain should take care to differentiate himself from other members of the health care team. In some hospitals chaplains wear lab coats; this is not appropriate when working with children. Chaplains should avoid carrying around objects which look "medical": clipboards, charts or folders, or anything resembling instruments. Younger children tend to think concretely, and they attach great weight to what they see; the five year old who meets a chaplain wearing a white lab coat may be completely unable to believe that he is anyone but a doctor, no matter what the chaplain tells him. Ministers who possess a doctorate should not use that title with children in the hospital (the exception is when the child knows the minister from church, and calls him "Doctor" there).

As the chaplain introduces himself to children, he may wish to use a title. Non-medical titles such as Chaplain, Reverend, Mr., Mrs., Miss, Ms., Father, Sister, and Brother are appropriate. The use of a title is by no means necessary; some highly successful chaplains work with hospitalized children on a first-name basis.

Having introduced himself to the child, the chaplain should briefly explain his role as a member of the health care team. To a younger child he might say, "Hi Steven! I'm Chaplain Jones. I'm a minister who works in the hospital. Do you know what a minister is?" Often in response to such an introduction, children will say, "A minister is somebody who works in church," or "Oh, you teach people about God and stuff." At other times, the child will exhibit some confusion about the chaplain's role. It may be impossible to explain to a child with no religious background what a minister is. In such cases the chaplain may be content with a *via negativa* approach; he can at least make sure that the child understands that he is not a doctor, nurse, or other medical worker: "Well, Steven, I'm not a doctor or a nurse or anything like that. I work in the hospital and I go around to see sick kids and ask them how they are doing. I talk with them and ask if I can be their friend."

Working with small children, the chaplain must at times be content with some confusion or even outright error on their parts concerning his role. The chaplain may visit a five year old who simply cannot understand that he is not a doctor. In such cases, it is enough that the child experience the chaplain as a friendly person who cares and is warm.

Even when the child understands clearly that the chaplain is a minister working in the hospital, he may ask the chaplain to fulfill a variety of roles. For example, prayer or discussion of his plight may be the farthest thing from a child's mind during the chaplain's visit. He might instead ask the chaplain to play a game, find a better television channel, empty the urinal, cut his meat, get the nurse, scratch his back, or tell him a story. Children do not compartmentalize peo-

ple and their roles as adults often do. The chaplain who is flexible
and willing to relate to patients in a variety of roles will find his ministry more effective (see Chapter Two, "The Chaplain's Role with Patients and Their Families").

The patient who is in isolation presents special problems for the
chaplain. Patients are placed in isolation either to protect them from
disease or infection, or to protect others from their own disease.
When this happens, a sign stating that the patient is in isolation is
placed on the door of his room. Before entering the room, the chaplain
who encounters such a sign should check with the nurse in charge,
who can explain to him what precautions are required. Different
kinds of precautions are used; the chaplain may be asked to put on a
surgical mask, vinyl gloves, a gown, or a combination of these items.
Special handwashing procedures may be in effect. The chaplain may
be asked not to touch the patient or bed. When the chaplain enters
the patient's room clothed in such garb, establishing his identity and
role for the patient is still important, but may be more difficult because now the chaplain looks like a doctor or nurse. When meeting
a child in isolation for the first time, it is helpful for the chaplain to
wave from a distance or through a window before donning gown and
mask; this lets the child know what the chaplain looks like, and thus
helps to establish rapport. In introducing himself under such circumstances, the chaplain should take special care to state clearly, and
repeatedly if necessary, that he has not come into the room to perform a medical procedure. Chaplains who are confronted with an isolation sign on a patient's door may shy away from their intended
pastoral visit, not wanting to go to the trouble of preparing properly,
or not wishing to cause extra work for busy nurses. But rather than
hesitating, they should make the extra effort to visit such patients;
it is precisely the child in isolation who may be most lonely and in
need of company and support, and the busy nurse may well be relieved that someone else can give the patient some attention.

Hospitalized children have been taken from their homes and
placed in a different environment, one that is new and strange to
many of them. They may feel threatened and invaded by what is
going on around them; this is particularly true of adolescents, whose
privacy needs are greater than those of younger children. Their space
is invaded by various workers who come and go at will, usually without asking permission. Even their bodies are invaded by outside elements: pills, injections, thermometers, medical instruments, and
perhaps even the hands of examining physicians. The chaplain can
help by not becoming yet another person who invades the personal

space of the patient. Chaplains should knock on the door if there is one, and, after introducing themselves, seek the child's permission to enter his bed area and to stay a while. This should be done even with pre-school children, for they, too, need to maintain their sense of autonomy and integrity. The vast majority of younger children will be quite agreeable to a visit from the chaplain, but occasionally one will not, and his wishes should be respected. Adolescents more frequently will indicate a lack of interest in a pastoral visit. In such cases, the chaplain may wish to explain briefly before he leaves how he may be contacted if they change their minds.

The following exchange is typical of how a chaplain may secure an invitation into the child's space. The patient is a ten year old boy, recovering from an appendectomy.

Chaplain: Hi, Walter. My name is Chaplain Norris. I'm a minister who works here in the hospital. How are you doing today?
Walter: Fine.
Chaplain: Do you know what a minister is? Have you been to church and seen one?
Walter: Yeah. We go to church. Our minister is Reverend Jones.
Chaplain: Good. Well, I'm a minister who works in the hospital. I wanted to see how you were doing and talk with you about being in the hospital. May I stay and talk with you a little while?
Walter: Yeah, sure.
Chaplain: Great! (Looks around briefly.) Where do you think I should sit?
Walter: Oh, you can just sit on the bed.
Chaplain: Okay. Good idea. I'll sit right here. (Sits down.) That okay?
Walter: Sure.

This exchange might appear to be a rather protracted way to take a seat, but it has several important advantages. It communicates clearly to the patient that his wishes are important, and that, to the extent possible, they will be respected. It gives him a measure of control over the situation in a setting where most of his control may have been taken away from him. It gives him an opportunity to take some responsibility for the character and limits of the new relationship. In this case, for example, Walter was able to invite a certain degree of closeness and intimacy by asking the chaplain to be seated on the bed; he could as well have asked the chaplain to take a seat several feet away. Chaplain Norris' approach helped Walter to state his own needs at the time of the visit and to set the pattern for the entire conversation, i.e., that the chaplain would address Walter's concerns rather than pushing to cover his own agenda.

It is actually a good rule of thumb to avoid sitting on patients' beds. The risks involved are several: There could be some risk of spreading infection this way; more importantly, one risks interfering with traction equipment or other items such as intravenous lines or wires which may or may not be easily visible; furthermore, for a patient who has just had surgery, a shift in bed position caused by a person sitting on the bed could be quite uncomfortable. When visiting smaller children, it may seem natural to sit on the side of the bed while the patient sits or reclines, especially if the child invites this. Still, standing at the bedside or taking a chair is a safer approach. Obviously, far fewer adolescents will invite the chaplain to sit on their beds, and chaplains must take especial care to avoid even the appearance of impropriety as they visit adolescents of the opposite sex.

If the patient's bed is raised high off of the floor it usually has the side rails up, and the chaplain might find it more comfortable to stand at the bedside so that he and the patient may see one another easily. Whatever the height of the bed, he may want to ask the child's permission to lower the rail so that they may see one another better. But once the chaplain moves the bedrail, he is responsible for making sure that the patient does not fall out, and he must replace the rail as soon as he is ready to leave the bedside!

Claiming Time and Space

The chaplain who wants to have a quality pastoral visit with a patient will most easily achieve this if he is able to meet with the child in privacy. The chaplain may feel most awkward about securing this privacy when the child's family members are present in the room. However, once the patient indicates his desire to talk with the chaplain, most family members will understand the latter's desire to have the conversation in private. Indeed, parents often welcome a chance to get out of the hospital room for a while, but feel uneasy about leaving the child unattended. In such cases, they may leap at the chance for a coffee and stretch break while the chaplain visits with the child. The chaplain should not be shy about stating his desire to speak with the patient alone. The following statements, made to parents or other family members present, have proved helpful:

- I usually see patients alone for a little while. When would be a convenient time for me to see Becky?
- Perhaps Becky and I could be alone for a few minutes.
- Could Becky and I have a talk together, just the two of us?

If the patient's parents are reluctant to allow a private meeting with the chaplain, then of course their wishes must be respected.

Other actions may need to be taken to ensure at least some measure of privacy while visiting a patient. The chaplain should not hesitate to draw curtains between the patient and other patients in the same room or on the ward. When two hospitalized children are playing together and the chaplain wishes to speak with one of them, he may ask the other to return to his own bed: "Steven and I are going to have a little special time together now. I'd like you to wait for us on your own bed. If you like, I'll have a special time with you, too." It is a kindness, time permitting, to give some attention to other patients in the room or ward, even if this is just a quick hello and a pat on the head; this helps to keep the other children from feeling left out.

Gus was a seven year old boy hospitalized with a dog bite on his leg. Stitches had been required and Gus was kept in the hospital overnight for observation. Chaplain Klaer had come to visit, and was hearing the story of the accident, when a nurse came into the room. She announced, "It is time for Gus to have his medicine. Would you wait in the hall for us, please?" The chaplain went out into the hall and stood. After a moment, the nurse came out and said, "I need to change his sheets, too. We'll be just a few minutes longer." In a moment she returned with the sheets. From his place in the hallway, Chaplain Klaer heard Gus and the nurse engaging in animated conversation, apparently enjoying one another's company. Finally, she emerged to say that she was finished. Chaplain Klaer had stood waiting in the hall for twenty-five minutes.

Such interruptions can be avoided to some extent if the chaplain checks in with the patient's nurse before visiting. The nurse will be able to say whether any medical procedures are scheduled and she can aid the chaplain in finding quality time with the patient which will not be interrupted.

Chaplain Klaer should have been more assertive about claiming his time with Gus. The chaplain's work with patients is important, and it is not to be shunted aside unless this is truly necessary. The chaplain who believes in the importance of what he does will feel secure in insisting that he be allowed to spend time with patients. Chaplains should not hesitate to ask other members of the health care team to return later or to give them a few more minutes with a patient. At times, however, this will be impossible, especially in the case of physicians whose time in the hospital may be quite limited. Like all members of the team, the chaplain must be willing to cooperate and compromise. The chaplain who is able both to claim his time with patients and to be flexible about scheduling this time will find that other team members come to respect the significance of his work more and more.

At times when the chaplain feels that a pastoral visit is particularly important and that uninterrupted privacy is needed, he should schedule the visit with the patient's nurse and if the patient may be moved, ask to use a conference room, which is available on or near most hospital units. It may take some time to set up such a visit, and it may be inconvenient to move the patient to the conference room, but often the results are well worth while. Here again, the chaplain will do his work more easily and effectively if he believes in its importance and in his unique contribution to the health care of the patient.

What To Look For and What To Talk About

It would be unrealistic to attempt to provide a comprehensive outline of the pastoral visit. Each visit will be unique, and no pattern holds for all cases. However, the following items may be kept in mind and used as a checklist which will help the chaplain to attend to important areas during his visit with a hospitalized child.

• *Observe the environment.* The patient's environment can provide many important clues about his situation. Get-well cards, gifts, or toys indicate that there are people who know that the child is hospitalized and who care about him. The chaplain can check out the child's support system by asking who sent the various cards and gifts. This provides an easy and natural way for him to find out about the patient's family and friends, information which may be helpful. Unless the patient is a new admittance, a notable lack of cards or gifts, on the other hand, will alert the chaplain that the child may lack a substantial support system and may be largely on his own while in the hospital; such children will need all the more care and attention.

Dolls with bandages or make-believe casts are significant because they almost always indicate treatments that the patient himself will be undergoing. The chaplain can ask about such dolls and the treatment they received, and then move into a discussion of what the patient expects to have happen to himself. Other medical toys are tip-offs: play needles, or a real syringe and an orange to stick it into, suggest that the patient must learn to give himself injections, perhaps because of diabetes; charts or dolls showing numbered puncture sites suggest the same thing; special dietary charts may tell the chaplain a lot about the kind of life the patient will be leading. Any such items may be observed by the chaplain in an effort to invite the patient to talk about his situation.

The chaplain may learn a lot by taking a close look at the patient himself. He may see bandages, traction apparatus, intravenous lines, catheters and urine bags, wounds with or without sutures, or even missing limbs. Taking notice of such things helps the chaplain to understand the patient's experience, and mentioning them to the patient is an effective way to invite significant conversation.

• *Ask the patient how he is.* Besides being a basic expression of care and concern, inquiring about the patient's present status gives the chaplain important information that may shape the rest of the interview. For example, the child may report that he is in a great deal of pain, or is extremely sleepy; this would cause the chaplain to watch carefully how the patient tolerated the visit, and to be prepared to end it quickly. Or, the chaplain might plan to spend extra time with a patient who reports that he feels fine, but is bored and lonely. The chaplain who inquires should be ready for any response: one child replied that he felt like vomiting, which he promptly did!

• *Check out the child's understanding of his illness or injury.* This is best accomplished through the straightforward question, "Why are you in the hospital?" With younger children the chaplain should not attempt to be subtle. Questions such as "What brings you here to Mercy Hospital?" may receive answers such as, "My mom drove me." Even though the chaplain knows the reason for the child's hospitalization, he should still ask the child why he is there; regardless of the true reason for hospitalization, the chaplain should find out why the *child* believes he is hospitalized. This is particularly true of pre-school children, whose egocentric and magical thinking patterns may lead them astray of the truth. The four year old hospitalized for abdominal surgery may believe that he is being punished for misbehavior. Other pre-schoolers may relate bizarre fantasies to the inquiring chaplain; these may concern bodily mutilation. For example, the five year old hospitalized for corrective surgery on her ankles may tell the chaplain that her legs will be cut off. The chaplain can quickly help children by dispelling their fantasies and correcting their erroneous impressions about their hospitalizations. Here again, the aid of a nurse may be enlisted to explain medical procedures to the child or to help correct misinformation. Even older children may have mistaken ideas about their medical situation, and the chaplain can help to straighten this out.

In asking children why they are hospitalized, the chaplain accomplishes more than merely obtaining information and evaluating the child's knowledge of his true status. He is able to watch the child as he tells his story, looking for signs of feelings which are present; in telling his story, the patient may show anger, fear, or, if the news is good, happiness and relief. The chaplain can aid patients in articulating their feelings and can discuss with them their significance and management.

• *Be concrete.* This is especially important with younger children who are not yet able to reason abstractly. The chaplain should take advantage of the significant aspects of the patient's environment to aid in the discussion. He should invite the child to show him the site of injury or sickness, especially if there is a visible wound or bandage there. Many children delight in showing and telling, and being asked to show helps them be able to tell. In the same way, the chaplain can ask the child to explain a bandaged doll, or to tell about the person who sent a certain get-well card. Even in working with older adolescents, referring to concrete realities helps to focus the pastoral conversation and move it to more significant levels.

• *Look for feelings.* Knowing how a child feels about his illness and hospitalization is at least as important, and sometimes clearly more important, than knowing the simple medical facts. The chaplain should look for the patient's feelings and gain some impression of their significance. The fact that a six year old boy is hospitalized for a circumcision is not particularly important; the fact that the impending operation terrifies him is, and urgently needs attention. The chaplain should also be alerted by the patient whose medical situation is quite serious, but whose feelings about the matter appear to be absent.

• *Find the defenses*. It is important to determine how a child is defending himself from the stress of being in the hospital (see Chapter 5). Some defenses are effective and helpful, and others are not. The strength and number of the patient's defenses will give the chaplain some indication of how stressful the situation is to him. The chaplain can support defenses which help the child to cope with his hospital experience. For example, he can play "doctor" or other medical games with the younger child (identification) or talk with the adolescent about the facts of his illness (intellectualization) or about choices that the teenager has about his treatment and life in the hospital (controlling). Or, when a child employs an unhelpful defense tactic, such as extreme regression, the chaplain can help him to use a more helpful, or at least a less harmful defense. He can do the same for a child who appears to have little or no defense against stress. Understanding a child's defense system will help the chaplain to support him better throughout his hospital stay.

• *Check out support systems*. A support system is a network of people or structures which give a person needed protection, emotional warmth, and personal support. A strong support system in the form of a close family or group of friends can make the hospital experience much easier for any patient, but especially for children. Part of the chaplain's work can be to evaluate a patient's support system, to strengthen it where possible, and even to provide some substitutions.

Ernie was an eight year old boy hospitalized for the surgical repair of hypospadias, a defect in the urethra, or the "tube" which drains urine from the bladder out through the penis. Chaplain Butler visited him in his room the day after surgery, and in their conversation learned that since Ernie's parents were both employed, they came to see him only in the evening after work, at which time they stayed for about thirty minutes. Asked whether he received any telephone calls during the day, Ernie responded negatively. Chaplain Butler was still in the hospital when Ernie's parents came for their visit that evening. When he entered Ernie's room, he saw them seated together across the room from Ernie, who was in his bed. As he introduced himself, the parents were polite, but somewhat cool.

He invited them to step out into the hall for a moment to talk, to which they readily agreed. After inquiring about Ernie's condition and progress and asking his parents how they were managing with the hospitalization, he told them that in his visit earlier, he had noticed that Ernie seemed to be very lonely. His mother, seeming to be surprised, said, "Really? Why, we've come to see him each day." Chaplain Butler observed that children love to receive telephone calls, and suggested that his parents might call him several times each day from work or home. He suggested further that other relatives or close friends be encouraged to call or visit, or at least to send Ernie some cards. Finally, having noticed on his earlier visit that Ernie's room seemed a bit bare, he suggested to his parents that they bring him a small gift, such as a coloring book, comic book, or toy car, each day when they came to visit. They received these suggestions gratefully, and thanked the chaplain for his interest. On subsequent visits, Chaplain Butler noticed that Ernie was getting more attention and support from his family.

Through careful observation and tactful communication, Chaplain Butler was able to give Ernie's parents some hints about being more supportive of their son. He sensed that the family was not close emotionally, but was able to suggest simple and non-threatening ways for them to give Ernie better support during his hospitalization. Chaplain Butler felt that the family's lack of closeness and inability to support one another were signs of possible pathology. But given the brevity of his contact with them, he chose not to pursue this possibility. He did, however, note in the patient's chart that the family did not seem to be emotionally close. His choice not to intervene further may not have been the best choice; he might, for example, have simply asked Ernie's parents if they were a close family. This could have opened the door for some deeper work with them.

The chaplain will at times find a hospitalized child whose support system has broken down. In this situation, a temporary substitute support system is helpful.

Faye was a twelve year old girl hospitalized with a broken leg. She and her parents lived in another state, and were traveling through the city when they had a serious automobile accident. Both of her parents were placed in another hospital, where they were in critical condition. Faye had no contact with family or friends for her first several days in the hospital. The entire staff of her unit was aware of the situation, and they went out of their way to spend extra time with her. The child life department was able to obtain some small gifts, such as books and cosmetics. Efforts were also made to introduce her to other children on the unit and to foster these friendships.

Hospitalized children may be left without support systems because of similar catastrophes, or because they never had a good support system in the first place. The chaplain may come across such a lonely child and be deeply moved by his plight. The chaplain, however, as well as other individual members of the health care team, must resist the temptation to assume total responsibility for the emotional support of such a patient. Rather, this responsibility is more appropriately shared among many members of the health care team, from the attending physician on down.

The following queries are helpful in evaluating a patient's support system:

- Who comes to visit you in the hospital?
- Do you ever get phone calls here?
- Who sent you this card (or gave you this book, or plays this game with you, etc.)?
- Has someone come to see you today?
- Whom do you live with at home?
- What are your friends' names?
- Do you have a favorite friend?
- Do you have a favorite teacher at school?
- When you leave the hospital, where will you go? Who will take care of you there?
- What is it like sleeping in the hospital? (The child may express feelings of fright or loneliness, or may talk about who spends the night with him.)
- Do you have a favorite nurse here?
- Have you made any friends in the hospital?
- Has someone done something nice for you today?

- *Check the patient's relationship to the staff.* It is important for the patient's well-being and recovery that he have a good relationship with the health care team. The chaplain can evaluate this relationship, support it when it is good, and take steps to improve it when needed. He may ask a child, "Who is your favorite nurse?" When the child is able to name a nurse in reply, or at least to say that he likes some nurses, the chaplain can support this relationship: "Why, yes, I think she is nice, too. How has she been helping you?"

At other times, the patient's reply may reveal his feelings of anger toward staff members, or may indicate that there has been a breakdown in communications.

Ben was a sixteen year old boy hospitalized on the adolescent unit for evaluation. He had been brought to the hospital after fainting in school. He had a history of drug abuse. Soon after arriving on the unit, Ben began to complain of headaches and demanded that his doctors prescribe narcotic pain relievers. They refused, offering him only over-the-counter-type pain relievers. Ben's behavior toward the staff was belligerent and abusive. When Chaplain Gomer came to visit him, he launched into a tirade about how bad and unfeeling his doctors were, and he expressed a great deal of anger toward them. Chaplain Gomer listened sympathetically, and acknowledged Ben's anger by saying, "You certainly are angry about a lot of things. You feel really mad!" Ben continued talking about his anger, and when he finished, she began to talk with him about what might be its source. Ben began to realize that he had been angry for a long time before entering the hospital, and that he was more angry at his parents and some of his schoolmates and teachers than at the hospital staff. Chaplain Gomer observed, "One of the nurses told me you're so mad that you've even been yelling at the ladies who bring your meal trays." This paved the way for a long discussion about Ben's relationship to the hospital staff. He began to realize that his stay would be more pleasant, and that he could even make new friends, if he became less abusive. He also agreed with Chaplain Gomer that his anger was important, and that it should receive further attention through the counseling that the hospital offered. Chaplain Gomer was careful to acknowledge his angry feelings and to affirm his need to express them. Rather than attempting to pave over this anger, she tried to help Ben to understand its source and to express it in ways that would be less destructive to himself and his relationships.

Chaplains are often able to support patient/staff relationships because they function in a more neutral role. For example, chaplains do not have to administer or withhold treatment, medicine, food, etc. They do not have to cause patients pain or attempt to control their behavior. When the chaplain is able to help the patient to see the medical staff in a more positive light, he helps the patient to progress in his recovery.

• *Offer to help.* At this point the chaplain should have a fairly clear picture of the patient's situation in the hospital. He may then offer to be of help. If the chaplain has discerned that the patient has certain needs which he can help to meet, he should make a specific offer to do so. It is to be remembered that children may not have a clear idea about what a chaplain does, and that therefore when asked how he may help, they may be confused. And we have stated repeatedly that the chaplain should be flexible in his role with patients. The following sorts of invitations have proved helpful:

- It sounds as though you're pretty scared about your operation. Could we talk about that some?
- It seems as though you're really bored today. Would you like me to play one of your games with you?
- You really miss your mother. Would you like me to help you make her a card?

The chaplain may also offer to pray with the patient. This is particularly appropriate if the patient has religious beliefs with a tradition of prayer. But even children who are not being raised in an organized religion sometimes show a surprising level of religious sensibility, and prayer may mean a great deal to them. (For a discussion of prayer in the hospital, see Chapter 6.)

- *Check the patient's time orientation.* The chaplain should check to see if the child's awareness of the flow of time is accurate. This is important because the hospitalized child has been taken out of his normal environment and has discontinued his normal schedule. He may become disoriented about time, losing track of days and falling into confusion about the length of time until his release. This is particularly true with younger children.

After checking with the nurse to find out the length of time that the patient has been hospitalized and the anticipated date of release, as well as other important factors such as upcoming surgery, the chaplain can talk with the patient to see if his impressions about these facts are accurate. He may begin by determining if the patient is oriented to present time. Helpful questions are:

- Do you remember what day it is today?
- What meal did you just have? (Or, what meal are they going to bring you next?)
- Do you know what time it is now?

Younger children may not yet be able to conceptualize time as minutes, hours, and days. Referring to more concrete daily events, such as meals or favorite television programs, may be more effective than trying to talk about "six hours." The chaplain might ask, "Has the Popeye show been on yet today, or will it come on later?"

Next, he should check to see if the child is clear about past events. He may ask:

- How many days have you been in the hospital?
- What day did you come to the hospital?
- What day did you have your operation?
- How many weeks have you been in traction now?

Finally, the chaplain should ask the patient about the future, but with an awareness that this may be indeterminate. He should focus not only on the anticipated date of release from the hospital, but on other important events as well, for example, surgical procedures, casting, the beginning or conclusion of therapy, return to school, etc.

The chaplain should not be surprised to discover gross misunderstandings of time on the part of patients. The child who has been hospitalized for two days may say that it has been a week. The child who has been in traction for six weeks may report that it has been two. The child about to be released from the hospital may believe that he is to remain there for another week; his roommate, who has just arrived to begin a long stay, may opine that it is time to go home. Children may not know what day it is, whether their last meal was breakfast or dinner, or when it will be nighttime again.

As the chaplain seeks to help children understand important time factors, he should remember that younger children, especially pre-schoolers, are not able to think abstractly. The concept of "three days from now" may be entirely meaningless to a four year old. The chaplain can help younger children by speaking concretely about such matters: "The nurse said you can go home in three days. Today is Monday. When today is over and you go to sleep, that's one day. Then it will be Tuesday. When Tuesday is over and you go to sleep, that's two days. Then it will be Wednesday. When Wednesday is over and you go to sleep, that's three days. When you wake up then, it will be time to go home." Pre-schoolers may understand ideas such as "after three sleeps" or "after three wake-ups in the morning" more easily than descriptions like "in three days" or "next Tuesday." Calendars on which days can be counted and marked off are most helpful; if the child has no calendar, a simple one can be drawn in a few moments.

Helping patients become oriented to time is part of the chaplain's role. Time disorientation can become frustrating to the child, who may not be able to tell when his favorite television show will be broadcast, or who may not know when his next meal will come. It can produce anxiety for the child who anticipates some medical procedure, but does not know when it will happen. The chaplain can help to prevent the patient's unnecessary disappointment when a falsely anticipated event, especially release from the hospital, fails to take place. In most cases, other members of the health care team, especially nurses, help patients to establish and maintain proper time orientation. But especially with younger children, this can require repeated communication before the message really gets through. Hospitalized children often need frequent reassurance, and helping them to understand and cope with the flow of time is an important aspect of the chaplain's ministry.

• *Communicate expectations about further visits.* The chaplain who has spent time with a child has established a relationship. The child deserves to have some information about the future of this relationship. If, for whatever reason, the chaplain does not expect to visit the child again, he should state this forthrightly: "Well, Jimmy, this has been a nice visit. I won't be coming to see you again because you're supposed to go home tomorrow. But I'll be thinking about you, and I hope that you get well real fast."

If the chaplain would like to see the patient again, it is appropriate to ask about that: "Since you are going to be in the hospital for a few more days, I'd like to come and see you again on another day. How would that be?" Usually, but not always, the patient will respond quite positively to the prospect of further visits from the chaplain; negative responses, though rare, are most likely to come from teenagers, and should be respected. When the chaplain is unsure about whether he will see the patient again, this, too, should be stated simply and clearly: "I'd like to come to see you again on another day. But I'm taking off a couple of days, and I'm not real sure whether you will still be here when I have a chance to come back. If it works out, I'll see you again. In case I don't, I'll be thinking of you, and I hope you get well real fast." It is better to err on the side of uncertainty than to promise future contact when it may not happen.

The Use of Games and Play in the Pastoral Visit

Children often find a face to face interview too intense, or even simply too boring, to endure. This is particularly true of the child who is naturally shy or who is experiencing a great deal of anxiety. The chaplain may find that his interviews with hospitalized children flow more smoothly and naturally if he plays a game with the patient and allows this activity to be the setting for discussion. This tactic has several advantages. It helps to establish a friendly relationship with the child in a short period of time. It communicates to the child the chaplain's interest and positive regard. It gives him something interesting to do, a relief to the boredom of hospital life. It provides the child with an outlet for his energy. For the anxious child, it provides a ready-made distraction when the discussion touches upon areas which are painful or frightening. Some chaplains carry a deck of cards with them on their rounds as a part of their standard equipment.

The following account illustrates the use of a card game during a pastoral visit.

Les was an eight year old boy hospitalized after being severely beaten by a male friend of his mother, who was a single parent. Les had been tied up and beaten with an electric cord until the outer layers of skin on his buttocks had been flayed away. Before visiting Les on the fifth day of his hospitalization, Chaplain Ingram spoke with his primary care nurse, who reported that Les was in surprisingly good spirits and had been a cooperative patient, but that he had been restless and bored in the hospital. When the chaplain entered Les' room, he found the boy standing beside his bed holding a toy. He appeared to be perky and glad to have a visitor. He was friendly and engaging, and talked easily.

Chaplain: *Hi, Les. I'm Chaplain Ingram. I'm a minister who works here in the hospital. Do you know what a minister is?*

Les: *Yeah. You work in church. We go there.*

Chaplain: *That's right, I'm like a minister who works in a church, except that I work here in the hospital. I come to visit kids who are patients here.*

Les: *Oh.*

Chaplain: *How would it be if you and I had a visit now? Would you like that?*

Les: Yeah, sure. *(Climbs onto the bed and lies on his stomach.)* Do you want to sit down?

Chaplain: Sure. I'll just sit in this chair here. *(Sits down.)* How are you doing today?

Les: Pretty good. I'm going to the playroom tomorrow. *(Looks excited.)*

Chaplain: Super! Would you like to play some cards with me now?

Les: Yeah! Can we play "Go Fish"?

The card game is begun. After a few minutes of playing, Chaplain Ingram asked about Les' hospitalization.

Chaplain: So, what are you in the hospital for?

Les: Well, you see . . . *(solemnly)* my daddy whipped on me with an extension cord. My mother tried to put medicine on it, but it got worse, so I came here.

Chaplain: Gosh, that must have been scary.

Les: No, it wasn't. Got any nines? *(The game continues for a few minutes.)*

Chaplain: Why do you think your daddy did that to you?

Les: He was just in a bad mood. He wasn't mad at me or nothing. Got any threes? *(The game continues.)*

Chaplain: Nobody ever whipped on me with a cord like that. What was it like?

Les: He hit me a long time. Almost all night. *(Looks serious, but calm and reflective.)*

Chaplain: Wow. That must have been real scary.

Les: Yeah.

Chaplain: Were you scared?

Les: Yeah. I was real scared *(stated with emphasis).*

Chaplain: I guess you or your mom couldn't stop him.

Les: No. He tied me up with electric cords around my hands. He held me down and whipped on me.

Chaplain: Man, I would have been really yelling and hollering.

Les: I was. *(Looks completely calm.)*

Chaplain: I guess so.

Les: Got any aces? *(The game continues.)*

Chaplain: Are you going home anytime soon?

Les: Yeah. In a few days.

Chaplain: How are you feeling about going home?

Les: Ok.

Chaplain: Do you think you might have any more trouble with your daddy?

Les: No. (*Stated emphatically.*) I'm going to live with my grandmother, where I used to live. He won't be able to hit me any more.

Chaplain: Good. I'm really glad you won't have to worry about your daddy hitting you again. That's good.

Les: Yeah. Got any kings? (*The game continues.*)

Chaplain: What about your mother? Will you miss her?

Les: Heck no! (*Looks as though he thinks it was a stupid question.*)

Chaplain: Can you tell me some more about that?

Les: She'll visit me in her car whenever I want; she'll be living real close by.

Chaplain: Oh, great!

Les: Got any sevens?

Chaplain Ingram and Les continued to talk, playing cards all the while. Les shared his concern that his mother was going to continue to live with a man who beat her also. The chaplain left, promising to visit Les again the next day.

The card game accomplished several purposes. It allowed for a rather extended conversation of almost an hour between Les and the chaplain by providing an interesting and entertaining setting. It provided a means for Les, when he felt the need, to retreat from the conversation about his trauma, a means that was both immediate and easy to utilize. Whenever Les became uncomfortable with the conversation, he simply retreated from it into the card game. Chaplain Ingram tried carefully to steer a course between encouraging Les to tell his story and express his feelings, and respecting his need not to deal with them all at once. The card game helped to keep the conversation going, but also prevented it from becoming too intense for the boy.

Working with the Patient's Family

The chaplain will want to make sure that he gives adequate attention to the patient's family as well as to the patient himself. If family members have been invited out of the room while the chaplain talks with the child, he may easily join them so that they may talk away from the patient. When this is done, he should avoid the appearance of going immediately from patient to the family to "report" his conversation.

The chaplain may be able to speak with the family easily enough right in the patient's room. The patient may be away from the room for a medical procedure, or may be too young to know what is being said anyway. The chaplain should exercise great care about speaking with family members in the patient's room while he is sleeping, even if medicated. Children often hear more than we suspect. When the patient is sleeping, it is still desirable to speak with family members outside of the hospital room.

The chaplain should take special care to find a place of relative privacy to speak with the patient's family. Most hospital units will have a consultation room, treatment room, or other waiting area where this can take place. Here again, nurses or unit coordinators can be of great help to the chaplain, and he should not hesitate to ask for their help in finding an appropriate place to speak with family members. This privacy is important because family members may need a chance to express some strong emotions: they may cry out of fear and frustration; they may vent anger at the disease, the staff, or even the patient; they may want to discuss other very personal issues.

In working with patients' families, the chaplain may utilize the same checklist of areas for discussion that was suggested for work with the patient. Even checking time orientation and making any needed clarifications is important. Sometimes the parents of a sick child, out of weariness or strained emotions, may lose track of the flow of time just as younger children do.

Working with families as well as with patients may seem like double duty, but it is an essential part of the chaplain's role. There are times when the chaplain can be of most help to the patient by ministering effectively to his family. Be that as it may, families of hospitalized children are people in stress who deserve the chaplain's attention.

Conclusion

Although a prefabricated outline of the pastoral visit would be artificial, certain techniques and patterns are regularly useful.

In establishing contact with a patient, the chaplain should be careful to clarify his identity and role, to respect the child's integrity and his need for privacy and control, and to secure a private setting for his interview with the patient. During his contact with the child, the chaplain should be aware of his environment, his status, his understanding of the illness or injury, his feelings, his defenses, his support systems (or lack thereof), his relationship to the hospital staff, and his orientation to time. The chaplain should strive to be concrete in his conversation, should offer his help and support, and should be clear about the character of his relationship with the child and the future of that relationship. The playing of games during the pastoral visit helps to establish rapport quickly, to keep the patient interested and the conversation flowing, and to provide the child with a ready means of withdrawing from subject areas which are too painful. The chaplain's work with families of patients can work along similar lines and is equally important.

RECOMMENDED READING

Bernstein, Joanne E. *Books To Help Children Cope with Separation and Loss*. New York: R. R. Bowker, 1977.

Clinebell, Howard. *Basic Types of Pastoral Care & Counseling*. Nashville: Abingdon, 1984.

Coleman, William L. *My Hospital Book*. Bethany House, 1981.

Elliott, Ingrid G. *Hospital Roadmap: A Book To Help Explain the Hospital Experience to Young Children*. Resources Children, 1984.

Kennedy, Eugene. *On Becoming a Counselor: A Basic Guide for Non-Professional Counselors*. New York: Seabury, 1977.

Klinging, Dennis R. *The Hospitalized Child: Communication Techniques for Health Personnel*. Englewood Cliffs: Prentice-Hall, 1977.

Lee, Ronald R. *Clergy and Clients: The Practice of Pastoral Psychotherapy*. New York: Seabury, 1980.

Natale, Samuel M., S.J. *Pastoral Counseling: Reflections and Concerns*. New York: Paulist, 1977.

Petrillo, Madeline. *Emotional Care of Hospitalized Children: An Environmental Approach*. Philadelphia: Lippincott, 1980.

Plank, Emma N. *Working with Children in Hospitals: A Guide for the Professional Team*, 2nd ed., rev. and enl. Chicago: Case Western University, 1971.

Stein, Sara Bonnett. *A Hospital Story: An Open Family Book for Parents and Children Together*. New York: Walker, 1974.

Thomas, Richard Howard. *Child Life in Hospitals: Theory and Practice*. Springfield: Thomas, 1981.

5.

Coping with Stress:
Defense Mechanisms

Hospitalization is nearly always a source of stress and anxiety about physical pain, unpleasant treatments, separation from family, friends, and other aspects of normal life, the course of the illness, and, often, death. Many times these fears are quite realistic and appropriate: illness and injury can be painful, as can medical treatment; for some patients, death is indeed a possibility or a likelihood. The fears and anxieties of patients are usually shared at least to some extent by their families. In the case of infants or very young children, the stresses on the family may be far greater than those on the child who is in this hospital.

Ministers who work in the hospital will see people every day who are undergoing stress, and they will also notice certain behaviors used by these people to cope with their stress. These coping behaviors often take the shape of defense mechanisms: behaviors which in some way help people to reduce the anxiety caused by the stressful situation, at least to some extent. Using defense mechanisms to reduce anxiety temporarily, people are better able to tolerate the stress of hospitalization. It is important for the minister to understand defense mechanisms and how to respond to them, since they may appear at times to be quite strange, even bizarre, and yet they can be very helpful to patients and families.

In psychoanalytic theory, "defense mechanism" has a specific and technical meaning.[1] Erik H. Erikson, trained as a psychoanalyst by Anna Freud, asserts that defense mechanisms "are unconscious

---

[1]The classic exposition is that of Anna Freud in *The Ego and the Mechanisms of Defense* (New York: International Universities Press, 1946).

arrangements which permit the individual to postpone satisfaction, to find substitutions, and otherwise to arrive at compromises between id impulses and superego compulsions."[2] It will be recalled that for Erikson, the ego is "a concept denoting man's capacity to unify his experience and his actions in an adaptive manner."[3] The ego organizes experience in such a way as to ensure the individual a sense of coherent individuation and identity. It enables the person to withstand shocks or unpredictable events which occur in the somatic and social processes.[4] In response to internal anxiety created by conflict between id and superego, the ego process employs mechanisms of defense to reduce that anxiety. In psychoanalytic theory, defense mechanisms are unconscious, meaning that the person employs them without an explicit awareness of them and the way that they serve to reduce anxiety.

The stress of hospitalization can produce a great deal of anxiety in patients and their families, particularly if they face the prospect of great pain or great loss. Losses may be as minimal as losing a few days of school, or may be as great as losing capabilities such as walking, losing a limb, or losing life itself. To reduce anxiety and to make the stressful circumstances surrounding hospitalization more tolerable, patients and families use defense mechanisms to distort their perception of reality and thus make it easier to handle. This distortion is unconscious—the person using a defense mechanism is not aware that he or she is doing so. A clue that a certain behavior is being used as a defense mechanism is that the person becomes emotional when this behavior is questioned. The use of defense mechanisms by patients and families is also often temporary. As the stress lessens, so does anxiety, and the defense is no longer needed and is dropped. The chaplain will also notice that defense mechanisms are used on and off as stress and the anxiety which it causes fluctuate during the hospital stay.

Defense mechanisms as coping behaviors are normal behavior patterns. Their presence indicates that people under stress are seeking to protect themselves from feeling too much anxiety, and that in itself is good. There are times, however, when defensive behavior becomes maladaptive, and in the long or short run causes more harm than good. Such would be the case when a patient denies so vehemently the reality of his illness that he refuses all treatment, even

[2]*Childhood and Society,* p. 193.
[3]Ibid., p. 15.
[4]See above, Chapter I.

though the probability of cure would be very high. In addition, the use of defense mechanisms consumes psychic energy, which at times could be better used to respond to a stressful situation more realistically. The minister who works in the clinical setting, therefore, must be able to recognize defenses, to evaluate their usefulness to the person, and, based upon this evaluation, to decide whether to support the defense, ignore it, or try to help the patient to let go of it.

A variety of defense mechanisms which are seen in the clinical setting will be described below. A discussion of how the chaplain may creatively deal with defensive behavior will conclude the chapter.

Denial

Henry was a seventeen year old youth in the last stages of terminal cancer. His cancer had metastasized (spread throughout the body) and his abdomen was grossly distended by the growths inside. Chaplain Keller began stopping in to see Henry on a daily basis. When he arrived one day for his visit, he knew that two hours previously Henry's doctor had told him frankly that he would die in the next few weeks. After exchanging greetings, Henry began to tell the chaplain about his church and the summer camp it ran. He went on to describe his plans to be on the staff of the camp the following summer (some eight months off).

Patients and families who are under severe stress are capable of denying the most obvious facts in an effort to reduce their anxiety. Henry's denial of his impending death, expressed by making plans for the following summer, brought forth a number of issues: Was he able to trust his doctor, or did he think that the doctor was mistaken? Did Henry really believe that he would recover, or did he know, at least at some level, that death was a certainty? What were Henry's primary emotions? What was he asking of the chaplain in bringing the subject up?

Rather than embroil himself in a medical debate with the patient about the possibility of recovery, Chaplain Keller began to talk with Henry about the history and course of his illness: the first discovery of cancer; the treatments and surgeries that had taken place; the pain that he had experienced; the things that he had had to give up. As the chaplain helped Henry to focus on the concrete reality of his experience, he was able to vent a tremendous amount of anger. He also expressed fear about the future. To the very end of his young life, however, Henry never admitted to anyone that he knew he was going to die.

What was important in Chaplain Keller's ministry to Henry was not an extraction from him of the whole ugly truth, but his presence as a caring and supportive person who was willing to share in Henry's pain and loss and give friendly support in his time of fear. His presence and interest were a great comfort to Henry, who had a lot on his mind that he wanted to share. He was able to respond directly to Henry's needs, and not to force upon the relationship his own agenda, or what he thought Henry's agenda should have been.

Quincy was an eleven year old boy hospitalized with third degree burns over ninety-five percent of his body. The damage to his lungs was also great, and the doctors made it clear to his parents that death was only a matter of days. Quincy's mother took the terrible news calmly and almost wordlessly. When she left the hospital a few hours later to go home, she bought an expensive motorcycle for Quincy. Taking a picture of it, she then brought the photograph to the hospital. Quincy was unconscious, but she showed the picture of the motorcycle to the nurses and to other visitors, explaining to all that as soon as her son recovered, he would come home and ride his new present.

Quincy was certainly near death, and his mother's actions seemed bizarre to other members of the family. It had appeared that she had accepted the terrible news with great strength. The reality, however, was that she blocked it out, denying the horrible reality. For her, the motorcycle became symbolic of her hopes, as unrealistic as they were. Perhaps at some level, she even thought magically that an expensive present would help her son to recover. Only when Quincy actually died a few days later could his mother begin her grieving and begin to accept what had happened.

Flight

Steven was a nine year old boy hospitalized with a broken femur, the large bone in the upper leg, the result of being hit by an automobile. During six weeks of traction, he was fretful and angry much of the time. Finally, he was placed in a spica cast, which he was to have for several more weeks. The cast began at his waist, extended down to the ankle of his broken leg and to the knee of the other, and had a steel bar connecting his thighs, so that both legs were immobilized. As the sedative began to wear off, Steven became more and more agitated, saying "I want to get out of here [the hospital]!" Finally he began tearing at the still-wet cast, literally ripping it away from his body.

Sarah Faust was a twelve-year-old girl hospitalized for the treatment of bone cancer in her leg. The leg had to be amputated just below the knee. Sarah weathered the surgery fairly well, but her mother, Mrs. Faust, left the hospital immediately after surgery and refused to come back to see her. Only after a week and two visits with a therapist was her mother able to return to the hospital.

Flight is a type of denial which takes on the form of an actual attempt physically to flee the source of stress. In Steven's case, this attempted escape was potentially disastrous, because it was imperative that his leg remain immobilized and that he stay in his cast for several weeks. His reaction was treated by the staff as a true emergency: a casting technician and the attending physician were summoned immediately to persuade him to cooperate with his treatment.

In the second case, the concern was for Sarah as much as for her mother. It was important that Sarah not interpret her mother's flight as a rejection of her. Instead, she was helped to see that this was her mother's way of coping with her sorrow, sorrow made all the greater because of her deep love for Sarah.

Regression

Ursula was a ten year old girl hospitalized with viral meningitis, a serious infection of the membranes around the brain and spinal cord. After a few days the viral infection seemed to have cleared up, but Ursula began to exhibit distressing behavior: she began to talk in baby talk ("Me want more!"); she refused to walk around her room or dress herself; she wanted to be fed.

Caroline was a ten year old girl hospitalized with third degree burns over much of her face and chest. After a number of weeks she was well along the road to recovery, but her appearance was shocking. The burn scars and skin grafts on her face were disfiguring; one ear had been burned away and would have to be reconstructed. Caroline had never been a particularly easy patient to manage, but her nurse was shocked to enter her hospital room one morning and discover Caroline smearing her feces on the walls.

People who regress are returning to behavior patterns which were more appropriate at a younger age. They may find some anxiety reduction and comfort in returning to earlier, familiar behavior patterns. Children who are sick or injured often regress to earlier patterns of behavior to help them cope with the upset. They may cry more than usual, cling to their parents, and seem generally less able to cope with daily life. This is usually not harmful, and can even be helpful to the children and their caretakers. A twelve year old boy with an abdominal surgical wound, for example, may readily submit to being bathed by his mother or a nurse, something he would never tolerate under normal circumstances. Thus, regression can be adaptive in a positive way, and a "good" patient is regressed. Such regression generally ceases naturally with the easing of stress, although it is not uncommon for caretakers to have to encourage the recovering child to "grow up" again: "You have been very sick, but you are perfectly capable of taking your own bath and picking up your room now."

Ursula's illness had been quite serious and for two or three days she had to be cared for to a great extent: she needed help eating, was bathed in bed, etc. The troublesome factor was her continuance in that regressed state when she began to recover. Subtly, her parents reinforced her continued regression. They gave in to her every whim and gave her all the attention that she desired. Not only did they not encourage her to act her age and exercise capabilities which she possessed, they actually discouraged it by doing so many things for her, such as bringing her toys and other articles that she could have reached for herself.

Feces smearing is an infantile behavior, and Caroline's return to it indicated great regression, suggesting that her anxiety was also great. Given the seriousness of the situation, a psychiatrist became involved to help her better to cope with her stressful accident and hospital experience.

As a person who visits sick children and spends time with them, the chaplain can help to keep their regression in balance. He can discourage children from attempting what they are truly incapable of doing, while at the same time insisting that they continue to perform those functions which they can realistically accomplish.

Controlling

Charles was a fifteen year old boy hospitalized for a kidney transplant. From the time of his admission, Charles seemed to take charge of his own case. He spoke directly with the members of the hospital staff with whom he came into contact, never allowing his parents to serve as intermediaries. His demeanor with doctors and nurses suggested that he viewed himself as equal to, or even superior to them. He argued with the surgeon about the proper time for surgery. He interrogated nurses about his medication schedule. He insisted on selecting the veins used for taking blood or for intravenous medications. People were at first impressed with his "grown up" attitude and behavior. Before long, however, the staff felt that he was being pushy and dictatorial.

Victoria was a nine year old hospitalized with an abscess in her liver. A major part of her treatment, which lasted several weeks, was the continuous administration of antibiotics through an intravenous drip. From the first day of her hospitalization, her father moved into her private room. As nurses and technicians came and went, he stood by her bed, carefully surveying all that they did and asking many questions. Each time medicine was brought to be placed in the intravenous line he insisted on inspecting it first. When a nurse made a slight error in dosage, he went into a rage, threatening to sue the hospital. He bypassed the usual lines of communication by calling and speaking directly with various departments or services of the hospital. He called the dietary department to instruct the dietician about his child's meals. He called numerous doctors to ask questions about their orders or to talk about the nurses. No one was able to get near Victoria without first passing his inspection. After numerous futile attempts to get him to change his behavior, the medical team had a meeting at which the attending physician wrote orders to restrict the father's presence in the hospital to normal visiting hours. In anger, the father asked to see a chaplain. Chaplain Nickels arrived on the scene, and after explaining the situation as he saw it, the father asked him to intervene with the medical staff in his behalf.

At first blush, Charles' behavior might seem to have been arrogant or childish. In reality, Charles was simply attempting to have some control over his own fate. He was quite aware that his surgery was dangerous; though death was not a likelihood, it was certainly a possibility. Even if the transplant surgery itself succeeded, there was no guarantee that the kidney would function properly or that his body would not eventually reject it, necessitating its removal. Faced with many uncertainties, Charles was able to take some comfort in being able to control various aspects of his treatment. Fortunately the staff understood this defense, and as much as possible they allowed Charles to have a say in his treatment procedures. They even supported this defense by creating choices which Charles could make: one phlebotomist pointed out two veins and asked Charles which he preferred to have blood taken from; a dietary technician suggested a number of possible choices for his meals. These tactics helped to bolster Charles' sense of security and supported a defense mechanism which helped to insulate him from the harsh reality of the uncertain outcome of his surgery.

In a similar way, Victoria's father sought to allay his fears by taking charge of his daughter's treatment. In his case, however, the defense mechanism exercised a harmful influence on his daughter's treatment. Victoria interpreted her father's surveillance of the staff as an indication that they were not to be trusted; her faith in the competence of her caretakers was undermined. The staff found the father's aggressive behavior to be an interference: his calling various departments directly tended to subvert normal lines of communication among the health care team; his threats about malpractice suits were disconcerting.

Chaplain Nickels was able to see that the father's behavior, instead of protecting his daughter, was actually hindering her treatment. It was most important in this case for him to avoid taking sides with the father against the medical staff. Yet, in order to support him, it was necessary to attempt to build some kind of alliance with him. He did this by inviting Victoria's father to share his fears and anxieties about his daughter's illness. He listened attentively, and responded to the feeling content of what he heard: "This infection has really scared you. You certainly are angry that the nurse was late with the medicine." After their visit, Victoria's father had another argument with a doctor and stalked angrily from the hospital, refusing to return. In so doing, he changed his defense from control to flight. His complete absence from the hospital created another set of problems, but at least did not sabotage the treatment of his daughter. An uneasy truce had been reached.

Identification

Ingrid was a seven year old girl hospitalized for corrective surgery on her foot, which had been deformed from birth. Chaplain Osborn stopped by for a visit before her surgery, and found Ingrid playing with a doll. She was holding the doll down on the bed and repeatedly jabbing its foot with a pencil. Invited to talk about her play, Ingrid explained that her doll's foot was broken and that she was fixing it with an operation. Chaplain Osborn seized this opportunity to observe that although the doll's foot was being cut, she felt no pain because the doctor had put her into a deep sleep. Ingrid happily agreed. Together, they rehearsed the operation a number of times from start to finish, with Ingrid playing the role of the surgeon each time.

Ingrid was afraid of her impending surgery, and she was able to reduce her anxiety by identifying with a person whom she viewed as important and powerful: the surgeon. In assuming the role of the surgeon in her play, Ingrid was employing a defense mechanism called identification; that is, she attempted to identify with another person, and through a feeling of oneness with him, she was able to reduce the anxiety she was feeling. Particularly in small children, identification can be a most helpful defense. Indeed, many pediatric units include medical role play with small children as a routine part of their preparation for surgery and other treatments. In this way, the child's helpful defense mechanism is supported and strengthened. Thus, a child about to be placed in a cast is often brought a doll and a small casting kit; in putting a cast on the doll, the child assumes the role of doctor and not only understands the procedures better, but is able to reduce his anxiety about it. Similarly, children are often encouraged to engage in "needle play" with dolls to reduce their fear of needles. Repetition of the play strengthens and reinforces the defense. In encouraging Ingrid repeatedly to play out her own operation with a doll, Chaplain Osborn assisted her in keeping her anxiety within tolerable limits.

Intellectualization

Wayne was a fourteen year old boy who was hospitalized with the onset of juvenile diabetes mellitus. His disease was severe enough to require stringent dietary rules and twice daily injections of insulin. When Chaplain Urban came to see him in his hospital room, she found Wayne poring over a small stack of literature about his disease and its management. After introducing herself, she asked him how he was feeling. Without really answering that question,

Wayne launched into a lengthy and surprisingly sophisticated discussion of his illness. When Chaplain Urban asked him how his illness would affect his daily life, he gave her a complicated explanation of blood chemistry and insulin therapy. His tone was objective and dispassionate; he showed almost no emotion.

Mrs. Altman's six year old son was hospitalized for surgical treatment of a congenital heart defect. The upcoming surgery was extremely rare and risky, and her son had less than a fifty percent chance for survival. When Chaplain Patterson came to see her, he asked, "Tell me about your son." Mrs. Altman began to describe in great detail the nature of his heart defect, using a great deal of jargon and medical terminology. She spoke only in terms of vessels, chambers, valves, blood gas levels, etc., while avoiding saying anything about her child as a person. It was clear to Chaplain Patterson from the ease and fluency of her lecture that she had rehearsed it many times.

Intellectualizing can be an effective way for a person to protect himself from an emotionally stressful reality. Speaking only in technical and objective terms distances the person from the source of stress. A constant flow of technical verbiage can create a wall between the person and his emotions, as well as blocking off the emotions of others around him. Intellectualization can be a seductive defense in the sense that others who come into contact with the intellectualizer can be drawn into the intellectual discussion. The territory there seems safe, and particularly if the intellectualizer is willing to do most of the talking (and he usually is!) his companion also enjoys the protection of this defense. Intellectualization is often supported by medical staff members, and rightly so to some extent. It is good for patients and families to have an accurate understanding of the illness or injury. They are better able to cooperate with treatment when they understand what it is and why it helps. In many cases, such as Wayne's, treatment and management of a disease can be successful only when the patient understands and actively cooperates.

At the same time, when intellectualization is used to block out powerful emotions, it can be harmful; the stifled emotional energy may be expressed or released in ways that create new problems. Chaplain Urban recognized that Wayne's disease would have a dramatic effect on his life. She knew that its side-effects could be dangerous. She was able to invite Wayne to talk about this by interrupting him and saying, "I am really impressed that you have studied your disease so well. I can see that you are going to be a good patient and take care of yourself. But I know that you must make a lot of changes in your life and give up things, like sweets. Don't you have some feelings about that?" In Wayne's case, he responded to this invitation by dropping the defense and speaking frankly about his anger and fear. As he spoke, he began to cry. The expression of these emotions was helpful to him and aided him in approaching his predicament in a more integrated manner.

Mrs. Altman was more reluctant to let go of her defense, even for a few moments. Her response to open-ended queries from the chaplain was highly rational and avoided emotional themes. Chaplain Patterson finally helped her to express some emotion by suggesting a feeling. He said, "You have told me that your son has less than a fifty percent chance of living through this. I think I would be very scared by that." This seemed to give Mrs. Altman the necessary permission to express her own fear, which she did briefly.

Chaplain Patterson could have attempted a forceful confrontation in his effort to break through Mrs. Altman's defensive behavior. However, the chaplain should remember that people generally use defense mechanisms because they *need* them; to shatter such defenses forcefully can do much more harm than good. A good rule of thumb is to think in terms of helping the person through *invitation* rather than through *confrontation*. Defenses do serve to protect people, and this is to be respected. It should also be remembered that in facing similar situations, different people need different levels of defenses; that is, some need to protect themselves more than others do.

Rationalization

John was a thirteen year old boy hospitalized for several weeks for the treatment of a broken femur (thigh bone). The long hospital stay was required because John was placed in traction, the broken leg hoisted up in the air. When Chaplain Quarrels came in to see him, they discussed the circumstances of John's injury. At one point, he said, "I'm really kind of glad I broke my leg. It's cold outside now, and it wouldn't be much fun to go out and mess around. I'm glad I have to stay in the hospital."

Mrs. Cramer's six year old daughter was hospitalized with leukemia. Previously the child had undergone chemotherapy and the disease had been in remission. Suddenly a new crisis had developed. At the time Chaplain Vine stopped in to see Mrs. Cramer, the outlook for her daughter was very bad. As they discussed her illness, Mrs. Cramer commented, "You know, in a crazy way I'm relieved that it finally happened. When she was in remission, every day was scary. Now at least I know what will happen."

Rationalization is a defense which may be characterized as "sour grapes" ("I didn't want it anyway") or "sweet lemon" ("This is really good after all"). In the former case, nothing can please a person; in the latter, the person makes up excuses to justify or to label as good almost anything, no matter how bad it really is. Carried to an extreme, people can create excuses which allow them to pretend that events such as serious injury or impending death are actually good, or at least not too bad. This helps them to insulate themselves from the pain which should accompany such tragic occurrences.

In the case above, John's rationalization was both "sour grapes" ("It wouldn't be much fun to go out anyway") and "sweet lemon" ("I'm glad I broke my leg and have to stay in the hospital"). His rationalization continued throughout most of his six week stay in the hospital, with occasional lapses. His situation was only temporary, and this defense served to protect him for that time period. Chaplain Quarrels saw no harm being done by this defense mechanism and chose not to challenge it in any way. He did, however, invite John to talk about things he was missing out on while being in the hospital, as well as any other negative features of the hospitalization. John responded accordingly, but kept his expression of dissatisfaction at a minimal level.

Mrs. Cramer's daughter eventually died. Her rationalization helped her as the death approached, but was dropped completely when it occurred. At that time, she gave in fully to her grief, and allowed Chaplain Vine as well as her family and friends to offer support and consolation.

Humor

Chaplain Yates was summoned to the hospital emergency room to be with a family whose eight year old son had just been accidentally electrocuted. She met the family and was surprised when, after a few minutes, the boy's father, Mr. Deardon, began to tell jokes and laugh hilariously. Clearly the family was shocked and dismayed by this behavior. Seeing that this was defensive behavior, Chaplain Yates commented quietly to him, "You are really going to miss your

son, aren't you?" Mr. Deardon looked slightly surprised, and then be-
gan to cry, finally breaking into racking sobs. As this happened, his
wife put her arms around him and they wept together.

Mr. Deardon's use of humor as a defense mechanism was blocking his grief over the death of his son. Humor was a way to deny the
pain or not let it come through. In addition to serving as a block to
his feelings, his joking dismayed the other members of the family
since it did not seem to them like appropriate behavior. However, the
wall was thin and fragile, and one probing comment from the chaplain broke through to the pain. It was important for Mr. Deardon to
get in touch with his pain, for only by feeling it could he begin the
necessary work of grieving for his dead son.

Compensation

Karl was a seventeen year old boy hospitalized with hemophilia.
Because he bled easily, Karl had always led a sheltered life. He was
never allowed far from home and could never play even mildly rough
games with other boys. Throughout his life his hospitalizations had
been frequent. His stature happened to be slight, and he appeared to
be weak. Karl arrived at the hospital dressed in blue jeans and
leather, with chains hanging off of his clothing. His hair was long
and unkempt. He became a management problem on the adolescent
unit when he constantly threatened other patients with violence and
tried repeatedly to coerce the staff into giving him narcotic drugs. In
his frustration, he asked to see a chaplain. When Chaplain Jacobson
arrived, Karl explained that he was "real bad" [slang for very tough]
but that the patients and staff "don't give me no respect." He stated
further that he wanted to punch one of the doctors.

Mrs. Post was in the hospital taking care of her sixteen year old
son. He was hydrocephalic and mentally retarded, and had required
constant care and supervision all of his life. Mrs. Post calculated that
in his sixteen years of life, he had spent at least four years in the
hospital. When Chaplain Farmer came by the room for a pastoral
visit, he noticed that Mrs. Post was dressed in well worn denim pants
and jacket. She wore no makeup, and had on a pair of very heavy
leather boots. Her response to him was friendly but a bit gruff. Mrs.
Post readily told the story of her son's birth defect and subsequent
hospitalizations. She spoke with pride of his accomplishments and
his will to survive. When Chaplain Farmer commented, "You have

had a very rough time with all of this," she replied, "That's true enough. But I'm tough as nails, and it doesn't bother me. I help the other parents [on the same unit] when they need support." "That's fine," remarked the chaplain, "but I'll bet there are times when you could use a little help and support yourself." Looking a little taken aback, Mrs. Post said, "I guess you're right, but I never get any."

When people feel inferior or weak and vulnerable, they may use the defense mechanism of compensation to negate the cause of those feelings of inferiority and thus reduce their anxiety. In Karl's case, his fear of being weak became an important issue during his adolescent identity crisis.[5] As he grew into manhood, it was important for Karl that he take on those characteristics which he considered to be manly. He felt inhibited in doing this by his illness and physical weakness, and this caused a loss of self-esteem and anxiety. In an effort to hide from his shortcomings and the pain which they occasioned, Karl compensated by imagining himself to be extraordinarily tough, a man to be feared by others, and by acting that way.

In their conversation together, Chaplain Jacobson and Karl discovered that he was constantly comparing himself to his father, a former Marine of burly physique. The chaplain helped Karl to see that as long as he equated manhood with a powerful and muscular body, he would never live up to the ideals which he set for himself. Over a number of sessions, they discussed the meaning of manhood, and Chaplain Jacobson pointed out that Karl could indeed attain important qualities of masculinity and adulthood, and that he already in fact possessed many of them. They spoke together about how men may also let their soft and gentle sides show, and that other people appreciated these qualities in men. The issue for Karl was neither his expressed desire to take narcotics nor his talk about aggressive behavior; rather, his concern was about his need and desire to be perceived as a man. Further time was spent with Karl exploring the notion that his disease would continue to be an important factor in his life, and that through acceptance of this real weakness, he could grow into a stronger person. Eventually Karl could see that his defensive pretensions of toughness actually hurt him more than they helped, and that they prevented significant others from liking and admiring him.

When Mrs. Post commented that she never received help or support from others, Chaplain Farmer pointed out that in her appear-

---

[5]See above, Chapter 1.

ance and mannerisms, she exuded a definite sense of strength, competence, and self-sufficiency. He spent some time affirming her strengths and expressing his sincere admiration of the way she had cared for her son all of his life. He then reflected with her on his own feelings about her: that she seemed to be so strong, so in control, and so unneeding of help. Together they explored ways in which she could ask for help or support from others in the future.

In each of these cases, a person adopted a defense mechanism which served as an insulation against pain, but which had a debilitating impact. For Karl, his acting tough held others at a distance from himself and solicited aggressive or angry responses. For Mrs. Post, this defense prevented others from seeing her own need to be supported and nurtured. In both situations, the defense mechanism isolated not only the pain, but the entire person as well.

Displacement

Donald was a five year old boy hospitalized with appendicitis. He was admitted to the hospital in the evening, with the plan that surgery would take place the first thing in the morning as long as his condition did not deteriorate during the night. The upcoming surgery was carefully explained to Donald, who had few comments or questions. Later, as his mother was preparing him for bed, she asked him to enter the bathroom and take a bath. Without warning, Donald began to cry hysterically, refusing to enter the bathroom, and saying that he was frightened to go in there.

Donald was apprehensive about his upcoming surgery. He displaced his fear of the operating room, however, onto the bathroom, i.e., he substituted a neutral thing for the true object of his fear—on an emotional level, he traded the operating room for the bathroom. Fortunately, the floor nurse recognized this defensive behavior as an indication of Donald's general state of anxiety. She helped him to focus on the real object of his fear by talking with him at some length about his surgery and the operating room facilities. She played doctor with him, encouraging him to assume the role of surgeon, thus helping him to substitute a better defense (identification) for the one he had been using. This tactic worked, and Donald was able to face his surgery in relative calm.

Projection

Nathan was a twelve year old boy hospitalized with Hodgkins Disease, a type of cancer which can be fatal and may occur in children. Chaplain Cooper came by for a visit, and Nathan readily told her about his disease and his upcoming course of chemotherapy. After a few minutes, Nathan beckoned her to lean closer, and, gesturing toward a child in the hallway, whispered, "See that kid? He's really afraid 'cause he's probably gonna die." The child to whom he referred was in the hospital with a broken forearm.

Nathan's implausible claim about another patient was a defensive maneuver. He knew that his own disease was extremely serious, possibly fatal, and of course this was a source of great fear for him. He attempted to insulate himself from this fear by projecting it onto another child. In short, fear was safer and hurt less if it was someone else's and not his own.

Chaplain Cooper recognized this defense mechanism, and instead of focusing on the obvious falsehood, she seized the opportunity to help Nathan begin to confront his own fear. After a serious nod, she commented, "Lots of kids in this hospital are afraid. I'll bet even you are afraid sometimes." This was enough of an invitation for Nathan to begin to open up. As he began to acknowledge his own fear of death, his eyes filled with tears. Chaplain Cooper said, "Sometimes when I'm really afraid of something, I just like to be held tight. Would you like me to hold you for a minute?" Nathan nodded and reached out for a hug. After a few moments, he indicated that he felt better. Chaplain Cooper then pointed out that there were a number of people who would give Nathan similar comfort and support if he were to ask them for it; she asked him if he could think of any. Nathan immediately named his parents and his grandmother. She then suggested that when he felt frightened, he could tell them about it and ask for a hug.

Chaplain Cooper was able to help Nathan to confront his fears and also taught him how he could ask for the kind of comfort which would make those fears more bearable. She did not challenge him on his judgment of the other child's prognosis; that was not the point. Instead, she helped to put him in touch with personal relationships that could serve as a source of strength for him.

Mr. Rose's fourteen year old mentally retarded son was hospitalized for treatment of hydrocephaly, a condition where too much fluid accumulates in the brain. His son had been in and out of hos-

pitals all of his life, and this was likely to continue. When Chaplain Pierce stopped in to see him, he mentioned that he did not like that particular hospital. When she inquired as to why, he explained that the nurses were all angry at his son. He was unable to explain their anger, and was unable to provide any convincing examples of it.

Chaplain Pierce recognized that Mr. Rose was feeling a great deal of anger himself. He was burdened with innumerable stays in the hospital and with appalling medical bills. Family life was constantly disrupted by his son's chronic illness. Even when his son was well, he required constant care and attention. At some level, Mr. Rose was angry with his son because he was ill. Admitting this anger, however, was not an easy thing to do. How could a father be angry at his own beloved son for circumstances that were entirely beyond his control? Mr. Rose avoided anxiety by projecting his own anger onto other people. It was easier for him to say that the nurses, who were virtual strangers, were angry at his son than it was to admit that he himself was angry at the sick boy.

Had Chaplain Pierce attempted to argue with Mr. Rose about whether the nurses were really angry, they might have become embroiled in an endless and fruitless debate. Instead, she reviewed with him the many stresses and inconveniences caused by the boy's illness, and suggested that such extreme problems could be reason for anger. She helped him to focus on his anger at the illness itself and on the situation, rather than on the boy as a person. It was her judgment that in a first interview it was not prudent to push the father into acknowledging anger at his son, even if this were the case (and such things are often not certain). Rather, she helped him to focus on his own feelings of anger in a safer way by inviting him to tell her how frustrating the years of hospital visits had been. Mr. Rose spoke at some length about his frustrations at the *situation:* financial struggles, missed vacations, multiple inconveniences, not being able to make long-range plans, etc.

Repression

Howard was a ten year old boy hospitalized with a broken femur (thigh bone), the result of being struck by a car as he crossed a street. He was fully conscious when he arrived at the hospital in an ambulance. During the next few hours, the doctors and staff took a number of x-rays, set the fracture, and placed the leg in traction. Making the leg ready for traction involved drilling a hole through Howard's tibia (shin bone) and inserting a small rod to which were attached weighted ropes. No general anesthesia was used, and throughout the procedures Howard was alert. He conversed intelligently with the staff, but also spent some time screaming in pain and fright so loudly that his parents could hear him down the corridor as they sat in the waiting room. On the second day of Howard's hospitalization, Chaplain Thorn came to visit him in his room. Having spoken with Howard's mother, the chaplain was aware of the harrowing experience two days before. He was surprised that when he invited Howard to talk about the experience of having his leg set, he claimed not to remember. He attempted to jog Howard's memory by recalling for him some details ("They took a lot of x-rays, didn't they?" "I heard from your mom that it hurt to have your leg set"), but Howard simply would not acknowledge any detailed memory of the experience.

People sometimes push painful memories out of their conscious memory and thinking. When this is done *consciously,* it is called suppression; when it is done *unconsciously,* it is called repression. Howard used the defense of repression in order to protect himself from the memory of a very painful and frightening experience. In this case, Chaplain Thorn decided not to attempt to challenge this defense since it did not seem to be causing any immediate harm and Howard seemed fairly tranquil about his hospitalization. Instead, he focused his conversation with Howard on other stresses which he was experiencing: six to eight weeks in the hospital, being in a body cast for a number of weeks, missing several months of school, etc. In this was he able to support Howard without hindering the defense mechanism which was reducing his anxiety.

The Chaplain's Response to Defensive Behavior

Ministers, or those learning to be ministers, seek to develop skills in hospital work through various means. They may take courses in pastoral counseling, engage in actual hospital work under formal or informal supervision, attend workshops, seminars, etc., or seek to learn through reading. In such experiences, they often hear about the value of the minister probing beyond surface level conversation with people, and of attempting to see with them their critical life issues, their pain, their need to grow, etc. Often ministers or students are exhorted, "Stay with the feeling level! Go for the emotions!

Do not skirt around areas that seem to be painful, but instead expose them and talk about them."

For those who seek to minister effectively and thereby reduce suffering and promote personal and spiritual growth, this is excellent advice. Yet, the inexperienced minister may, without being aware of it, make a mere caricature of this good counsel. He may interpret it to mean that his job is to make people confront their deepest pain, no matter how forcefully. He may recognize a person's defenses, but regard them merely as blockades to growth, walls that should be torn down expeditiously so that the whole painful truth is revealed in all its ugliness. He may believe that his function is to help people see the whole truth about themselves (at least as *he* sees it), and that harsh confrontation is a great act of love and liberation.

Such an attitude betrays on the minister's part an ignorance of at least two realities. First, defense mechanisms are normal behaviors. All people, healthy or not, employ some defenses not only in their day to day living, but in times of crisis. Second, these defense mechanisms are actually necessary. Their function is to protect the person against realities which are anxiety producing or difficult to bear. Life is filled with stressors, and some of the resulting anxieties are intolerable; defenses shield people from them and allow them to continue with life. Defenses help people by reducing anxiety, at least temporarily. An attempt to dismantle all of a person's defenses is an attempt to render him defenseless, totally vulnerable to overwhelming anxiety. Far from being an act of love, this would constitute an act of aggression, setting a person up to be dysfunctional.

Having said all of this, it remains true that the chaplain should approach defensive behaviors critically. After recognizing a defense mechanism, he should attempt to evaluate its helpfulness for the patient or family member. To do this, he can ask himself several questions. First, does this particular defense actually function so as to reduce anxiety? One situation which yielded a negative answer to this question was that of Donald, who traded his fear of surgery for fear of the bathroom, but was still overwhelmed with anxiety.

Second, the chaplain may ask: Is this defensive behavior harmful to the patient, or neutral, or helpful? When Steven attempted to tear away his cast and flee the hospital, he was harming himself. In the first place, such an act simply could not be allowed by the staff. But even if Steven had succeeded in getting out of his cast, he would have been utterly unable to move about, and probably would have caused himself tremendous physical pain.

Third, one asks what effect the defensive behavior has on other people who are part of the situation. Does this behavior promote or interfere with important relationships? Mrs. Faust experienced great anxiety when her daughter's leg was amputated. However, by fleeing the situation, she put distance between herself and her daughter, as well as making it difficult for her to support the child and for the medical staff to keep in touch with her so as to provide the best medical care. When Caroline regressed and smeared her feces on the wall, she elicited in others responses of anger, revulsion, disgust, etc. Her actions strained her relationship with the health care team and with her family. On the other hand, defenses may promote important relationships. Mild regression may reinforce the bond between parent and child. Intellectualization may help the patient relate well to the medical team and to participate more fully in treatment.

Another way of approaching the evaluation of defenses is to ask whether the defense is functional or dysfunctional, i.e., does it work to reduce anxiety? Also, does the defensive behavior create new problems, and, if it does, are these greater or lesser evils than the original anxiety? It should be obvious that such evaluation requires judgment calls. Chaplains should by no means take it upon themselves to judge the value and helpfulness of every defensive behavior they encounter. Remembering that they function as members of a health care team, they should freely consult with other members when they have doubts.

When a certain defense is obviously beneficial to the patient, the chaplain can be helpful by reinforcing that defense. Perhaps the outstanding example is that of identification by means of playing doctor. In many pediatric units, this activity is standard procedure with patients. It is easy for the chaplain to support this behavior by playing with children he sees or at least by encouraging them to do so. Even when the chaplain has helped the patient to move beyond the defense, the defense can still be supported. Wayne dealt with the stress of his diabetes by intellectualizing. When the chaplain invited him to discuss his feelings, he did so and expressed his pain appropriately. At the same time, however, continued support of his intellectualizing was also appropriate: it encouraged Wayne to continue to learn about his disease and its treatment, and thus to be able to cooperate more effectively with the treatment plan.

In a similar vein, the chaplain will find patients under great stress who are inadequately defended against it. In such situations, the chaplain can help the patient to find and use defenses which reduce stress. Again, identification through playing doctor is particularly helpful for younger children. Intellectualization can be a helpful defense for older children and adolescents. At times, a certain amount of regression is to be encouraged, as in cases when it helps the patient submit to necessary treatment or other care. Van Ornum and Murdock have pointed out that in order to enable children better to cope with crisis situations, the helper needs to assist the child in marshaling positive forces, in both the child's life and self. Specifically, this involves improving the child's relationships with others, affirming positive relationships with important caretakers, and looking for mature coping efforts on the child's part.[6] It should be apparent that the chaplain can often work in precisely these areas. He can improve the child's relationships with staff and family by encouraging him to communicate openly, by praising appropriate behavior, and perhaps by acting as liaison.[7] He can affirm positive relationships with caretakers by assuring the child that the medical staff is there to help and that they are good people. He can look for mature coping behaviors on the child's part and praise and support them; he can help the child to choose the defensive behaviors which are more helpful than others.

When the chaplain encounters defense mechanisms in patients or families which seem harmful or counter-productive, he may be able to help them let go of these defenses or to substitute in their place more helpful ones. In deciding how hard to push, this author finds the following rule of thumb helpful: Invitation rather than confrontation. The chaplain may invite the patient to let go of a defense. For example, Chaplain Farmer observed to Mrs. Post that in choosing the defense of compensation by acting tough, she was giving the impression of not needing help. He suggested that it was all right to appear weak at times and to ask for help. He encouraged her to be freer about trying this in the future. He did not, however, attack her behavior, or describe it in a blaming or accusing mode. Similarly, Chaplain Urban invited Wayne, who was intellectualizing about his diabetes, to express himself on a different level, the emotional one. She did not accuse him of hiding his feelings or belittle his attempts to intellectualize. Her approach took on the character of an invitation to explore new areas.

---

[6]William Van Ornum and John B. Murdock, *Crisis Counseling with Children and Adolescents* (New York: Continuum, 1983) pp. 11–14.

[7]See above, Chapter 2.

There are times when a defense mechanism is so strong and so harmful that it does real damage to the patient. In such situations it might be appropriate to attempt to confront this mechanism, perhaps even harshly to do so. When this is done, however, the helper must concomitantly take on the responsibility of helping the patient to construct new defense mechanisms which are more helpful and less harmful. This falls within the purview of the psychiatrist or psychologist, and is clearly not the function of the chaplain unless he has specialized training in one of those fields.

A second rule of thumb that will help the chaplain is: When in doubt, consult. The chaplain must remember that he is part of the health care team, a group of experts who specialize in different areas of patient care. He should never be hesitant to consult other members of the team when he is in doubt about how to approach a given situation.

Conclusion

Defense mechanisms are ways of thinking or behaving which protect people from the anxiety associated with stressful situations. They are normal behavior patterns which the chaplain will encounter often in the clinical situation. Types of defense mechanisms were discussed by way of example: denial, flight, regression, controlling, identification, intellectualization, rationalization, compensation, displacement, projection, and repression. After recognizing defense mechanisms, the chaplain should evaluate their helpfulness, and, based on his evaluation, ignore the defense, support it, or invite the person to let go of it, even if only temporarily. Consultation with other members of the health care team should always take place in questionable cases.

RECOMMENDED READING

Freud, Anna. *The Ego and the Mechanisms of Defense*. New York: International Universities, 1946.

Petrillo, Madeline. *Emotional Care of Hospitalized Children: An Environmental Approach*. Philadelphia: Lippincott, 1980.

Vernon, David T. A. *The Psychological Responses of Children to Hospitalization and Illness: A Review of the Literature*. Springfield, Ill.: Thomas, 1965.

6.

Prayer as a Form of Pastoral Care

The ability to help hospitalized children and their families to pray will be one of the chaplain's most important assets in the exercise of pastoral care. This prayer may well take the form of spoken words, whether this entails the recitation of memorized prayers or simply "talking" to God. But prayer can and should move well beyond these words and become the occasion for experiencing God's presence and for listening for his voice. As will be seen, even younger children can be helped to pray more deeply through forms of meditation. Finally, ritual as a very special type of prayer will be discussed; religious ritual may be uniquely effective in fostering a believer's relationship with God.

What is Prayer?

If chaplains are in the habit of asking patients and their families how they may be of help during the hospital stay, a frequent request will be for prayer. This is truer of parents and older children than of younger children. Prayer can be a powerful tool in ministry, and prayerful moments often have powerful healing effects.

Prayer derives its power from its very nature: prayer is the carrying on of a relationship with God, however one might conceive of God. Like all other relationships, a person's relationship with God must flow in two directions: toward God and from God. Prayer, therefore, involves not only communicating thoughts and feelings *to* God, but also an openness to listening, an inner personal stillness that permits receptivity to what God might want to communicate to the person.

117

A relationship between two human beings can never be completely defined or totally structured. Relationships are by their very nature dynamic, not static. They change and evolve constantly. They involve many levels of interaction, some conscious and intended, others unconscious and unintended. Relationships are affected by external circumstances: their context affects their substance. But relationships may also transcend their context and grow in ways that no one could foresee; great literature has long explored this mystery (see, for example, Shakespeare's *Romeo and Juliet*) and a mystery it remains. The more fully human a relationship is, the more dynamic, complex, multi-faceted, and mysterious it becomes.[1]

In a similar way, our relationship with God is dynamic, complex, multi-faceted, and mysterious. It may never be completely defined or laid out in a diagram. Prayer, therefore, understood as the carrying out of our relationship with God, may never be exhaustively described. Any explanation of prayer will be incomplete. But that does not mean that such explanations are empty or useless, for they can tell us some of the truth about prayer.

A useful description of prayer is offered by John Macquarrie in *Paths in Spirituality*.[2] He presents prayer as *thinking*. Macquarrie understands each person as having a religious dimension. This might be described as an inner strength or inner depth, both dynamic and stable. It is a sort of inner serenity and inner peace in the face of the world. Macquarrie's thesis is that "a fully human, fully personal being is one in whom the religious dimension has been developed, and that the capacity for religion belongs to all of us."[3] This dimension can grow and develop, but if left unattended and unnourished, it will wither away.

For Macquarrie, prayerful thinking has four characteristics. First, it is passionate thinking. Rather than a detached analysis of the world, prayer is a form of thinking that enters "feelingly" into the world and knows itself to be deeply involved there. Second, prayer is compassionate thinking. We consciously regard ourselves as standing alongside of others, sharing their feelings and aspirations. Concretely, this takes the form of intercessory prayer for others. Third, prayer is responsible thinking, whereby we accept responsibility to go outside of ourselves. We acknowledge the claim that the world makes upon us. Fourth, prayer is thankful thinking,

[1]See Martin Buber, *I and Thou*.
[2]New York: Harper & Row, 1972, esp. pp. 25–39.
[3]Ibid., p. 5.

wherein we gratefully acknowledge what is good in the world and what hopes for good things are held out to us. These four elements comprise a fundamental style of thinking which, even if it is not explicitly prayer, leads a person toward belief in God. Thus, agnostics or atheists may be said to "pray" in this way.

In the chaplain's relationships with patients, families, and hospital staff, there will be frequent occasions for experiencing all four types of prayerful thinking. Prayer is first of all *passionate* thinking. Passions often run rife in a hospital setting, especially when there is a life-threatening crisis. Those who face a possible loss often feel great fear and anger. There may be an atmosphere of tension and pressure. Feelings of helplessness and depression may soon follow. On the other hand, there are situations which elicit in those involved feelings of tremendous joy and exultation: when surgery is successful, when a baby is born, when an excellent prognosis is anticipated, when the day of release from the hospital at last arrives. The chaplain will also encounter more placid passions, which does not mean that they are any less strong: the peaceful acceptance with which some are blessed as they prepare for death, be it their own or a loved one's. The expression of any of these passions may be the stuff of prayer and may become the occasion for a deep awareness of God's presence.

Prayer is, secondly, *compassionate* thinking. In the hospital setting, its locus would seem to be primarily within the ones who choose to be present to those who suffer. "Compassion" means "feeling with" or "feeling together." It involves a sharing in the life experience of another to the extent that part of the other's reality becomes one's own. Prayer as compassionate thinking takes form as the chaplain enters into the patient's experience of suffering and then offers support and comfort. In this compassionate prayer, the chaplain affirms God's love and the church's concern for those who suffer. Compassionate prayer means finding a way to let those who suffer know that they are not alone in their pain. It should be obvious that other caregivers in the hospital setting may choose to have a share in this compassion which is prayerful; they, too, share in the patient's journey and they, too, offer support, comfort, and reassurance. At times patients begin to care for one another, if not medically, at least in other authentically human ways. Fast friendships can form between roommates, and it is often the support of others who share the same tragedy which is most helpful.

Third, prayer is *responsible* thinking. Authentic prayer is never detached in the sense of being uninterested and aloof. Prayer ties people together, constituting at times new relationships, at other times strengthening those which already exist, or introducing into them new facets. As the minister is drawn into the patient's world, a new alliance is created; the minister becomes someone who is for and with the patient. This new alliance creates new responsibilities. Ministers do not operate in a vacuum. They represent their churches, seen both as gatherings of the faithful and as institutions, and they may, in the eyes of the patient, represent God. They are, therefore, responsible to patients precisely because they are powerfully symbolic. They bring into the relationship a reality which transcends and surpasses the mere personal encounter of two human beings.

Prayer, is, lastly, thankful thinking. Patients often have much to be thankful for, and at times may be fairly bursting with gratitude. This may stem from relief at having avoided something painful or onerous, such as a painful medical procedure. At other times, patients wish to celebrate successful treatment. Patients and chaplains both may be thankful for the new-found relationships with one another. They may rejoice also in the experience of the closeness of God. Whatever the context, thinking with gratitude becomes the opportunity for prayer.

Prayerful Thinking with Patients and Families

Most children conceive of prayer in one or two forms: "talking to God," and reciting memorized prayers. Many adults also view prayer primarily in this way, and most who pray are comfortable with putting their prayer in the form of words, even if these words are unspoken and only thought. Macquarrie's view of prayer as different types of thinking meshes nicely with an understanding of prayer as comprised of words. Chaplains will find that using words to express thinking which is passionate, compassionate, responsible, and thankful will be an effective prayer form. At times, and especially when the one who prays believes in God, these words will be addressed explicitly to God. At other times, with both believers and non-believers, the words which express thinking that is passionate, compassionate, responsible, and thankful will not be explicitly addressed to a higher power. And yet, this thinking is at least prayer-like.

> This passionate thinking, that is open to feeling the world as well
> as knowing it, is at least the threshold of prayer. To think of the

world with longing for its perfecting is a step toward praying for the coming of the kingdom; to think of the world with rejoicing for all that is good is inarticulately to hallow the name; to think of the world with shame for our failures is implicitly to ask forgiveness for our sins and trespasses. Wherever there is the kind of passionate thinking described above, there is something that has an affinity with prayer.[4]

Prayer is a fundamental style of thinking, passionate and compassionate, responsible and thankful, that is deeply rooted in our humanity and that manifests itself not only among believers but also among serious-minded people who do not profess any religious faith. Yet it seems to me that if we follow out the instinct to pray that is in all of us, it will finally bring us to faith in God.[5]

As has been mentioned, chaplains often become involved in praying with others because they are asked to do so. At other times, the chaplain may sense that it is appropriate to suggest that prayer take place; in this case, the chaplain must be prepared to accept the unwillingness of others to enter into prayer if that is their wish. When a patient or family has indicated a desire not to become involved in prayer, comments from the chaplain such as "Okay, but at least *I* will pray for you" are not helpful; rather, they seem to the author to be a form of religious one-upmanship that is an affront to the wishes of others.

In beginning a time of prayer with others, the chaplain should first of all give some attention to the environment and the comfort (or discomfort) of those present. For example, a child patient may have a real willingness to pray with the chaplain, but also may need urgently to go to the bathroom; at other times, patients will be in a state of pain, and the chaplain should be aware of this. Privacy for those who wish to pray is important. Some people would be embarrassed to pray with a minister in the middle of a day room or hallway; a more private space is preferable. In a similar vein, the time of prayer should not be imposed upon unwilling or hapless bystanders: roommates or visitors, for example, should be invited either into or out of the prayer; simply ignoring them while they sit several feet away produces an uncomfortable situation. The chaplain may take steps to secure privacy such as drawing curtains around the bed or closing the hospital room door, but this should be done with the ap-

---

[4]Ibid., p. 26.
[5]Ibid., p. 30.

proval of the patient: "I'd like to close your door now so that we can pray without being disturbed. Is that okay with you?" Similarly, the chaplain may seek to eliminate distractions as much as possible. Hospital room televisions are a big offender here. Child patients and even adult family members may not think to turn them off or even turn the volume down when the chaplain arrives for a visit. In this situation, the chaplain should ask permission to deal with the problem: "I'm ready to pray with you now, but it's hard for me when the television is going. Could we turn it off while we pray?" Chaplains may also find their prayer time with a patient interrupted when hospital staff or visitors enter the room. In such cases, it is good to say, "We're having a little prayer together now. We'll be finished in just a minute (or a few minutes, or whatever)." Rare indeed is the visitor who is unwilling to respect the time of prayer. Some may even wish to join in, and this is entirely appropriate if the patient desires it.

It is helpful to invite patients or other family members to begin the prayer. This helps the chaplain to gain some idea of their relationship with God, and to respond in a way that is appropriate. For example, a small child who has been hospitalized with appendicitis may pray, "I'm sorry, God, for being bad. Please let me go home soon." This gives the chaplain a tentative idea of the child's concept of God (punisher?) and alerts him to an important issue to be addressed (the patient's feelings of guilt, and possible misunderstanding that bad behavior caused the illness). In order to invite prayer in this way, the chaplain may say, "Would you like to begin our prayer? Then I could finish up."

In many cases such an invitation will be readily accepted, and the patient will begin a prayer. At other times, the patient may exhibit a faint unease with the idea, and yet, with a little encouragement, be able to articulate a prayer. In some cases, however, patients will state flatly that they prefer not to have to pray, but want the chaplain to do it for them; these wishes should always be respected.

The chaplain's prayer should not be created in a vacuum. Rather, it should have as its context the life experience of the patient, particularly with regard to the hospital visit, and the patient's religious beliefs insofar as the chaplain has been able to discern them. Prayer should come after the chaplain has spent time with the patient, getting acquainted and hearing the patient's story. It can then be a more accurate reflection of the relationship with God which the patient actually has. It is even better when the patient is able to pray first, for this gives the chaplain a far better sense of how the patient relates to God. If prayer *is* one's relationship with God, then it cannot take on form or content which does not reflect the reality of the relationship. When chaplains, for whatever reason, are asked to pray when they still have little or no sense of the patient's relationship with God or religious beliefs, then they should not attempt to make the prayer that of the patient; rather, they should make the prayer their own, with its own context established by the chaplains' belief systems. We turn now to illustrations and discussion of these principles.

William was an eleven year old boy hospitalized with Hodgkins Disease, a type of cancer which can be fatal. When Chaplain Yearly visited him, the boy had already been told about his illness and its seriousness. During their conversation, William expressed clear feelings of fright about his upcoming chemotherapy and about the ultimate course of his disease. When asked about his religion, William indicated that he and his family were members of a Protestant church, and he went on to say that he believed that God would help him to be cured. When invited by the chaplain to pray together, William readily agreed.

Chaplain: Would you like to take a couple of minutes now and pray together?
William: Yeah, I'd like that.
Chaplain: How about if you start us off, and then I'll finish.
William: Okay. (Pause) I'm not sure I know how.
Chaplain: Well, why don't you just tell God how you feel, and ask him to help you?
William: Okay. (Pause) God, I'm real sick. I have Hodgkins. I'm scared 'cause I don't want to die. (Pause) Please don't let me die, God. (Pause)
Chaplain: God, William is really scared right now. He knows that you love him, and he wants your help. Help William. Help him to get better. Help the doctors to cure his sickness. Help William not to be so afraid. (Pause) Amen.
William: Amen.

The prayer shared by Chaplain Yearly and William reflected accurately the medical situation, William's feelings about it, and William's concept of God. The objective situation was that William was dangerously ill, and was faced with the possibility of death as well as with the certainty of unpleasant treatment. William did not attempt to avoid this reality, and neither did the chaplain. The life or death seriousness of William's condition was reflected in the prayer. To such a harsh objective reality, William reacted subjectively (and appropriately) with fear. He was able to express his feelings of fear forthrightly to the chaplain, and to God in his prayer, making it a form of thinking which was passionate. In his prayer, the chaplain acknowledged this fear and asked God to help—his prayer was compassionate. He was willing to enter deeply into William's experience, to share his feelings, and to walk along with the boy on his journey of pain and fear.

It can hardly be stressed enough that prayer should acknowledge and validate a patient's reality and that prayer should not turn into an effort to hide the reality, to deny it, or to attempt to distract the patient from it. William's reality during this time of prayer was danger and fear, and for the prayer to be authentic, it had to acknowledge this. Once this took place, God could be invited into the experience. In this case, God was seen as one who protects and helps those in need. Because William already viewed God as protecting and helping, it was easy for Chaplain Yearly to support this idea with his own prayer. Thus, he was nurturing a relationship which already existed between William and God, a relationship which the chaplain evaluated as healthy and supportive for the boy. God was invited to be present precisely as helper, as one who might alleviate pain and fear.

The chaplain's intervention with prayer had several facets. It acknowledged clearly the experience of illness and fear already articulated by William; thus, it gave William a clear message that he had been heard. It also acknowledged and supported William's relationship with God, a relationship which the chaplain deemed helpful. Finally, it was a means for the chaplain to express his own personal support for William and to let him know that he did not face his illness or even his possible death alone. This solidarity, expressed in a time of prayer, and in the presence of God, if you will, became a powerful support and comfort for William.

When the chaplain first invited William to speak his own prayer, he initially showed some hesitation. Wisely, Chaplain Yearly was not too quick to accept this as a final answer, but instead invited William once more to begin, this time offering a couple of practical suggestions. In this case, William was able to accept the second invitation and to pray in a way that was meaningful to him. In other cases, however, patients will insist that they do not wish to pray aloud, but prefer the chaplain to do so for them. They may say, in response to a repeated invitation, "I don't know how" or "I wish you would pray for me." These wishes should be respected. In such cases, as the chaplains begin their prayer, they might invite the patients to pray with them in silence: "Okay, I'll be glad to say the prayer. If you want, you can pray quietly in your heart."

Olivia, eleven, and Cathy, fifteen, were two girls with serious kidney disease. They had met during their thrice-weekly visits to the hospital dialysis unit, and over time became fast friends. One day when Chaplain Mayo visited the unit, it happened that Cathy was there as usual, but Olivia was not. Cathy explained that Olivia was in surgery receiving a new kidney. She expressed her hopes that the surgery would be successful and that the new kidney would function properly. When Cathy asked Chaplain Mayo to pray for Olivia, the chaplain invited her to pray also.

Chaplain: *I think it's a great idea to pray for Olivia. Would you like to take a minute now and pray with me for her?*
Cathy: *Yeah. Sure.*
Chaplain: *Would you like to start us off, and then I'll finish?*
Cathy: *Okay. (Closes eyes.) God, please help Olivia. Make sure the doctors do the transplant right so she will have a new kidney. (Pause)*
Chaplain: *God, we know that you love us and look after us. Cathy and I ask your help for Olivia. Help the doctors, the nurses, and the staff to do their work well. Help Olivia to be strong during surgery. We ask also that her new kidney work for her. Whatever happens, please be close to Olivia now and always. Amen.*

Cathy expressed her concerns very well in her prayer, and Chaplain Mayo mirrored them accurately in her own prayer that she added. In this way, solidarity was reinforced between the chaplain and patient. At this level, Chaplain Mayo was ministering effectively to Cathy. At another level, she was also ministering to Olivia. Given our Christian belief that prayer for others is good, the prayer shared in the dialysis unit was also a way to minister to Olivia in surgery. Their prayer together was compassionate thinking.

Chaplain Mayo not only mirrored Cathy's prayer, but she added a new element: "Whatever happens, please be close to Olivia now and always." This was a tacit acknowledgement that unsuccessful surgery was a possibility to be reckoned with. As they prayed together, chaplain and patient were aware that it was possible that Olivia's new kidney would not function properly or would be rejected; it was even possible (but less so) that Olivia would die during surgery. Chaplain Mayo was trying to leave a door open for Cathy. Often children, and sometimes even adults, attach a magical significance to prayer; they believe that prayer is necessarily efficacious, that it will always receive the effect which it seeks. When people who have convinced themselves of this find an important prayer unanswered, they may take it very hard. At times they experience this as rejection by God, and may even begin self-recrimination: "If only I were a better Christian, God would have answered my prayer" or "If only my faith were stronger, my prayer would have been answered." At other times, the experience of having a prayer go unanswered may elicit from a person recriminations against God, or even a denial of his existence. Such thinking traps Christians into a corner which is difficult to exit while leaving their faith intact. Chaplain Mayo was attempting to leave Cathy with another exit: even if Olivia were to die, or even if her surgery were unsuccessful, she could still trust that God was close to Olivia and still cared about her.

Chaplains will invariably run into people who insist that their prayers must be answered. Sometimes these prayers are completely unrealistic:

Quincy was an eleven year old boy hospitalized with third degree burns over ninety-five percent of his body. The damage to his lungs was also great, and the doctors made it clear to his parents that death was only a matter of days. Quincy's mother took the terrible news calmly and almost wordlessly. When Chaplain Gerber came to visit her, she expressed her firm belief that Quincy would be able to recover soon, despite the poor prognosis given by the doctors. She reminded him of a New Testament verse which she found highly significant for her situation: "I assure you, if you had faith the size of a mustard seed, you would be able to say to this mountain, 'Move from here to there,' and it would move. Nothing would be impossible for you." She asserted that her faith was sufficiently strong to cause God to cure her son. When she prayed with Chaplain Gerber, she asked God to heal Quincy quickly so that he could come home and ride his new motorcycle.

Chaplain Gerber wanted to respond to this mother in a way that would be supportive, but also realistic. At the same time, he did not want to dash the hopes to which she so desperately clung, however unrealistic they might be. He recognized that she was using the defense mechanism of denial to protect herself from the horrible reality of her son's impending death. He wanted to respect her need for this self-protection. At the same time, he could foresee the possibility that the boy's death would cause his mother to blame herself for not having sufficient faith to save him. In the end, he decided not to challenge her unrealistic hopes at that time, but to help her deal with the problem of guilt later on, if it arose. He decided to make his own prayer ambiguous vis-à-vis the expectation of healing:

Chaplain: God our loving Father, we need your closeness very much now. We ask that you ease Quincy's sufferings and bless him and his family with your loving presence.

Elizabeth was a thirteen year old hospitalized with a brain tumor. The medical staff had evaluated her condition exhaustively and concluded that surgery to remove the tumor offered the only hope for her recovery. They knew that the surgery would be extremely difficult and risky. Chaplain Bateman had been involved with the case from the beginning, and at his suggestion the neuro-surgeon and a dozen other members of the health care team gathered on the day before surgery to pray.

Chaplain Bateman began by reading Psalm 86:1-10, which speaks of God's power and asks for his help in times of need. He then invited those present to voice aloud any prayers which they wished to share. After several had done so and there was a pause, he concluded: "Lord God Almighty, you have promised us your love, and you have assured us of your presence in our times of need. Be with us now. We care so much about Elizabeth, and we ask your help as we seek to restore her health. Guide our minds, our hearts, and our hands. Help us to help her. Help us above all, Lord, to put our trust in you and in your will for Elizabeth and for us." Knowing that all present happened to be Christian, Chaplain Bateman led them in the Lord's Prayer as a conclusion to their prayer service.

Elizabeth's critical situation and the staff's desire to do everything possible to help her created an opportunity for risk-taking and trust-building among them. Chaplain Bateman took a risk by suggesting that they gather for prayer. Other members of the health care team took a risk in participating; it is sometimes difficult to acknowledge that one is not completely in control of a situation in a professional setting. In this case, the health care team shared a mutual awareness that Elizabeth was in great danger and that their very best efforts might not be enough to save her. They were willing to gather and to place this awareness before God, asking for his intervention. Their gathering took on great importance as each felt God's presence and found comfort in it. Afterward, when Elizabeth came through her surgery safely, they looked back on their prayer experience and considered it to have been even more significant. The prayer which the staff shared was both passionate and compassionate thinking, but it was especially responsible thinking. They looked upon the prayer experience as a means of being nurtured by God so that they could all fulfill their professional duties better. Impressed, even overwhelmed by the extent of their responsibilities and the risk they were undertaking, they turned to God for help. Their desire to pray seemed to arise directly from their feeling of responsibility for Elizabeth.

Ivan was a twelve year old boy hospitalized for a kidney transplant. Chaplain Huber had met him and his family during previous admissions, and she had spent time with them just prior to the transplant, which was successful. Two weeks after surgery, as Ivan was preparing to be released the next day, his mother asked that Chaplain Huber lead them in a prayer of thanksgiving for the successful surgery. They waited until Ivan's father, older sister, and his surgeon could be present.

To begin their prayer, Chaplain Huber invited each person to say aloud what he or she was most thankful for. Each mentioned the success of the transplant, and most went on to describe specific aspects of the experience for which they were thankful. Chaplain Huber concluded with a prayer of thanksgiving.

Chaplains may become so involved in desperate situations in the hospital setting that they forget to celebrate the many happy events which also take place there. One of the chaplain's greatest joys can be the time spent with patients, families, and staff in thanksgiving. There will be many events for which to be thankful, such as successful surgeries, effective treatments, the announcement of cures, the ruling out of serious medical problems, and especially, the birth of children. These are appropriate times for the chaplain to help others turn to God as their thankful thinking becomes the stuff of prayer and worship.

Meditation for Children

As we noted above, most children conceive of prayer as "talking to God" or as the recitation of memorized prayers. Yet, if prayer is the carrying on of a relationship with God, then saying prayers is only part of it. A relationship between two beings must flow in both directions; a unidirectional "relationship" is no relationship at all. Certainly "talking to God" can be prayer. But prayer must also involve an openness to "hearing" what God is communicating. Prayer also means listening to God.

Learning to listen to God involves the cultivation of an inner quietness so that his voice may be better heard over the background noise of daily life and our own mental energy. Priest-psychologist Henri J. M. Nouwen calls this inner quiet *solitude*.[6] Solitude is different from loneliness, according to Nouwen, yet the quest for solitude must begin with a willingness to embrace loneliness and change it to solitude. This is a process of conversion, a process which Nouwen calls the movement from loneliness to solitude.

Loneliness is a universal human experience, but we find it highlighted especially in our modern technological society. In our crowded, complex society people are often reduced to anonymous numbers and their uniqueness becomes lost in a sea of humanity. Everyday conversation reveals attempts to counteract this anonymity and loneliness: people use first names and their diminutive forms with virtual strangers; social amenities speak of our love and concern for and intimacy with others. But these habits are mere attempts to cover up and deny the deep and pervasive loneliness which all feel. Many other attempts are made to deny loneliness and to avoid its painful emptiness: people distract themselves with constant sensory input from television, radio, newspapers, conversations, and fictional writings; they try always to be busy, to have something to do every spare minute of the day; they avoid having nothing to do. But such attempts at denial and cover-up are dysfunctional. For one thing, they are doomed to failure, because people can never completely block out loneliness no matter how desperately they attempt to fill up their lives. Furthermore, the pain of loneliness is a prerequisite for creativity. The fear of encountering the void of loneliness severely limits the person's possible self-expression.

---

[6]*Reaching Out: The Three Movements of the Spiritual Life* (Garden City: Doubleday, 1975), esp. pp. 13–44.

One false but prevalent idea is that people are responsible for taking away each other's loneliness. The result of attempting this is disastrous. A frantic clinging to another person so as to avoid one's own loneliness and to prevent his results in a suffocating relationship. This is one trouble some married couples experience as their compulsive togetherness begins to stifle the spouses as well as the relationship. Friends must be together, yet not too near. Human closeness cannot neutralize loneliness.

The response to loneliness which leads to spiritual growth is a response of accepting and embracing loneliness with an effort to change it into solitude. This is a difficult road, the road of conversion.

> Instead of running away from our loneliness and trying to forget or deny it, we have to protect it and turn it into a fruitful solitude. To live a spiritual life we must first find the courage to enter into the desert of our loneliness and to change it by gentle and persistent efforts into a garden of solitude. This requires not only courage but also a strong faith. As hard as it is to believe that the dry desolate desert can yield endless varieties of flowers, it is equally hard to imagine that our loneliness is hiding unknown beauty. The movement from loneliness to solitude, however, is the beginning of any spiritual life because it is the movement from the restless senses to the restful spirit, from the outward-reaching cravings to the inward-reaching search, from the fearful clinging to the fearless play.[7]

In the conversion to solitude, it is probably true that no one can progress very far without some withdrawal from the busy world. However, physical solitude is not primarily what is meant. Rather, the person seeking conversion should learn to cultivate an inner sense of solitude that is independent of his environment.

This involves learning to listen to oneself. So much emphasis has been placed recently upon interpersonal sensitivity that a person might forget that he must also learn to listen to his own inner voices. The development of such inner sensitivity is the beginning of the spiritual life. Each person has a vocation, an inner necessity, and it is only through creating some quiet inner space that this necessity can be discovered.

This listening to oneself, this turning inward, need not necessitate a narcissistic or solipsistic turning away from others. Indeed, it is precisely by virtue of creating our own inner space and finding

---

[7]Ibid., pp. 22–23.

our vocation that we can develop deep fellowship with others. It is the discovery of the self that enables a person truly to love another. Solitude embraces others and community becomes an inner quality. One way that this is occasionally experienced is the awareness that we are closer to a friend during his absence than in his presence. A person's growing and deepening solitude gradually embraces a wider circle of others. In the realm of solitude love for another can abide in freedom rather than being crippled by the person's desperate attempts to deny loneliness. Thus solitude is receptive.

Similarly, solitude turns the person toward the world and precipitates his action in the world. The person overcome by loneliness will relate to the world in a "reactionary" way. That is, he will nervously and anxiously react to events in the world, mostly without reflection. But the person who acts from solitude acts in a thoughtful, purposive way.

> The movement from loneliness to solitude should lead to a gradual conversion from an anxious reaction to a loving response. Loneliness leads to quick, often spastic, reactions which make us prisoners of our constantly changing world. But in solitude of heart we can listen to the events of the hour, the day and the year and slowly "formulate," give form to, a response that is really our own. In solitude we can pay careful attention to the world and search for an honest response.[8]

Thus there is alertness in solitude. Rather than causing a turning away from the world, solitude reacts to history as a constant call to action.

The response to the world which is born out of solitude is less frustrating and more hopeful than the response from loneliness, for the latter is expressed in a burdensome need to "fix" the world, to end suffering. But the person who knows solitude can reflect upon evil and suffering in the world that is much too great for him to prevent and for which he is not responsible, and he can realize that he is called to respond to this suffering and evil through compassion for and solidarity with others. For the compassionate person the experience of evil becomes the opportunity for his own conversion and that of others. His solidarity with others in pain becomes the beginning of healing, even though concrete solutions are not achieved. The movement from loneliness to solitude, then, is a movement toward deeper engagement with the burning social issues of our time. It enables a person's responsibility toward the world to become a vocation

---

[8]Ibid., pp. 34–35.

rather than a burden. The movement frees up our healing power for others.

As lofty as the movement from loneliness to solitude may sound, it remains true that children, even children in their early elementary years, may learn to cultivate a sense of solitude and to practice, within the inner stillness they create, prayerful meditation. The hospital setting by its very nature subjects child patients to alternating experiences of invasion by others and the loneliness of being left alone. Situations which children experience as invasive are many and varied in the hospital: losing one's clothing, receiving injections, having body orifices probed, losing privacy in the bathroom, questioning about personal matters, receiving oral medications, etc. These are quite disturbing for some children, and in many cases create in them a strong desire to be left alone, to have time by themselves to become collected and once more to assume the mantle of at least some dignity. But all too often, the periods of being alone in the hospital become oppressive to children. They may summon the nurses unnecessarily in order to have some company or insist on leaving their hospital rooms even when asked to stay in bed, or they may simply weep in lonely misery.

Times of aloneness, whether sought after by patients or forced upon them by their circumstances, provide the opportunity for them to begin to develop a sense of inner stillness which can become prayer. But they need to be taught how to do this, and it is here that chaplains may be of great service. The first step is to help children to relax and to become attuned to their own inner voices. Only then can the second step, learning to listen to God's voice, be taken.

Children may be taught these steps of meditation either individually or in groups. They should be invited to enter into the experience of learning to meditate: "I'd like to teach you about a kind of prayer that I think really helps a person get closer to God. It takes a few minutes to try. Would you like me to teach you?" Of course, answers in the negative should be respected.

Body posture is significant in meditation. It is best to sit, either in a chair or on the hospital bed. The child should sit upright, with the spinal column vertical. It will probably be necessary for the chaplain to demonstrate the difference between a back which is straight and vertical and a back which is stiffly arched; children often confuse the two positions, and the latter is quite uncomfortable. The chaplain may demonstrate by sitting in a chair and turning sideways with respect to the patient. Legs are best loosely crossed, or the feet may be placed on the floor, or at least hang downward if the child is sitting in a chair. Some children may be interested in trying the classic "lotus" position, with legs tightly crossed; the resulting tension caused by discomfort in the legs is usually more of a distraction than a help. Hands should be placed loosely in the lap, either clasped together or side by side. Nothing should be held in the hands because this, too, creates a distraction. This sitting posture is advantageous for meditation because it combines relaxation and alertness. However, meditation may be done in virtually any posture, and patients who may not sit up may learn to meditate while reclining.

Now instruct the patients to close their eyes and begin to concentrate on their breathing. Tell them simply to notice the flowing in and out of air. After a moment, have them open their eyes once more. It is now time to teach them about breathing. We may draw air into our lungs by means of two kinds of muscular action: lifting the shoulders and ribs in order to expand the chest, or lowering the diaphragm. Usually the two methods are used in combination. Learning to breathe from the diaphragm is important for meditation. As the diaphragm lowers, the belly will bulge out slightly, and so it is helpful for children to describe this movement as "belly breathing." Demonstrate the two methods of breathing and invite the children to try each briefly. Then ask them to resume their prayer posture, close their eyes, and begin to breathe from the diaphragm. As they begin, ask them to breathe very deeply, taking in as much air as possible and then exhaling all of it. Ask them to slow their breathing down as much as possible, making it as slow, gentle, and quiet as possible. There should be no pause between the inhalations and exhalations. The air should move in one smooth, continuous action. Tell them that if they notice any jerkiness in their breathing they should smooth it out. It may help the children to concentrate on the flow of air if they imagine it to have a color, such as red or blue; they can visualize the colored air as it flows in and out of their bodies. Have them practice several short drills of this breathing and concentration, perhaps thirty seconds to one minute each.

It is now time to teach them to deal with noise distractions. Hospitals can be very noisy places; it is unlikely that a patient will be isolated from all noise even in a private room. Have them begin their breathing exercise once more, and invite them to hear the various noises which are in the background. The chaplain may point out some of the obvious ones such as a television or a conversation. Then ask the children to allow the noises to pass through them. "Don't try to hold on to those noises. Let them go. Let them pass through you just as light passes through a clear pane of glass." Allow the children to practice this once or twice.

The advantages of this first step in meditation are several. The sitting posture combines alertness with relaxation, allowing people to concentrate on their prayer, but also helping them to rest. The smooth, slow, deep breathing has a tranquilizing effect. It helps people to rest, to rid themselves of tension, and to become more relaxed; indeed, patients who do this lying down may find that they quickly go to sleep. This step also helps people to become more self-aware, to become more attuned to their own inner voices. It helps them to find their own inner powers which may be stronger than they ever imagined. It helps them to focus these personal energies, and in the hospital setting these may be applied to problems of pain, physical therapy, anxiety, etc. In consolidating their personal strengths and giving them focus, patients may be able to bring them to bear where they are needed most. Finally, this first step prepares patients for the second: listening to God's voice.

The following are first-step exercises which are designed to help children to practice their breathing and concentration. Each exercise must begin with the chaplain helping the children to assume an adequate posture, close their eyes, and begin their slow deep breathing. Directions from the chaplain should be given in a voice which is soft and gentle, but clear. At the end of each exercise, the chaplain should invite the child to open his or her eyes. This should be said softly and gently.

Melt Your Body[9]

After helping the child to relax and establish smooth breathing, the chaplain continues: "As you breathe quietly, feel the muscles in your face and forehead. There will be some stiffness there. Let the muscles in your face just melt away. Pretend they're made of molasses, and they flow slowly downward. [Pause] Feel the muscles around your eyes melt. [Pause] Feel your mouth and jaw melt. [Pause] Now the melting is going on down. Feel your neck melt away. [Pause] It spreads to your shoulders and back. The tension and stiffness just slowly flow downward, leaving you totally relaxed. [Pause] Feel your

---

[9]This exercise may not be appropriate for children under the age of seven or so, since pre-schoolers are susceptible to worries about the loss of body parts.

stomach. Let the tension melt away. [Pause] Feel your arms and hands. The tension melts downward, into your hands and out through the tips of your fingers. [Pause] Feel your hips. Let them melt. [Pause] Feel your legs. All the stiffness flows downward into your feet. [Pause] Feel your whole body. Any tension just flows on down into your feet and out through your toes. [Pause] When you are totally melted, just rest and concentrate on your breathing." Have the patient continue his deep breathing for another minute or so.

Float Away

After helping the child to relax and establish smooth breathing, the chaplain continues: "Each time you breathe in, imagine that your body gets a little lighter. [Pause] Feel the push of the chair (or bed) on you. [Pause] Each time you breathe in, the push is less. [Pause] Less and less. [Pause] Finally, you are weightless, and you drift up off of the chair (or bed) into the air. [Pause] As you continue to concentrate on your breathing, just float in the air and rest." Have the patient continue his deep breathing for another minute or so.

Jesus Prayer

This is an excellent exercise for children of the Christian faith. After helping the child to relax and establish smooth breathing, the chaplain continues: "Each time you breathe in, think the word, 'Jesus.' Each time you breathe out, think the words, 'Come to me.' Keep breathing in and out, concentrating on your breath and the words." Have the child continue the deep breathing for two or three minutes.

After leading children through meditation exercises, the chaplain should spend a little time talking about the experience. The children should be invited to talk about their experience of the exercise. To facilitate this, the chaplain may ask whether it was mostly good or mostly bad, what feelings the patients had during the exercise, what thoughts they had, whether they learned anything from it, etc. Children will continue to learn from their prayer experiences if they are able to talk about them afterward and reflect upon them. Finally, the chaplain should point out to children that once they have learned a certain meditation exercise, they may do it whenever they wish, and for whatever duration; they do not need the chaplain to lead them all of the time.

The second step of meditative prayer occurs when one experiences God's presence in prayer or somehow hears his "voice." This is not something which can be caused by either the patient or the chaplain, for God himself chooses the time to speak. It has always been a mystery for religious persons to ponder that at times God's voice is heard quite clearly and that at other times his silence is devastating. The encounter between God and humans is both mysterious and powerful. Prayer, understood as a relationship with God, is his gift to us. It is a gift which can transform lives forever, but it is a gift which humans can never control or own completely. Through the teaching of some techniques of meditation, chaplains may teach patients how to cultivate an openness to hearing God's voice. That openness is a kind of prerequisite, and once we learn it, when God does choose to speak, our prayer takes a quantum leap and our relationship with God deepens in new ways. If chaplains can assist patients in cultivating the inner stillness which leaves them open and receptive to God's presence, their ministry will have been most fruitful.

Applications of Meditation
in the Clinical Setting

The following clinical situations and meditation exercises are intended to be illustrative. In each case, an actual hospital experience is described, followed by a meditation exercise which was deemed helpful. The reader wishing to help a youngster to employ these or similar exercises must be ready to adapt them to the age, intelligence, religious background, and life situation of the child. The chaplain or minister should not hesitate to be creative in further adaptations or in the creation of wholly new meditative exercises which might be of help to patients or their families.

A ten year old boy was hospitalized with a broken leg which he received when he was struck by a car. He was in traction and would remain so for several weeks, a prospect which he found distressing. The chaplain encouraged him to meditate on freedom and to ask God for his help:

After helping the boy to relax and establish smooth breathing, the chaplain continued: "Imagine yourself on a high mountain peak.

You look all around, and you can see for miles in every direction. [Pause] You are so high up, you feel as though you can do anything you want. [Pause] After a minute, you spread your arms and begin to fly away. [Pause] You fly and fly and fly, going everywhere you want to. [Pause for one minute.] Now take a moment, quietly in your heart, and ask God to help you get well soon." [Pause for one minute.]

A fourteen year old girl had been hospitalized for several weeks with leukemia. She told the chaplain that she had always been a church-goer, and that her faith was important to her, but that she felt that God had abandoned her. The chaplain invited her to meditate about Christ's presence and to ask him to be with her:

After helping the girl to relax and establish smooth breathing, the chaplain continued: "Imagine Jesus standing in front of you. [Pause] See how he looks, the color of his hair, the kind of clothes he has on, the look in his eyes. Watch him. [Pause for one minute.] Now imagine Jesus in your hands. Hold him there and watch. [Pause for one minute.] Now imagine Jesus in your heart. [Pause] Feel his closeness to you. Let him become a part of you. [Pause for one minute.] Now take a minute or so to ask Jesus to be with you and to help you while you are sick." [Pause for one or two minutes.]

A sixteen year old girl was awaiting open heart surgery. She told the chaplain that she was quite frightened that she might not live through the surgery. Noticing a bottle of baby oil on the bedside table, the chaplain led the girl in a meditation exercise using some of the oil:

After helping the girl to relax and establish smooth breathing, the chaplain continued: "Keep your eyes closed, and cup your left hand. [The chaplain poured a small quantity of baby oil into the cupped hand.] Now with the fingers of your left hand, begin to feel the oil. [Pause] Rub it between your fingers. Feel its smoothness. [Pause] Now put your hands together, and slowly, very slowly, rub the oil all over them. Rub it into your skin. [Pause for one minute.] Feel the oil sinking in. It becomes part of your skin, a part that will not wash off. [Pause] God is like the oil. He sinks into us deeply and becomes part of us. [Pause] God stays with us always. He never leaves us alone. [Pause] Now take a minute, in your heart, and ask God to be close to you during your surgery." [Pause for one or two minutes.]

A twelve year old boy was hospitalized with third degree burns on his legs. He had several months of treatment ahead, including de-

bridement and skin grafting. He expected to experience a great deal of pain and other discomfort. The chaplain gave him a pad of paper and a pen, and helped him to meditate on his treatment and to ask for God's help. He had the boy make a list of the various events which he dreaded. When the list (six items) was finished, they continued:

After helping the boy to relax and establish smooth breathing, the chaplain said: "Now, slowly, open your eyes and look at your list. Read just the first item, and close your eyes again. [Pause] Now take a moment and ask God to help you during that time. [Pause] Now open your eyes again just long enough to read the second thing. Ask God to be with you when that happens. [They continued until all items on the list had been similarly covered.]

A thirteen year old girl was hospitalized with a broken leg. The cast had been put on, but she had to demonstrate her ability to use crutches before she could be discharged. During her first session in physical therapy, she had been unable to walk successfully with the crutches. When the chaplain visited her, she expressed her fear of continuing to be unable to pass the crutch test. The chaplain helped her to meditate about the test and to ask God for help:

After helping the girl to relax and establish smooth breathing, the chaplain continued: "Picture the physical therapy room where they teach you to use crutches. See the walls, the railings, the little staircase. [Pause] Look all around the room and see the things in it. [Pause] Now imagine yourself sitting on a chair. You are holding crutches in your hands. [Pause] The physical therapist is there to help. Is it a man or a woman? [Pause] Imagine yourself holding the crutches, getting ready to stand up with them. [Pause] Slowly, pull yourself upward. It feels hard, but you make it. [Pause] You begin to walk around the room. See yourself doing it, step by step. [Pause] Now you go over to the little staircase. You look at it. [Pause] One step at a time, you begin to climb. You go up. [Pause] And up. [Pause] Now you come down. [Pause] And down to the floor. [Pause] You have passed the test. Now take a minute and ask God to help you when you go back to physical therapy. Ask him to help you with your crutches." [Pause for one minute.]

A nine year old boy was hospitalized with an inoperable brain tumor. He was receiving radiation treatments in the hope that they would shrink or even destroy the tumor. The chaplain taught him a meditation exercise which he could use as often as he wished during his illness:

After helping the boy to relax and establish smooth breathing, the chaplain continued: "Imagine that tumor in your head. Picture it in your mind. [Pause] What color is it? How big is it? [Pause] Now imagine a tiny little Pac-Man. He begins to bite away at the tumor. [Pause] Here come other little Pac-Men. They all start biting at the tumor. They are eating it up. [Pause] Thousands and thousands, millions and billions of Pac-Men are eating up the tumor. Chomp! Chomp! They keep on going until the tumor is all gone. [Pause] When you are ready, ask God to help make your tumor go away. Ask God to help make you well."

A fifteen year old boy was hospitalized with spina bifida. This was yet another in a long series of hospitalizations going back to his birth. In his conversation with the chaplain, the boy indicated that he had never prayed much about his illness because he had never thought it mattered. The chaplain suggested that he try the following meditation:

After helping the boy to relax and establish smooth breathing, the chaplain continued: "Think back over the years and remember some of your trips to the hospital. Just take a minute and make a mental list of what you can remember. [Pause for one minute.] What events in the hospital were more important? List them. [Pause for one minute.] What hospital events were not so important? List them. [Pause for one minute.] What made you sad? [Pause] What made you happy? [Pause] When did you have a celebration? [Pause] Were you ever mad? [Pause] Scared? [Pause] Now open your eyes. Take this pad and pen and write a letter to God about what it's like to have spina bifida. Tell God about your experiences."

Two eight year old girls shared a room in the hospital. When the chaplain visited one, her roommate had gone to surgery. She asked the chaplain to help her to pray for her roommate. The chaplain taught her this meditation exercise:

After helping the girl to relax and establish smooth breathing, the chaplain continued: "Think of your friend Aggie. Imagine her standing in front of you. [Pause] Now imagine Aggie down in surgery. She is covered with a blue sheet. [Pause] The doctors and nurses are all around. The lights are bright. [Pause] Now take a minute, and ask God to help Aggie and make her well again. [Pause]

Religious Ritual as Prayer in the Hospital

Religious ritual can take many forms. Generally speaking, a religious ritual is a customarily repeated act or acts addressed to a meaningful transcendent. There is a formal or ceremonial quality to religious rituals, indeed to rituals in general. They possess a certain structure, and tend to stand out sharply from the normal everyday activities of people, possessing a special intensity and significance. Rituals are special times in the lives of the participants. They may happen every day, but they are not everyday events. Three functions of rituals may be readily identified.

First, rituals communicate a culture's most cherished values to individuals—particularly to children as they mature within that culture. These most cherished values are especially the values which the society in question considers to be ultimate. For Christians, this can be called salvation; others may have other ultimate values. The communication of cherished values protects the very existence of a culture. Aidan Kavanagh states that "if a culture has any root in the real order, it is to be found in the patterns of repetitive behavior by which a group of people conceives of and enacts those values which enable the group to survive its own particular context of stresses and threats that would destroy it."[10] He further emphasizes that "myth and ritual . . . are the enactments by which that communication of values takes place on the deepest and most critical level for the future survival of society itself."[11] This is ritual's *didactic* function.

A second function of ritual is *supportive*. Rituals provide continuity between past, present, and future, thus making it easier for humans to cope with the present. This is accomplished by ritual's orientation to life as a whole. Rituals address the whole span and flow of life. But continuity is also achieved through the repetitive nature of rituals. Because of this repetitiveness, rituals give people a sense of security in time of crisis, such as serious illness. When crisis occurs, ritual enables humans to integrate the present crisis with past crises, and with the flow of life. It enables them "to draw on their own memories of those around them, and the faith of those around them. It is by drawing on such memories that a sense of identity, security, and continuity is assured."[12]

---

[10]"The Role of Ritual in Personal Development," in James D. Shaughnessy, ed., *The Roots of Ritual* (Grand Rapids: Eerdmans, 1973), p. 147.

[11]Ibid., p. 151.

[12]Margaret Mead, "Ritual and Social Crisis" in James D. Shaughnessy, ed., *Roots*, p. 95.

Third, ritual has an *integrative* function. It is a tool for socializing new members of the community. This function is closely related to the two just mentioned. Erik H. Erikson asserts that it is through ritualized behavior patterns that the child is able to develop a sense of security and identity, to learn to function in a peer group, and to extend this learning process to society writ large.[13]

Religious rituals can function as powerful forms of prayer in the hospital setting. Their didactic, supportive, and integrative functions may all work to strengthen patients and their families in their faith and to bring about a prayerful experience. Some church traditions may not employ acts or ceremonies which they would call rituals, but most, if not all, do employ customarily repeated actions or words which are addressed to God. Other religious traditions provide specific rituals for the pastoral care of the sick, and even for the pastoral care of sick children.

The Roman Catholic Church offers a brief ritual of prayer which is suggested for use during visits to sick children.[14] This consists of a reading from the Bible, a prayer response, the Lord's Prayer, a concluding prayer, and a blessing. After the minister (this may be a priest, deacon, or other minister) becomes acquainted with the sick child and his invitation to pray together is accepted, there is a brief reading, or at least a brief quotation, from the Bible. Mark 9:33–37 (Jesus calls his followers to be humble like children) and Mark 10:13–16 (Jesus blessing the little children) are suggested. After the reading, there may be a time for silent reflection and prayer if the child is capable of this. The minister may also lead the child and others who are present in a litany-style prayer:

Minister: *Jesus, come to me. (All repeat)*
           Jesus, put your hand on me. (All repeat)
           Jesus, bless me. (All repeat)

Next, the minister introduces the Lord's Prayer in these or similar words: "Let us pray to the Father using those words which Jesus himself used." All pray the Lord's Prayer together. The minister then says a concluding prayer. Two suggested prayers are provided:

---

[13]Erik H. Erikson, "Ontogeny of Ritualization in Man," *Philosophical Transactions of the Royal Society of London,* Series B, No. 772, Vol. CCLI (1966), pp. 337–50.

[14]*Pastoral Care of the Sick: Rites of Anointing and Viaticum* (New York: Catholic Book Publishing Co., 1983), pp. 53–62.

God of love, ever caring, ever strong, stand by us in our time of need. Watch over your child N. who is sick, look after him/her in every danger, and grant him/her your healing and peace. We ask this in the name of Jesus the Lord. (All respond: Amen.)

Father, in your love you gave us Jesus to help us rise triumphant over grief and pain. Look on your child N. who is sick and see in his/her sufferings those of your Son. Grant N. a share in the strength you granted your Son that he/she too may be a sign of your goodness, kindness, and loving care. We ask this in the name of Jesus the Lord. (All respond: Amen.)

The ritual continues with a prayer of blessing for the sick child. Two forms are given, each of which calls for the minister to make a sign of the cross on the child's forehead:

N., when you were baptized, you were marked with the cross of Jesus. I (we) make this cross on your forehead and ask the Lord to bless you, and restore you to health. (All respond: Amen.)

All praise and glory is yours, heavenly God, for you have called us to serve you in love. Have mercy on us and listen to our prayer as we ask you to help N. Bless your beloved child, and restore him/her to health in the name of Jesus the Lord. (All respond: Amen.)

After this prayer, each one present may in turn make the sign of the cross on the child's forehead in silence. Finally, the ritual concludes with a blessing. If the minister is a priest or deacon, he prays:

May the blessing of almighty God, the Father, and the Son, and the Holy Spirit, come upon you and remain with you forever. (All respond: Amen.)

If the minister is not a priest or a deacon, he or she prays as follows:

May the Lord bless us, protect us from all evil, and bring us to everlasting life. (All respond: Amen.)

For older children, the Catholic ritual provides the possibility for additional elements. Children who are old enough to derive some comfort from the anointing of the sick may receive this sacrament. The ritual consists of readings from the Bible and prayers, followed by the priest laying hands on the sick children and anointing their foreheads and hands with the oil of the sick, which has been blessed especially for this purpose. In addition, sick children who are old enough may receive the sacrament of Holy Communion.

The notes to the minister included in the ritual book instruct him or her to be prepared to make adaptations that will make the ritual more meaningful to the particular child. For example, the minister may choose to employ any suitable prayers with which the child is already familiar, or may invite the child to suggest suitable prayers. The language used by the minister should be adapted for the particular age and mental capacity of the child, and the child's age and condition should be taken into account as the minister decides how long the ritual should last.

The Roman Catholic ritual for visiting a sick child functions didactically, supportively, and integratively. As a teaching device, it creates the opportunity for the minister to remind sick children of God's love and concern for them. It models the idea, born of faith, that prayer in a time of need is good. It may also provide the occasion to teach the children new prayers or to acquaint them with the sacrament of the anointing of the sick. This ritual also serves to offer support to sick children and their parents. It communicates to them the support of the church as well as the loving care of God in a time of need. It reassures them with words of comfort. In recalling stories of sickness, healing, and God's care from the Bible, it helps believers to draw on the faith-filled memories of the religious community and to draw strength from this reflection. The ritual is an acting out of a supportive statement: You are not alone in your suffering. Finally, the ritual functions as a means of integration. It names and specifies the sick child's new and unique position within the faith community, and does the same for others who are encouraged to join the community in prayer for the sick.

Even faith communities which have no explicit ritual for the pastoral care of the sick often have religious actions or prayers which are customarily repeated. When the minister is able to draw upon a body of known religious practice, the familiarity of certain actions or prayers can be supportive and reassuring to believers. There may be a certain sequence of prayers, a particular reading from the Bible, or a song which is especially meaningful; the minister may take good advantage of this situation by making use of such familiar prayers, readings, or songs. Even the simple "ritual" of reciting the Lord's Prayer may fulfill didactic, supportive, and integrative functions in important ways. When the hospital chaplain is unfamiliar with a patient's religious tradition, he should make some effort to discover those religious actions or prayers which are particularly meaningful to the patient, and should endeavor to use them as a part of pastoral care.

Conclusion

Prayer is the carrying on of a relationship with God, and it is important for those who render pastoral care to foster this relationship among patients and their families. Prayer may be understood as thinking, either silent or spoken out loud, which is passionate, compassionate, responsible, and thankful. Chaplains may also help patients, even younger children, to move beyond merely spoken prayer to various forms of meditation. The inner stillness which arises from meditation may help people to be calm, to focus personal energies more creatively, and to cultivate an openness to hearing the voice of God. Prayer in the form of ritual may be particularly powerful and helpful for the sick by enabling them to learn more about their faith, by supporting them with the assurance of God's care and the community's presence, and by helping them to integrate their experience of sickness and suffering into their larger lives and their place in the faith community.

RECOMMENDED READING

Buber, Martin. *I and Thou*. Trans. by Walter Kaufmann. New York: Charles Scribner's Sons, 1970.

Caprio, Betsy. *Experiments in Prayer*. Notre Dame: Ave Maria, 1973.

Erikson, Erik H. "Ontogeny of Ritualization in Man," in *Philosophical Transactions of the Royal Society of London,* Series B, No. 772, Vol. CCLI (1966) pp. 337–50.

Hesch, John B. *Prayer and Meditation for Middle School Kids*. Mahwah: Paulist, 1985.

Link, Mark, S. J. *You: Prayer for Beginners and Those Who Have Forgotten How*. Niles: Argus, 1976.

Macquarrie, John. *Paths in Spirituality*. New York: Harper & Row, 1972.

Nouwen, Henri J. M. *Reaching Out: The Three Movements of the Spiritual Life*. Garden City: Doubleday, 1975.

Reid, Clyde. *Celebrate the Temporary*. New York: Harper & Row, 1972.

Shaughnessy, James D., ed. *The Roots of Ritual*. Grand Rapids: Eerdmans, 1973.

7.

Terminal Illness and Death

Ministers who otherwise feel confident in their roles and their ability to help may feel inadequate when faced with the situation of a dying child. This is understandable since the death of a child is certainly one of life's greatest human tragedies. Precisely because of the severely traumatic nature of such an event, the minister's presence and help may be extremely important. In this chapter we will discuss children's conceptions of death, their awareness of it in cases of fatal illness, stages or phases of dying, the process of grief, and the role of the minister in these circumstances.

Children's Conceptions of Death

Children under the age of three years generally have not grasped the idea of death.[1] Their intellectual capacities have not yet developed to the point that they possess concepts of beginning and end, existence and non-existence, much less a permanent cessation of life.

Children in the pre-school years tend to think magically and egocentrically (see above, Chapter 1), and their thinking about death follows these patterns. They see death, first, as a temporary event or condition.[2] Thus the pre-schooler who has seen a dead pet buried in the back yard may tell stories about its coming back to life sometime in the future, much as a seed which is planted later grows into a

---

[1]William Van Ornum and John B. Murdock, *Crisis Counseling with Children and Adolescents* (New York: Continuum, 1983), p. 70.

[2]Elisabeth Kübler-Ross, *On Death and Dying* (New York: Macmillan, 1969), p. 178.

plant, or as a plant flowers, wilts, and flowers again. They may also liken death to a deep sleep, expecting that at some point the dead person or animal will simply reawaken. Pre-school children, second, may personify death, describing it as a monster, a bogey-man, etc.[3] Seen in this way, death becomes for the pre-schooler an invasive, hostile outsider, a power to be feared and perhaps to be run away from. Third, because their thinking is not only magical but egocentric, pre-schoolers may believe that their own actions can decisively influence the occurrence or prevention of death. For example, when a loved one has died, the pre-schooler may claim personal responsibility for the event: "Aunt Bess died because I was bad and she is angry at me." They may also accept responsibility for their own fatal illness: "I have leukemia because I didn't button up my coat before I went outside to play."

As children enter the school age years, they begin to understand death in a more realistic manner, i.e., as a biological process with a permanent result.[4] They continue to grow in their awareness of death as a process and they come to understand clearly that death is irrevocable.

Adolescents are in the process of forming new self-concepts as they begin to assume adult roles in society (see above, Chapter 1). In the midst of this process of self-discovery and self-definition, their sense of personal identity may be tenuous and fragile. For a teenager in the midst of these personal concerns, death becomes a new factor to be integrated into the developing sense of self. This integration can be destructive. Adolescents who suffer from terminal illness may come to regard themselves as failed persons; thus the experience of illness becomes a severe blow to self-esteem.

Children's Awareness of and Reaction to Fatal Illness

Adults who are involved with a child who suffers from a terminal illness may expend a great deal of energy struggling with the question of whether the child should be told of impending death, or protected from knowledge of this harsh prospect. Research and clinical experience suggest that this is a moot point, since children who

[3]Ibid., pp. 178–79.
[4]Ibid., p. 179.

are terminally ill find out about their condition whether they are told of it explicitly or not.

Eugenia H. Waechter conducted a study about children's awareness of fatal illness in preparation for her doctoral dissertation and has reported some of her findings in the *American Journal of Nursing*.[5] Dr. Waechter hypothesized that children between the ages of six and ten years, inclusive, who suffer from fatal illness, do experience and express anxiety about their impending deaths. Since she believed that a false cheerfulness or evasiveness in those adults around them discouraged such children from openly expressing their anxieties, she chose two techniques to help children express their anxieties about death less directly. First, they were given the General Anxiety Scale for Children that measured concerns in many areas of living. Second, each child was shown a series of eight pictures and asked to tell stories about them; four of the pictures were chosen from the Thematic Apperception Test, and four were designed specifically for the Waechter study.

The subjects for Waechter's study were

> 64 children between the ages of 6 and 10, divided into four groups matched for age, race, social class, and family background. In one group were three children with leukemia, six with neoplastic diseases, six with cystic fibrosis, and one with progressive septic granulomatosis. In the second group were children with a chronic disease, but good prognosis; in the third, children with a brief illness. These groups were tested in the hospital. Testing of the fourth group, non-hospitalized children, was carried out at an elementary school selected after the data had been completed for the three groups of hospitalized children.[6]

Waechter found that children with poor prognoses scored twice as high as other hospitalized children on the General Anxiety Scale for Children, and that they told substantially more stories relating to the threat of bodily integrity. She concluded that they were more preoccupied with death. Even though only two of the sixteen children with fatal illness had discussed death with their parents, sixty-three percent of this group's stories related to death. Dr. Waechter concluded that this dichotomy suggests that even though impending death was not discussed directly with these children, they were able

---

[5]"Children's Awareness of Fatal Illness," *American Journal of Nursing* 71 (1971), pp. 1168–72.

[6]Ibid., p. 1168.

to discern the seriousness of their illnesses by means of clues from their environment, such as changes in the emotions of those around them. For example, one six year old boy in the terminal stages of leukemia had discussed his disease with his parents in terms of "tired blood." Yet, after looking at a picture of a woman entering a room with her face in her hands, he told this story:

> This is about a woman. She's somebody's mother. She's crying because her son was in the hospital, and he died. He had leukemia. He finally had a heart attack. It just happened . . . he died. Then they took him away to a cemetery to bury him, and his soul went up to heaven.
>
> The woman is crying. But she forgets about it when she goes to bed. Because she relaxes and her brain relaxes. She's very sad. But she sees her little boy again when she goes up to heaven. She's looking forward to that. She won't find anybody else in heaven—just her little boy that she knows.[7]

One might have assumed that this child would have had little or no awareness of his impending death, and indeed he did not tell the story in the first person. Yet the fact that he told the story about the mother of a little boy with his own diagnosis (leukemia), and his graphic images of death and emotional trauma, are quite striking, and they belie any claim that he was ignorant of his prognosis.

The study surfaced certain feelings that children with fatal illness tend to have. There is, first, the feeling of helplessness. In the above story, the sense of helplessness involves the impossibility of changing the course of events. At other times, children may feel that they have lost control, and their feeling of helplessness is about the hospital environment which they experience as invasive and painful:

> One girl was reading a book in the hospital. The nurse was over by the bed. The girl's name was Becky. She had the bad coughing. She had trouble with her lungs. She had lung congestion. The nurse is looking at her chart. Becky is thinking they're going to do an operation. Becky is only 8 years old. She thinks they're going to hurt her and she doesn't want it. And they did give the operation. They gave her a sleeping shot. She didn't like shots. The same nurse always came in, because she knew what to do. Becky died. Then her

---

[7]Ibid., p. 1170.

mother came to see her and they told her she died. But the mother didn't like to hear that.[8]

Such feelings of helplessness are appropriate in the sense that a child's desire to be well can rarely avert the eventual course of a fatal illness, and that hospitalized children will have to undergo any number of procedures that they might wish not to endure.

A second set of feelings which fatally ill children expressed involved their distress in not experiencing the hospital environment and personnel as supportive and helpful. At times they viewed members of the health care team as actively hostile, punishing, and not willing to help the child to recover a sense of body integrity. A seven year old boy with cystic fibrosis said in a story:

> The little boy had to stay in the hospital because the doctor wanted it. He got a shot in the back; a big needle. He was scared of shots, and didn't want it. And the doctor did it hard. His lungs are gone— he can't breathe. His lungs got worse and he didn't get well. He died and he was buried with a big shovel.[9]

Some children add guilt to this complex of feelings, blaming themselves for their own predicament. A little girl with cystic fibrosis commented that the girl in her story "got sick by not coughing up the mucus," a comment from which Waechter inferred not only that the child had been instructed about the nature of her illness, but that she may have assumed responsibility for causing it.[10]

A third feeling common in terminally ill children is that of loneliness. Their hospitalizations may be extended, and the time periods between visits from parents may seem interminably long to them. A six year old girl said in her story, "She has to be in the hospital for long days and never gets to see her Mommy and Daddy. She's very lonesome."[11]

Fourth, terminally ill children may feel anger about their situation. This anger may be directed toward members of the health care team, or it may even be directed toward persons who would seek to hide the seriousness of the disease from the child. The mother of an eight year old girl who had been diagnosed as having a malignant tumor in her leg attempted to keep this information from her daugh-

---

[8]Ibid., p. 1171.
[9]Ibid., p. 1172.
[10]Ibid.
[11]Ibid.

ter. That the child nevertheless discovered the truth can be seen in a story which she told:

> She's in the hospital, and the doctor is talking to her mother and father. She's sick—she's got cancer. She's very, very sick. She's thinking she wishes she could go home. She had an operation at the hospital, but she didn't want it because she wanted to get out of the hospital. This little girl dies—she doesn't get better. Poor little girl. This girl at the hospital—she has cancer. Her hip is swollen and her bone's broken. This little girl in the picture died, and then they buried her. And then she went up to heaven. She didn't like it there—because God wasn't there.[12]

This child mentioned death in all eight of her stories. In one she commented, "She was very lonesome before she died, because nobody cared"; and in another, "And nobody cared—not even her mother!" Thus, the mother's attempts to protect her child from the terrible truth not only failed, but helped to create in the child a sense of doubt about her mother's concern and a great deal of anger about that perceived lack.

Waechter also investigated the influence of religious instruction on the children's attitudes about death. She concluded:

> The data about religious instruction . . . lacked a variability suitable for drawing conclusions about specific effects. . . . Trends, however, indicated that [religious training does] affect the response of children with fatal illness. The religious devoutness of parents does not seem to affect the quantity of anxiety as expressed by children, but does influence the quality of their concerns and the manner in which they cope with their fears.[13]

Waechter concludes by noting that the efforts of parents and others to prevent terminally ill children from learning the truth about their condition may not prevent them from gaining this knowledge, and may not be helpful in reducing the children's anxiety levels. She adds:

> The question of whether a child should be told that his illness is fatal is meaningless; rather questions and concerns which are conscious to the child threatened with death should be dealt with in such a way that the child does not feel further isolated and alien-

---

[12]Ibid.
[13]Ibid., p. 1170.

ated from his parents and other meaningful adults. There should be no curtain of silence around his most intense fears. . . . They need support that allows introspective examination of attitudes and fears related to death in general and to the death of children in particular.[14]

We can see from Waechter's study that the question of whether or not to tell children who are fatally ill the truth about their condition is in reality a red herring which can distract from the real issue, namely: How can a child who is facing death be helped to articulate his thoughts and feelings about the experience in a manner that allows parents, friends, and members of the health care team to be supportive? As a member of the health care team, and precisely because of his religious orientation, the chaplain can become a key figure in offering support to dying children and their families. The religious faith which chaplains bring to bear upon such situations can help people to find meaning in suffering and hope in the face of impending death.

Phases of Human Reaction
Along the Way to Death

In a now classic study, the psychiatrist Elisabeth Kübler-Ross describes five reactive stages through which terminally ill persons progress.[15] She calls these *coping mechanisms*,[16] and asserts that these have become even more important to patients who live in a modern technological society where death is greatly feared and not spoken about. Our society attempts to deny the reality of death in a variety of ways. There is the "cult of youth," where we purchase many products and engage in many activities in order to forestall the natural aging process. When a person has died, the body is usually altered with cosmetic devices to make it appear as though the person still lives, but is, perhaps, just sleeping. Some who face death even arrange to have their bodies frozen and stored against the day when a cure will be found for their ailment and they may be revivified. So strong is our denial of death that "in our unconscious mind, we can

---

[14]Ibid., p. 1172.
[15]*On Death and Dying* (New York: Macmillan, 1969).
[16]Ibid., p. 37. See above, Chapter 5, "Coping With Stress: Defense Mechanisms."

only be killed; it is inconceivable to die of a natural cause or of old age."[17]

Kübler-Ross laments the deleterious effects of this denial of death. Death becomes something to be feared, an evil power which works against us, rather than a natural part of living. In addition, our fear of death and our need to deny it work to increase our destructiveness and aggressiveness; we act out our hostilities to the point of killing others in order to avoid the reality of facing our own death. Kübler-Ross fears that this destructive reaction in the face of death is so severe that society could end up destroying itself.

In working with dying children and their families, chaplains may be of help by respecting their need to deny impending death while at the same time being ready to help them move beyond this denial toward an acceptance of the inevitable reality. In terms of their relationship with the chaplain, the greatest need of people facing death may be simply to talk about it. There are times when the well-meaning health care worker may actually frustrate the fulfillment of this great need by defensively avoiding the topic of death. This may reflect more accurately the fears and needs of the worker than of the patient. For example, Kübler-Ross asserts that ". . . doctors who need denial themselves will find it in their patients and that those who can talk about the terminal illness will find their patients better able to face and acknowledge it."[18] Indeed, we have learned from the Waechter study[19] that dying children are not helped when those around them exhibit a false cheerfulness and refuse to talk about death; rather, children treated in this way may become even more anxious about death and may feel isolated from others or even rejected by them.

But even as dying patients have a strong need to talk about the course of their illnesses and their impending deaths, they also have a need to view that death as not quite certain. They need to have a sense of hope, and this hope, however faint, is usually present through all of the stages of dying which Kübler-Ross describes.

> In listening to our terminally ill patients we were always impressed that even the most accepting, the most realistic patients left the possibility open for some cure, for the discovery of a new

---

[17]Ibid., p. 2.
[18]Ibid., p. 32.
[19]See above.

drug or the "last minute success in a research project" . . . It is this glimpse of hope which maintains them through days, weeks, or months of suffering. It is the feeling that all this must have some meaning, will pay off eventually if they can only endure it for a little while longer. It is the hope that occasionally sneaks in, that all this is just like a nightmare and not true; that they will wake up one morning to be told that the doctors are ready to try out a new drug which seems promising, that they will use it on him and that he may be the chosen, special patient, just as the first heart transplant patient must have felt that he was chosen to play a very special role in life. It gives the terminally ill a sense of a special mission in life which helps them maintain their spirits, will enable them to endure more tests when everything becomes a strain—in a sense it is a rationalization for their suffering at times; for others it remains a form of temporary but needed denial.[20]

Kübler-Ross goes on to note that patients put greater trust in doctors who gave them some reason for hope and appreciated this gesture, whether or not it was realistic.[21] The chaplain who works with the dying should expect to encounter feelings of hope in them and their families, and may strengthen his bond with them by affirming and supporting these feelings of hope, even when they are unrealistic. Attempts to force the issue by demanding that patients or family members "face up" to the entire ugly truth are not helpful and will alienate them from the chaplain.

Family members of dying patients often experience the same reactions to death as the patients themselves; this may be called anticipatory grief. The timing of these reactions may be synchronous with those of the patient, or may be entirely different. In the case of children, the chaplain should remember that they often pick up clues about how to act from their elders; therefore, they may imitate the responses of their parents. In the following presentation of the stages of dying as described by Kübler-Ross, examples of each stage as it was seen in both a dying child and a related adult will be given. However, the reader should be aware that the application of "stage-thinking" to the dying and grieving processes will be criticized and found wanting in a number of respects.[22]

---

[20]Ibid., p. 139.
[21]Ibid.
[22]See below.

THE FIRST STAGE OF DYING:
DENIAL AND ISOLATION

*Gary was a twelve year old boy hospitalized with cystic fibrosis,
a chronic and ultimately fatal childhood disease characterized by serious congestion of the lungs. He had been admitted to the hospital
because his lungs became dangerously congested. When Chaplain
Cutler came to see him for the first time, their conversation included
the following interchange:*

Chaplain: So, what brings you to the hospital this week?
Gary: Well, I have this bad cough, and my lungs got all clogged
          up. I was having trouble breathing. So my mom had to
          bring me here to get medicine.
Chaplain: I see. Well, how are you doing now?
Gary: Oh, a lot better. It's just a cold. See, the doctor says I have
          C.F. [cystic fibrosis] but it's just a cold.
Chaplain: The doctor says you have C.F.?
Gary: Yeah.
Chaplain: What does that mean?
Gary: Oh, it's cystic fibrosis. It's a bad disease that kids get and
          can't breathe. But I'm not that sick. It's just a cold. Even
          if I do have C.F., I'm getting better. My mom even says I
          can go home tomorrow.
Chaplain: It would be really great if you can. You must be breathing
          better than when you had to come in.

*While visiting patients, Chaplain Newton met Mrs. Little,
whose six year old daughter was hospitalized for evaluation. The little girl had suffered an accident which caused extensive brain damage, and her condition had deteriorated steadily. As Mrs. Little told
her story, she related that when the accident had happened about
one year prior, doctors had told her that her daughter's eventual
death was a certainty. Since that time, Mrs. Little had had her
daughter admitted to four major hospitals for evaluation, and in each
case received the same prognosis. She commented, "I hope that this
time around I will finally find some decent doctors who won't just
give up. I know that this child can be helped, and I just have to find
the right hospital."*

Often when patients first find out that their illness is fatal, they
enter a numbing state of shock. As this begins to wear off, their first

reaction is usually, "No—this is not happening to me." Gary was a chronically ill child who had been told about his illness and that it would ultimately be fatal unless a new treatment were found. He voiced explicit denial of this grim prospect, but at the same time maintained a minimal acknowledgement of its reality: "The doctor says I have C.F." "Even if I do have C.F., I'm getting better." Gary's use of denial to help him cope with his illness had endured for an extended period of time (several years), and helped to give him the hope which strengthened him and made his life bearable. The mere fact that he even mentioned cystic fibrosis showed that he was letting down his defense of denial and beginning to face the truth. Chaplain Cutler decided wisely not to challenge Gary's denial with comments such as "You know the doctors are right" or "You know good and well that this is not just a cold." Instead, she acknowledged the situation as he related it and encouraged him to talk more about it. As their conversation proceeded, the degree of his denial lessened somewhat and he spoke more openly about his feelings of fear and the misery of being chronically ill. Such verbalizations are helpful.

A somewhat less obvious form of denial was exhibited by Mrs. Little. She acknowledged the severity of her child's injury, but engaged in a protracted and virtually pointless quest for the one doctor who could accomplish what all others could not. She faulted some of the doctors who had worked with her child: they were not "decent" and they gave up too soon. Chaplain Newton opted not to attempt to challenge her claims, which would have been pointless and would probably have alienated Mrs. Little. Indeed, a strong challenge might have done harm by taking her coping mechanism away. Instead he invited her to reflect on the tremendous pain she had been experiencing by commenting to her, "This whole thing must be like a terrible nightmare for you." At that Mrs. Newton began to pour out her anguish, weeping as she told him about the accident and about her child's steady decline since that time. Ultimately, with the support of the entire health care team, she was able to accept her child's impending death and even began to make funeral arrangements as it became imminent.

THE SECOND STAGE OF DYING: ANGER

Lana was an eleven-year-old girl suffering from muscular dystrophy, a degenerative disease that is fatal. Chaplain Underwood had gotten to know Lana during previous hospitalizations, and when she stopped by Lana's room for a visit, she noticed that the child was angry.

Chaplain: Hi, Lana. How are you doing?
Lana: Oh. It's you.
Chaplain: How are you getting along today?
Lana: (Angrily) I don't know!
Chaplain: Seems like you might be mad about something.
Lana: Well, I have to be in the hospital again! Why is God doing this to me?
Chaplain: Pretty mad about it, huh?
Lana: Yeah! (Starts to tear.)
Chaplain: Have you told God how you feel today?
Lana: No.
Chaplain: Would you like to do that?
Lana: I don't know if I can.
Chaplain: Why don't you give it a try? Just tell God how you are feeling right now.
Lana: (tentatively) I'm mad. (Pause)
Chaplain: Mad about what?
Lana: I'm mad at you. (Pause)
Chaplain: Who?
Lana: I'm mad at you, God. (Pause)
Chaplain: Hmmmm. Could you show God how mad you are?
Lana: (Shouting) I hate you, God! Why are you making me be sick? I hate you!

Chaplain Echols stopped in to see Mrs. Morris, whose two year old daughter was hospitalized with leukemia. During their conversation, Mrs. Morris suddenly said, in great anger, "Will you tell me something, Chaplain? Just why is this happening to my baby? Why in the hell would God hurt an innocent child?" She broke into sobs.

As people begin to give up their denial of fatal illness, they sometimes begin to feel angry. As in the two cases above, this may be coupled with the idea of: Why me? Fatal illness brings with it the prospect of tremendous loss, the loss of one's life, which may begin to happen long before death as the patient loses first one, then another capability or freedom. People feel anger in the face of loss, and a great loss may engender great anger. Anger is a difficult emotion for others to deal with; it is a powerful emotion and it can be threatening. Angry patients or angry family members may lash out at anything or everything around them, without regard to whether others deserve this anger. They may shout that the doctors don't care, the nurses are cruel and lazy, the food is inedible, the room is poorly lit, etc. The angry persons may also find the anger difficult to accept, particularly as they begin to realize that it has caused them to mistreat others. It is common for feelings of guilt to arise along with the feelings of anger. Religious persons who direct their anger at God may place themselves in a double bind: even as they feel angry at God, they feel guilty that this feeling is sinful, and may even fear that God will punish them.

When the chaplain finds that people are angry at God, it may be tempting to try to "fix" that, either by arguing persuasively that anger at God is logically unwarranted, or by judging this anger to be sinful and trying to bring the patient to feelings of remorse. Such approaches are distinctly unhelpful. Not only are they judgmental, but they miss the point: the person feels anger and needs to voice it, no matter where the anger is directed.

As Lana began to shout angrily at God, Chaplain Underwood simply remained silent and let her finish. Then she remarked that it was all right for Lana to feel angry, that many sick people felt angry at one time or another. She encouraged Lana to express her anger further by asking her to say more about what losses made her feel that way. As Lana talked, the chaplain nodded and listened carefully. Later, Lana asked, "Is God mad at me?" Chaplain Underwood responded by saying that God was not angry, that God knew why Lana was angry and that God was not hurt by her anger. She concluded, "God loves you and wants to be your friend, even if you are really, really mad sometimes." It was only after Lana's opportunity for catharsis that this teaching could take place. Had the chaplain short-circuited the process by attempting to stop Lana's voicing of her anger, the attempt to teach her about God's love might well have fallen on deaf ears. It was also important for her to help Lana to discover that anger, even very powerful anger, can be expressed safely and without fear of punishment or rejection.

Although Mrs. Morris was expressing her anger in the form of a direct question to the chaplain, she really was not looking for an answer so much as finding a way to express the tremendous anger and resentment that she was feeling. Rather than assuming responsibility for answering her question or for speaking for God, he remained silent and attentive as Mrs. Morris continued to speak angrily at some length. After she paused, he observed, "You really feel a lot of anger right now," and she resumed her voicing of rage. Finally, when she seemed emotionally spent, he said, "I really don't have any answers for you. But I am here to be with you and to help you in any way that I can." They began to talk about how she had stuffed her feelings inside for so long, and how relieved she felt to begin to get them out. A real alliance was created between the two, and Mrs. Morris readily accepted the chaplain's ongoing support during her child's hospitalization.

The anger of patients or their families can be frightening to witness, but it remains true that one of the most important services a chaplain can offer is to listen to the expression of anger and even facilitate it when it is being held back. Encouraging people to give voice to feelings of anger is not "upsetting them." It has, rather, the opposite effect, enabling them to give vent to emotions and thus obtain some measure of inner peace. When a chaplain senses that a person is ready to ventilate anger, it is wise to find a more private setting for this to take place, so that the expression of anger will not be cut short by the appearance of visitors or other hapless witnesses. When helping a patient to express anger, it is wise to alert the nurse first, so that crying or shouts will not cause undue alarm.

THE THIRD STAGE OF DYING: BARGAINING

Debbie was a seven year old girl hospitalized with cystic fibrosis. As Chaplain Miller was talking with her about her desire to go home soon, she commented, "I prayed to God and I promised that I would listen to my mom better. So maybe he won't let me get sick anymore."

Mrs. Caldwell's pre-school son was hospitalized with leukemia, and his death was anticipated within a week or two. As she spoke with Chaplain Insbrook, she confided, "I have begun a fast. I am fasting and offering it up to Jesus so that he will cure my baby. I really have faith that if I just fast long enough, Jesus will take pity on him." When the chaplain asked how long it had been since she had eaten, she told him that it had been three days.

People who have been angry with God may arrive at the point where they begin to reason, "Being angry did not help. Maybe if I put on my best behavior, then God will listen." This may take the form of a real bargaining attempt, where the person promises God certain concrete behaviors in exchange for definite rewards: I'll read the Bible every day if only you will let me live until Christmas; I'll give half of my savings to the poor if I can avoid more surgery. The aim of this bargaining is to avoid the inevitable, even if only for a short time or in very small ways. There is a magical character to this kind of reasoning, and as can be seen from the above stories, it is by no means confined to the pre-school years, when magical thinking is the norm.

Chaplain Miller sensed that Debbie needed her belief in the efficacy of her bargaining to help her cope with her anxiety and suffering. He did not attempt to explain the fallacy of her reasoning, but instead continued to encourage Debbie to talk about her experience of illness and her hopes for better health.

The case of Mrs. Caldwell presented another problem as Chaplain Insbrook judged that her fasting could harm her if it continued. He began to explore with her the feelings which lay under her desire to fast, only to find that she was feeling a great deal of guilt. At one point she commented desperately, "I must have sinned very badly for God to take my baby away. I have let evil run my life. I just hope I still have time to make up for it." Chaplain Insbrook suggested that God would not punish a mother's sins by making her child sick. He observed that continued fasting would hurt Mrs. Caldwell, and said that he could not believe that God wanted her to hurt herself. He added, "Your baby really needs you now, and he needs you to be strong and healthy, not sick." As they talked, Mrs. Caldwell talked more about her feelings of guilt, and began to realize that they did not make sense to her; she had always believed that God was loving and kind. She appeared to change her attitude about her bargaining behavior and said that she would resume eating. They prayed together, and the chaplain left. Because Mrs. Caldwell was remaining in the hospital twenty-four hours a day, he stopped by the nurses' station to tell them what she had been doing and to ask that they make sure trays of food were sent to the room at mealtimes.

Bargaining behavior should not be actively promoted, but neither should it be challenged unless it is clearly harmful to the patient. It should be recognized as a coping behavior which suits the person at a particular point in time. Kübler-Ross does warn that it may be associated with feelings of guilt over past infractions, real or imagined, and therefore bargaining should not be ignored by the health care team. The bargainer may fall into a destructive cycle of feeling guilty, promising reform, failing to reform, and feeling even more guilty. When this happens, intervention is appropriate.[23]

---

[23]*On Death and Dying*, p. 84.

THE FOURTH STAGE OF DYING: DEPRESSION

James was a fifteen year old boy hospitalized with inoperable cancer. When he was visited by Chaplain Krisak, he was obviously depressed. His mouth was turned into a frown; he was listless and spoke monosyllabically in a low voice that was barely audible. Acknowledging that he seemed to be very down, even more so than his physical condition would cause, the chaplain encouraged him to talk about his sadness. Slowly, and with constant encouragement, he began to enumerate his many losses. He could no longer attend school. He had lost his girlfriend. He could not play at sports or even ride his bicycle. He was not allowed out of the hospital to go see a movie or to go shopping. The list was a long one. He also added morosely, "I just don't think I'm going to get well."

Mrs. Sanders' ten year old daughter was dying of cystic fibrosis. When Chaplain Orcutt visited her, the child had been in the hospital for several weeks, declining gradually. Mrs. Sanders looked exhausted and listless. She told the chaplain that she had been unable to sleep more than an hour or two each night and that she had no appetite for food. She said, "I'm on an endless treadmill and there is no end in sight. I am so tired." She also talked about her feelings of guilt: "I keep asking myself whether I should have done anything different. Maybe I should have gone to another doctor. Maybe there is another hospital."

As a person's defenses begin to weaken and break down, and the impending loss of death looms threateningly, depression often results. Kübler-Ross identifies two different types of depression which are associated with impending death, and recommends a specific reaction to each.[24] One type is called *reactive,* and concerns depression over past losses. The person may feel responsibility for some of these losses, or may be worried about how others will be able to manage the death. Chaplains can be helpful by reassuring the sick persons that they are not responsible for the development of fatal illness (if, indeed, that is true) and by helping them to attend to the tasks which must be accomplished, such as reorganizing the family, looking after finances or other arrangements, etc. Another kind of depression concerns not so much past losses as anticipated losses; the person begins to grieve in anticipation of death which is now inevitable. Listening carefully to such persons and avoiding attempts to cheer them up is

---

[24]Ibid., pp. 86–87.

appropriate and helps them to come to an acceptance of death and its loss.

In each of the above cases, there is some mixture of these types of depression, but there are also clear emphases. Mrs. Sanders was more concerned with reviewing past losses and sorting out feelings of guilt. James focused more on the brute fact of many losses, and the anticipation of not recovering any of them. In each case, the chaplain was helpful in listening attentively. In addition, Chaplain Orcutt was able to offer support to Mrs. Sanders by assuring her that she had acted appropriately and responsibly in seeking care for her child. In neither case did the chaplain attempt to cheer up the depressed person, for this would only serve to belittle the losses which each expressed and possibly to instill guilt over being depressed in the first place.

THE FIFTH STAGE OF DYING: ACCEPTANCE

Natalie was a fourteen year old girl hospitalized in the final stages of cancer. Over a period of two years, she had endured several operations, including the amputation of one leg, several courses of chemotherapy, and many months of hospitalization. As she neared her death, she came to possess a great calm, which was quite different from the periods of depression which she had experienced. Her family and the hospital staff noticed that she backed away from interpersonal relationships and turned inward more and more. She was able to speak of her impending death calmly and at one point spoke with her mother about what would be done with her bedroom at home after she had died.

Mr. Young was the father of a twelve month old child who had numerous serious birth defects. The little boy had been hospitalized much of his short life, and was finally dying of heart failure. When Chaplain Wolfe stopped in to see him, Mr. Young began to talk about the long ordeal. He described the anguish and fear that he and his wife had felt when they had been told of their son's problems and poor prognosis. He talked about the many hospitalizations, the endless tests, the fruitless treatments. Finally he commented to her, "You know, I guess I should be falling apart right now. But, really, I'm ready for him to die now. He's been through so much, and it's time for it to be over. Do you think I'm cruel to feel this way?"

As fatally ill people near death, they are fortunate if they are able to come to accept their situation. Such acceptance should not be understood as a feeling of happiness, but simply as a readiness at last to face what is inevitable. With acceptance comes a cessation of both the denial of death and the desperate struggle against it. The sick persons begin to prepare themselves to die in peace. At the same time, they often begin to bring closure to some of their more important interpersonal relationships. They may "say the things I've always wanted to say" or begin to discuss plans for what will take place after death, such as funeral arrangements, changes in family life, the inheritance of property, etc. Gradually they begin to withdraw from relationships with others and to decrease interpersonal communication, a process called *decathexis*. As they prepare to leave the world, they let go of some of their meaningful relationships, which makes the leave-taking easier.

Natalie came to the point of accepting her impending death, and she began to experience a certain serenity as she found herself able to face it realistically. It was fortunate for her that her family understood her need to say some things about her death and its aftermath, and they did not discourage this conversation. However, they were hurt, at first, by what they interpreted as Natalie's rejection of them. When she began to talk less and to withdraw more and more from her loved ones, they wondered what they had done to deserve such treatment. It was only after the medical staff had explained decathexis to them that they began to understand that this was Natalie's way of letting go of her earthly ties more gradually, thus making the moment of death easier and more peaceful. They began to see that it was part of her own grieving process.

Mr. Young had also come to accept death, in his case, the death of his child. But it was this acceptance itself which caused him to feel guilty. Chaplain Wolfe helped him to see that his feeling of acceptance was not at all a heartless lack of interest or a cruel abandonment of his child, but simply a coming to terms with the real inevitability of death. As he reviewed the history of the child's treatment, she supported him by observing that the family and medical team had gone to great lengths and taken heroic measures to try to save the baby's life. No one could have done more, she said, but the best efforts of all were powerless to avert death. She helped Mr. Young to see that his feeling of acceptance was a sign that he was continuing to cope well with the stress of his child's fate and that it was a good place for him to be at the time.

Not all fatally ill patients or members of their families will come to an acceptance of death. Some continue desperately to deny its inevitability and will struggle against death to the very end. With loved ones of the patient, this struggle can continue even after death has occurred, and rather than grieving the loss, they continue to deny it. But when acceptance of death does come, it is a blessing.

Chaplains can be supportive to those who have come to accept impending death by listening carefully to what they say and by encouraging them to speak freely. When chaplains themselves are not ready to accept death, they can impose their own denial upon the patients, stifling free and honest communication. This is especially true in the case of children, who pick up cues about what responses are "right" from the behavior and attitude of adults around them. When an adult continues to exhibit a false cheerfulness and optimism, for example, it may prevent the child from mentioning his own fears or thoughts about death, and it may engender in the child a sense of isolation. This forced cheerfulness is not supportive to the child, but is instead distancing.

THE LIMITATIONS OF "STAGE-THINKING"

Valerie was a sixteen year old girl who was hospitalized during the final stages of cancer. Her attitude about her illness could be described as anything but peaceful, and in the week before her death she experienced tremendous inner turmoil. Although her doctors had told her clearly that she would die from her illness and that no further treatment was possible, Valerie continued to deny even the possibility of impending death. She expressed tremendous anger, accusing members of the medical team of lying to her about her condition; it was common for her to speak in an abusive manner to the nurses on the unit. Valerie had strong ties with her church, and she had placed many religious objects such as a Bible, pictures, and inspirational literature in her room. She told the chaplain who visited her that if only she had enough faith and learned the Bible well enough, God would cure her. In between bouts of anger, Valerie experienced periods of depression. She would refuse to eat, would not talk to others in the room, and would cry for long periods of time. Although Valerie's weakness progressed until she finally lapsed into a coma and died, her denial, anger, bargaining, and depression never seemed to leave her.

There are at least three important inadequacies in "stage-thinking," if by that is meant that dying people progress in an orderly manner through five distinct periods. The first limitation is that this simply does not coincide with reality. Patients and their families may experience some of the five stages of dying, but not others. They may not experience them in the order in which they have been described here. It is also quite common, even expected, for them to fluctuate back and forth, for example, going from total denial one day (or even one hour) to anger the next, and then back to denial after that. And, as in the case of Valerie, people may experience the various stages of dying in a mixed fashion, with little or no separation or pattern. For this reason, the experiences of those facing death might better be called "phases" or "modes" rather than stages. These should be understood as fluid and mixed rather than as having clearly defined termini or boundaries.

A second limitation of stage-thinking is that it may become evaluative in tone. It is easy to fall into the trap of thinking of the stages of dying as levels in a progression that one must accomplish. This attitude leads to thoughts such as "You're moving along nicely; you should be arriving at depression any day" or "It's a shame that you're stuck in denial, since most people would have reached bargaining by now." Worse yet, one could look at a person like Valerie and see her inability to accept her impending death as a kind of failure. Such evaluations are out of place in working with the dying.

A third limitation of stage thinking is that it can engender a rigidity on the part of the helper, who may expect dying people or their families to progress in an orderly manner through clearly defined stages. Thus the chaplain may fail to notice a patient's anger if he is under the assumption that anger has already been "accomplished" and now the patient is "doing another stage." Those who work with the dying need to be constantly open to whatever the patient is experiencing and expressing, whether or not this seems to be logical or correct. Only in this way can helpers respond directly to needs rather than imposing their own game plan upon others.

The "stages" of dying, then, have been presented not as a road map, but as an aid to helping chaplains understand the experiences of the dying, and to give some hints about how to be supportive.

The Chaplain and the Aftermath of Death

Ministers who work in the community know well the importance of ministering to bereaved families. Those who work exclusively in a clinical setting as hospital chaplains should not operate under the impression that their ministry to patients' families ends with their death. On the contrary, ministry and follow-up care for grieving families may be the most important work that a chaplain does throughout the course of terminal illness. During the time that a critically injured or terminally ill child is hospitalized, family members have rather extensive contact with members of the health care team. This is a necessity simply because the team must communicate with them about the treatment process. This necessary communication provides the context for staff members to be supportive of families, to listen to their concerns, and perhaps to see to some of their needs, be they emotional, financial, educational, etc. But after the death of a patient, the family may lose all contact with health care team members, and may feel abandoned and adrift at sea. Many hospitals offer after-care for grieving families in the form of counseling or support groups, but not all do. In any event, the hospital chaplain may attend to a great need by continuing to minister to families after the death of a loved one. Chaplains and families may find it very meaningful for the chaplain to officiate at or participate in the dead child's funeral services. Chaplains may help families begin to make necessary arrangements and to contact relatives, friends, and their own churches. But families may need the help of a chaplain even more after the funeral services are over and they are forced to return to the concerns of normal life, but now without a loved one. At this time, the grieving process has only begun, and the chaplain's ministry to those who grieve is important.

The death of a loved one is rarely easy to accept, but when the one who has died is a child, the pain and grief are even more severe. The death of one's child may produce the most painful grief of all.[25] The death of children is particularly hard to accept because they seem to have been cheated out of a full and happy life. One has the sense that they were just beginning, or perhaps even had no opportunity to begin life, when death cruelly struck them down. The obvious innocence of children makes justification of their deaths seemingly impossible (although the view that *anyone's* death is punishment for sin is not a Christian one). Parents, caretakers, and even members of the health care team may experience feelings of severe guilt and loss of self-esteem at the time of a child's death. They may rehearse events leading up to the death over and over, in an endless

---

[25]C. M. Parkes, *Bereavement* (New York: International Universities Press, 1972), pp. 122–23.

quest for identifying wrong choices or errors which caused the death. They may come to see themselves as failures: they were responsible for a child's welfare, and they let him die.

When the fatal illness has been a long one, families may have begun their grief work prior to the actual death. Even so, death always comes as a painful shock. Chaplains who are involved with families who have lost a child should plan to continue their ministry to them. As we discuss the form of this ministry, we begin with a discussion of the grieving process.

The Process of Grief

Grief is the pain associated with loss. Persons may grieve over the loss of a cherished possession, a personal failure, a disappointment, a death, etc. As a process, grief has certain typical and clear manifestations which people experience. Although some have attempted to name "stages" of the grieving process, the phenomenon of grief is even less suited to this kind of description than is the experience of dying. The limitations of "stage-thinking" which were described above as applied to the dying process are even more pressing in the case of the grieving process which is more individualistic, thus making stage-thinking difficult. Attempts to describe stages of grieving have suffered from a lack of clarity and have been susceptible to variant interpretations by professional clinicians.[26] Therefore, as aspects of the grieving process are described below, the reader should understand them not as progressive stages, but simply as varied reactions which grieving persons normally experience. Grieving is understood here to be a healthy and necessary reaction to a major loss. Grieving is therefore to be embraced rather than avoided, and, indeed, attempts to avoid or abort the grieving process after a major loss may lead to illness and debilitation. Aspects of the grieving process include an initial period of numbness and shock,

---

[26]Ibid. This is a now standard work which attempts, in my view, unsuccessfully to describe distinct stages of the grief process, although Parkes' description of grief as a human experience remains immensely edifying. Attempts to summarize Parkes' stages seem only partially successful, as a comparison of two such attempts demonstrates: cf. Harold I. Kaplan, M.D. and Benjamin J. Sadock, M.D., eds., *Modern Synopsis of Comprehensive Textbook of Psychiatry/III* (Baltimore: Williams & Wilkins, 1981), "Grief, Mourning, and Simple Bereavement," pp. 383–85; and Eugene Kennedy, *On Becoming a Counselor* (New York: Seabury, 1977) pp. 249–52.

panic and confusion, painful longing for the lost loved one, depression, and recovery.

Mr. Yuban's young daughter was hospitalized and undergoing dangerous brain surgery. As he was waiting in her hospital room, the surgeon came in and informed him that his daughter had died during surgery. Mr. Yuban said nothing, but turned and stared intently at the television. The doctor stayed with him for several minutes, attempting to talk, but he continued to stare at the television, apparently in a daze.

Mrs. Train's teenage son had been killed instantly in a motorcycle accident. She had been informed at her home by a policeman. She took the news without apparent reaction, and when the policeman left, she went into the kitchen where she quietly began to wash the dishes.

When people first hear of the death of a loved one, it is common for them to experience a sense of complete numbness. They may have no feelings, either emotional or physical, and the external situation takes on for them a sense of unreality. People who experience this numbness may withdraw into a shell, as did Mr. Yuban, or they may become absorbed in everyday routines, like Mrs. Train. This initial numbness may be understood as a form of denial. The external reality is too terrible for some persons to accept, at least at first and so suddenly, and they simply build a sort of wall or capsule around themselves and refuse to let the pain sink in. This denial functions as a defense which allows the person to become better prepared to be confronted by a painful event. As such, it is a good and helpful phenomenon as long as it does not become prolonged. Attempts should not be made to "shake the person out of it" or "force them to confront the death." Usually the person will do this when ready. This period of numbness may last anywhere from several minutes to about a day, or even longer. If it persists longer than this, a mental health professional should be consulted.

Mr. Ornby's young son had been struck by an automobile and taken to a hospital emergency room. Shortly after the father arrived, the doctor came in to tell him that his son had been killed almost instantly and was dead on arrival at the hospital. After a few moments, Mr. Ornby became restless and agitated. He began to pace rapidly and aimlessly, and suddenly cried out, "I've got to get out of

this place!" With that, he ran from the emergency room to the park-
ing lot.

Mrs. Peterson was waiting with the chaplain in a conference
room while her daughter was undergoing open heart surgery. The
surgeon came in to inform her that her daughter had not survived
the procedure. They spoke for a few minutes, and after the doctor left,
she began to sob violently. She clung to the chaplain, and said over
and over, "Oh help me, please! I'm so scared! Please help me!"

The loss of a loved one changes a person's life drastically and ir-
revocably. As this reality begins to sink in, the person's reaction may
be similar to the kind of reaction one would expect to see in the face
of danger. Such people begin to feel agitated and panicky, and may
also be confused. Their hearts race, their blood pressure soars, their
nerves become taut, and they may need a physical release for the im-
mense energy which begins to build up inside them. Mr. Ornby reacted to these feelings by fleeing the scene; it was only after he
calmed down and walked around the parking lot for a while that he
was able to come back into the hospital and see his child's body. Mrs.
Peterson experienced severe alarm as well, but in her confusion she
reached out in desperation to the chaplain who was with her. When
grieving people have such a reaction, it is usually best to allow it to
run its course as long as they are not harming themselves. For example, any attempts to restrain Mr. Ornby and prevent his leaving
the emergency unit would have been counter-productive (and might
have resulted in an actual scuffle). The author does not advocate the
administration of tranquilizers or sedatives to persons who are grieving in this manner, although he does recognize that this ultimately
must be a medical decision which chaplains do not make.

Mr. Wilbur was grieving over the loss of his ten year old nephew,
who had died suddenly in an accident three days before. He and the
boy had been very close and the shock was severe. In speaking with
his minister, Mr. Wilbur sighed from time to time and described his
grief as an actual physical pain in his chest, in the area of the ster-
num. He related that he was constantly preoccupied with thoughts
of the boy, and that with these thoughts came the pain. He had been
crying frequently since he heard of the boy's death.

Harriet was a seventeen year old girl whose younger sister had
died of leukemia. The day after the death, Harriet went with her
family to the funeral home to see her sister's body. As they entered

the viewing parlor, Harriet rushed to the coffin, grasped her sister's hand, and began to beg, "Please don't be dead! Please wake up!"

Mr. and Mrs. Lubbitch were in the hospital with their baby, who was having open heart surgery. The child died during surgery, but when the doctor informed them, Mrs. Lubbitch insisted that a mistake had been made. Despite the protestations of the doctor and Mr. Lubbitch, she began to call various departments in the hospital, asking if her baby were there.

Mr. Fisk's eight year old son had been struck and killed by an automobile. Several weeks later, while shopping in a large department store, Mr. Fisk noticed a little boy in the crowd and suddenly believed that it might be his son. He rushed after the child, and it was only when he got within several feet of him and saw his face that he realized that it was not his own son.

Mrs. Erlich's five year old son had died of cancer. Several weeks after the death, she was taking a nap at home when she awakened to hear the sound of children playing in the back yard. She was quite certain that she heard the playful shouts of her own son until she looked out of the window and saw that he was not among the group of youngsters who were there.

After the initial shock and numbness of death wear off, the painful reality begins to sink in, and grief is experienced primarily as painful longing for the lost one. This pain may be quite severe, and is often accompanied by a great deal of weeping and physical sensations of pain or discomfort.

This phase of the grief process is described by Parkes as pining and searching. Thoughts of the lost one preoccupy the grievers, and they feel a deep and intense longing for him or her. The reality of the loss has begun to sink in, but denial persists in the form of a search which is carried on for the dead person. As the above stories illustrate, this searching behavior takes several shapes. As in the case of Harriet, a mourner may confront the corpse and talk to it as if the person were still alive, even to the extent of begging or demanding a response. After the burial or cremation, and sometimes even before, the mourner may have a feeling that somehow the dead person is still "present," perhaps attempting to communicate with survivors. Actual searching behaviors may take place, as when Mrs. Lubbitch attempted to locate her baby in the hospital. Usually, however, this takes a more subtle form: the mourner begins to take in external stimuli in a selective and biased manner which perpetuates the illusion that the person is still alive. It is common for survivors to catch a glimpse of someone who looks like the deceased and believe that it is he, or to hear his voice in a crowd. Olfactory sensations can be particularly powerful, and smelling the deceased's favorite perfume on another person may elicit the sudden fantasy that she is still alive.

These searching behaviors are a normal part of the grieving process, and should not cause alarm as long as the mourner clearly understands that death has actually taken place, and that the mind is simply "playing tricks." Grieving persons often mitigate successfully the pain of loss by creating a pseudo-presence of the deceased. This, too, is a healthy and normal reaction and is actually to be encouraged. For example, it is most helpful for the mourners to tell stories about the dead person, and in so doing to relive important memories. They may tell the same favorite stories again and again to anyone who will listen. Along these lines, it is also helpful to tell the story of events surrounding the death itself. This helps mourners to accept the reality of death and begin to ventilate feelings about it. Such story telling is to be encouraged. Dreaming about the dead person also creates a pseudo-presence. It is common for persons who are grieving realistically and appropriately to have dreams that the dead one is still alive or has returned to life. At times such dreams are distressing; once understood they may be a source of great comfort. Mourners may want to have physical mementos of the deceased as well as memories. They may place articles owned by the deceased in prominent places around them, or clutch them tightly. Pictures of the dead person may be put out on special display. Acts of commemoration are also helpful. One woman placed a large photograph of her dead child on the living room table and placed fresh flowers in front of it each day. Visits to burial sites are common and may give comfort to mourners because they somehow make the deceased person seem closer.

Mr. Dirk was the father of a twelve year old girl who was killed in an accident. Several weeks after her death, he began to feel extremely tired and heavy-hearted. He was unable to eat or sleep well, and instead of performing well at work, he tended to wander aimlessly around the office. He came to see his minister to report that he had been having suicidal thoughts, and was contemplating driving off a bridge.

It is not uncommon for a mourner to experience depression. This is to be differentiated from the raw pain and intense sadness which is experienced soon after a loss. Depression may set in after the period of pining and searching, and may last several months. Symptoms of depression include an overwhelming sadness, a feeling of listlessness or, in some cases, of restlessness, inability to concentrate, disturbances in sleep or appetite—either too much or too little—a feeling of heaviness in the body and limbs, and, at times, suicidal thinking. Anxiety may accompany depression, with the sufferer worrying constantly about any number of things.

Ministers who are approached by depressed persons should be ready to give them a good deal of time. Because of the nature of the problem, depressed persons may speak very slowly and quietly, perhaps inaudibly, and may have great difficulty expressing their feelings and communicating accurately. It is fruitless to try to cheer up a depressed person by admonishing him to "look on the bright side" or by acting cheerful and lighthearted oneself. Rather, the minister should be prepared to listen carefully to the depressed person and to share the odyssey of pain. The expression of feelings is greatly to be encouraged, especially if the depressed person hints at feelings of anger, even if this is directed toward members of the health care team, God, or the deceased person; often it is stifled anger which actually has contributed to the onset of depression in the first place. Feelings of rejection, loneliness, and emptiness are also common.

When a mourner's depression interferes with work or personal life, referral to a competent mental health professional is appropriate. If the minister should pick up any hints of suicidal thoughts or overt expressions of these, great concern is called for. Suicidal talk must always be dealt with calmly, but with great seriousness. It should never be simply dismissed as unimportant. Persons having suicidal thoughts should be put in contact with a mental health professional immediately. They may require therapy, in-patient care, and medication to help them.

When a person's depression does not interfere significantly with life and does not seem to be dangerous, the minister may be of help by spending time with the person, which is itself a supportive act, and by encouraging him or her to talk about the deceased person, the experience of death, and the process of grief. Special efforts should be made to help the mourner express feelings.

Mr. Bean was the father of a teenage girl who died of cancer after a relatively brief illness. He experienced the shock, pining, and depression which are typical of the grief process. About eight or nine months after his daughter's death, his depression began to lift. He resumed his hobby of woodworking, in which he had not engaged since shortly after her death, and began to return to the lifestyle which he enjoyed prior to the death. He still had some days on which he became very sad and cried, but they were not as frequent as before. It was particularly painful for him to face the one year anniversary of his daughter's death, but he was able to spend this day with family and friends and to give and receive support from them. Things began to get back to normal for him.

"Getting back to normal" may be the best description of the recovery and reintegration experience which marks the end of the grief process. Mourners become less preoccupied with thoughts of their loss and more able to function as they did prior to the loss. The deceased is still remembered with sadness, but this is not a sadness which preoccupies or interferes with normal functioning. Mourners are able to get on with life, incorporating changes in their circumstances which the loss of the loved one may require.

Ineffective Grieving Patterns

We have noted above that grieving is to be regarded as a process which is both necessary and healthy. Aspects of the typical or "normal" grieving process were discussed. There are times, however, when the necessary grief process is avoided or aborted, to the detriment of the mourner. In such cases, grief therapy with a mental health professional is indicated.

Mrs. Monroe was the mother of a child who had been born with untreatable heart defects and had died at the age of three years. She showed little reaction at the time of his death; her eyes teared a little, but she did not cry. Her friends marveled at her stoicism during the funeral rites. Afterward, she dismantled her child's room, giving away all of his furnishings and possessions. She scoured her home for any pictures or other reminders of him and packed these away in a box in the attic. She refused to talk about her child or to allow others to do so in her presence. She never visited his grave.

Mr. Adler's seven year old daughter had been struck by a car and killed. He appeared quite sad when he learned of her death and remained so throughout the next few weeks. He did not, however, cry, or tell the story of her death over and over, as did other members of his family. Several weeks after her death, a neighbor's dog was

*struck and killed by a delivery truck. When Mr. Adler heard about
the event, he began to sob hysterically. He was unable to return to
work and was eventually hospitalized for treatment of depression.*

*Mrs. Jaspers was the mother of a fourteen year old boy who died
of leukemia. Her grief appeared to be normal for several weeks, but
she was not able to resume her normal life. One year after the death
she still cried several times each day for her dead son. She would
spend hours each day in his room, looking at his belongings and at
times talking to him as if he were there.*

At times mourners suppress the grieving process. In cases such
as Mr. Adler's, this is a temporary situation, and the work of grieving
is simply delayed for several days or weeks. Often in such cases an
event which is similar to the original loss triggers the full grief reaction. People who have delayed their grief reactions may react dis-
proportionately to the death of a stranger, or, in the case of Mr. Adler,
to the death of a neighbor's pet.

In other cases, such as that of Mrs. Monroe, the grief work is delayed indefinitely. It is not uncommon for people who do this to express their pain somatically through the development of a physical
ailment. This kind of inhibited grief is a form of denial. For Mrs.
Monroe, this entailed not only denial of her son's death, but denial
of his very existence in the first place. She systematically and thor-
oughly sought to eliminate every reminder of him.

The opposite problem can also be debilitating. When grief is prolonged, as in the case of Mrs. Jaspers, recovery and reintegration into
normal life are prevented. The mourner becomes "stuck" in a painful
and constricting pattern.

When grief reactions are inhibited, delayed, or prolonged in a
way that is painful or that interferes with a person's ability to function in family or at work, referral for loss therapy is indicated. John
G. Corazzini describes four tasks which the counselor and the bereaved share in such therapy.[27] The first is to share an openness to
the loss. It may be the denial of the loss which has resulted in the
abortive grieving pattern. Counselors must communicate their openness to acknowledge the loss, and the clients must perceive this openness. The second task concerns the expression of feelings about the
loss. The bereaved persons must come to an adequate expression of

---

[27]"The Theory and Practice of Loss Therapy" in B. Mark Schoenberg, ed., *Bereavement Counseling: A Multidisciplinary Handbook* (Westport: Greenwood, 1980), pp.
71–85.

these feelings, and the counselor must be ready to respond with empathy. A third task to be shared is reminiscing about the lost person. The counselor is to encourage this, and the bereaved must begin the process of reminiscing. Finally, the counselor must insist on the reality of the loss, and the bereaved must develop an ability to acknowledge this reality.

Some ministers and chaplains are well qualified to work as grief counselors. But since the physical health, mental health, and, in the case of suicidal persons, their very lives are at stake, those who do not feel confident of their ability to handle the situation adequately should not hesitate to make referrals to counselors who are trained to deal with aborted grief reactions.

Conclusion

Children's conceptions of death, their awareness of it in cases of fatal illness, stages or phases of dying, the process of grief, and the role of the minister in these circumstances have been discussed in this chapter. The minister may well find that his greatest gift to those who are involved in a child's death (including the dying child) is in giving permission and encouragement to talk freely about what is happening. The subject of death is so often taboo, as if it were obscene, and the suppression of communication about it can be extremely painful and harmful. In addition, the minister brings a unique perspective, that of faith, to the situation, knowing that for those who face death, hope may be the single factor which makes their pain bearable.

RECOMMENDED READING

Bishops' Committee on the Liturgy. *Study Text II: Anointing and Pastoral Care of the Sick.* Washington: United States Catholic Conference, 1973.

Bordow, Joan Wiener. *The Ultimate Loss: Coping with the Death of a Child.* New York: Beaufort, 1982.

Borg, Susan. *When Pregnancy Fails: Families Coping with Miscarriage, Stillbirth, and Infant Death.* Boston: Beacon, 1981.

DeFrain, John D. *Coping with Sudden Infant Death.* Lexington: Lexington Books, 1982.

Empereur, James L., S.J. *Prophetic Anointing: God's Call to the Sick, the Elderly, and the Dying.* Wilmington: Michael Glazier, 1982.

Gorer, Geoffrey. *Death, Grief, and Mourning.* New York: Arno, 1977.

Hollingsworth, Charles E. *The Family in Mourning: A Guide for Health Professionals.* New York: Grune & Stratton, 1977.

Kinast, Robert L. *When a Person Dies: Pastoral Theology in Death Experiences.* New York: Crossroad, 1984.

Knauber, Adolf. *Pastoral Theology of the Anointing of the Sick.* Collegeville: Liturgical Press, 1973.

Kübler-Ross, Elisabeth. *On Children and Death.* New York: Macmillan, 1985.

—. *On Death and Dying.* New York: Macmillan, 1969.

Kushener, Harold S. *When Bad Things Happen to Good People.* New York: Schocken, 1981.

Lancaster, Matthew. *Hang Tough.* Mahwah: Paulist, 1985.

Monson, Gabriele. *Say Hi to Jesus for Me: The Story of Young Todd & His Battle Against Cancer.* Augsburg, 1979.

Parkes, Colin Murray. *Bereavement: Studies of Grief in Adult Life.* New York: International Universities, 1972.

Pincus, Lily. *Death and the Family: The Importance of Mourning.* New York: Pantheon, 1975.

Reid, Clyde. *Celebrate the Temporary.* New York: Harper & Row, 1972.

Schiff, Harriet Sarnoff. *The Bereaved Parent.* New York: Crown, 1977.

Schoenberg, B. Mark, ed. *Bereavement Counseling: A Multidisciplinary Handbook.* Westport: Greenwood, 1980.

Schulz, Richard. *The Psychology of Death, Dying and Bereavement.* Reading: Addison-Wesley, 1978.

Van Ornum, William and John B. Mordock. *Crisis Counseling with Children and Adolescents.* New York: Continuum, 1983.

Waechter, Eugenia H. "Children's Awareness of Fatal Illness," in *American Journal of Nursing* 71 (1971), pp. 1168–72.

8.

Theological Reflections

What is presented here are the author's personal reflections on the experience of illness and ministry to the sick. Illness can easily become for the patient an experience of personal disintegration, alienation from other people, and weakening or even destruction of religious faith. The minister who works with the sick can address these aspects of their suffering, at times quite effectively. Ministers to the sick will find the locus of their power in their ability to make Christ present to patients.

For the sake of convenience, reference is made throughout this chapter to the minister's work with the *patient*. It should be understood, however, that the patient's family and loved ones also suffer, and that the aspects of the experience of illness which can be so oppressive to the patient burden them as well, often in the very same way. Therefore, the assertions made here about the minister's work with patients apply to work with their families and loved ones as well.

Phenomenology of Illness

Irene was a six year old girl hospitalized with infectious hepatitis. Because this is a potentially life-threatening disease and is contagious, Irene was put in isolation. This meant that signs were placed on the door of her hospital room, warning potential visitors to check in with the nurse before entering the room. Those who entered the room, including doctors and nurses, were to wear a gown and gloves. During the visit, they were to avoid touching Irene or her bed or items close around her. When leaving the room, visitors put their gowns and gloves in special containers which were marked "Contam-

176

inated Materials." Irene's four year old brother was not allowed to visit her because he was too young. Because Irene's mother was pregnant, she was not allowed to enter the hospital room at all, but could only wave to her daughter through the small window in the door.

Naturally, Irene was deeply distressed by her predicament. The hospital staff knew that it was important to help her to understand the reasons for placing her in isolation, and they took great pains not to make Irene feel dirty or bad. The reality, however, was that Irene's body was infected with a dangerous virus, and contact with her constituted a threat to the health of others. Because of her age and thus her tendency to think magically (see above, "Child Development and the Clinical Context"), it was difficult for Irene not to feel that she was bad and to blame for her illness and her threat to the health of others.

In addition to the feelings of guilt which Irene's predicament engendered, there were other distressing aspects of her experience. She was plucked suddenly, and with virtually no time to prepare, from her familiar home environment and put into a strange place. She was confined not just to her room, but to her bed. Visits from family and friends were severely restricted. The appearance of strangers entering her room garbed in mask, gown, and gloves was frightening to Irene. Many of her treatment procedures were painful, especially those involving needles: injections, intravenous treatment, the taking of blood samples. On top of it all, Irene felt physically weak and miserable.

It is granted that Irene's experience of illness is a fairly extreme case, although in a large hospital setting it is not a rare one. It was selected for presentation here because it illustrates clearly certain facets of the experience of illness which are common to most cases, especially cases of illness or injury which require hospitalization. Five features which are common to the experience of serious illness or injury will be discussed: change of environment; loss of control and power; the experience of pain; anxiety over the future; the feeling of uncleanness or contamination.

A sudden *change of living environment* can be distressing for anyone, but it tends to be even more so for children. Children gain a sense of security by experiencing constancy in their environment. The familiar, the predictable, that which can be relied upon, are comforting and reassuring. Smaller children often develop rather rigid patterns of behavior, which may take on a ritualistic character. Consider, for example, Irene's bedtime routine, which many parents will recognize as familiar and typical:

Each night after dinner, Irene and her younger brother watched their favorite television show from 6:30 to 7:00. After this program, Irene had her bath. In addition to the soap and water, Irene always had the following in the tub with her: her waterproof plastic doll named "Susie," two plastic ducks, one yellow and one blue, a toy tugboat, and a plastic mirror which could be hung over the side of the tub. The presence of her little brother was desirable, but optional. Following her bath, Irene put on her favorite pajamas, made of pink cotton flannel, which she called her "snuggies." Next, she sat on the bed while her mother or father read to her her favorite story; Irene always insisted on the same story; she knew the words by heart and would say them along with the parent who was reading them. Next, Irene would be tucked into bed along with certain stuffed animals: her large teddy bear, her small one, a white bunny, and a brown dog. Finally, her mother would make sure the night light was on, and kiss Irene first on the left cheek, then on the right, lastly on the forehead. Whenever her mother or father omitted one of the elements of this bedtime routine, Irene would remind them and insist on its proper observance.

It is usually upsetting to children to experience abrupt changes in environment and routine. Often they experience the hospital environment as not only strange, but frightening. They are surrounded by new sights, sounds, feels, and smells. A missing teddy bear, or a change in night wear, which may not seem significant to adults who are trying to save a child's life, may still be of great importance to the child. All of the sudden changes may combine to instill in children a deep sense of insecurity, fear, and misery. This distress may be even more severe in children who have never before spent a night away from home.

In many cases, hospitalized children also experience a diminished contact with their parents. This may be due to very practical considerations, such as the parent's inability to spend the night in the hospital, to be present during the child's breakfast time, etc. Other factors may be operative here as well, as in Irene's case, when fear of infection prevented her mother's close presence. This diminished contact with parents may produce in the child feelings of fear and apprehension, often called "separation anxiety."[1]

The hospital environment also tends to interrupt the child's usual pattern of communications. First, hospitalized children are often unable to communicate with their "usual" people. Although the advent of telephones in hospital rooms has been a great help here, hospitalized children are still often unable to talk with their usual playmates, their teachers, or even members of the family. Even when telephone communication is possible, it is not the same as being with others, being able to see, to touch, to be held. Second, children in the hospital must communicate with a large array of strangers who participate in their care. They may have to talk with strangers about very personal matters such as bathroom habits or hygiene. For some outgoing children this is not much of a problem; for some who are shy, however, coping with so many strangers may be intensely difficult.

Hospitalized children also experience a *loss of control and power*. Much of the independence which they normally enjoy may be taken away from them: they may be confined to bed; they may have to ask permission to go to the bathroom; they are forced to undergo procedures which are painful or invasive; they may have a strictly controlled diet, or they may be allowed no food or drink at all. This loss of control may develop into a sense of personal disunity. The powers and levels of independence which the child has worked to possess are now summarily taken away, at times even without explanation. The health care of children may require that they return to earlier behavior patterns, for example, allowing an adult to bathe or feed them. Being forced to give up some measure of their independence, children may complain of being "treated like a baby." This sense of personal disunity may be fostered by their being asked, on the one hand, to cope with new stresses in a mature and cooperative manner, and, on the other hand, to submit to infantile behavior patterns.

The *experience of pain* is usually part of a child's hospitalization. Even small procedures such as pricking the fingertip for a drop of blood can be quite threatening to a child. Often the fear of pain is worse than the physical pain itself.

Anxiety over the future is experienced by many hospitalized children. There are situations where a child will be afraid, quite appropriately, about certain procedures which are sure to take place.

---

[1] See J. Robertson, *Young Children in Hospitals* (London: Tavistock Publications, 1958, pp. 20–23).

Kevin was a thirteen year old boy hospitalized with viral meningitis, an infection of the tissues around the brain and spinal cord. Part of the diagnostic procedures included a spinal tap, which Kevin experienced as immensely painful and terrifying. When the chaplain saw Kevin on the third day of his hospitalization, the boy had been told that later that day he would have to undergo a second spinal tap. He was afraid and preoccupied with the upcoming ordeal.

Patsy was a ten year old girl hospitalized with third degree burns on her arms. Twice a day her bandages were changed, a procedure which caused a great deal of pain. Patsy lived in dread of the twice-daily torment.

In other situations, children will be apprehensive about their own unrealistic fantasies of what will happen. Pre-school children are concerned with bodily integrity and may have outrageous fantasies about losing parts of their bodies in the hospital. Older children may sometimes imagine that their disease is more serious than it actually is. Some may be thinking about death as they anticipate a routine procedure such as a tonsillectomy.

Older children and teenagers who suffer from life-threatening illness will experience anxiety as they are confronted with the hard fact of their own personal finitude. Even the child who is recovering from a serious illness may have been hard hit with the awareness that he is not immortal, and that even though death has been avoided in the present crisis, it will one day come. Even for children, a close brush with death or an experience of serious illness can result in a new awareness of the transitoriness of life.

Finally, hospitalized children may be burdened with *feelings of uncleanness or guilt.* At times these feelings have their basis in matters of fact. Even a small child who has an infectious disease can usually understand that it is possible to pass the illness on to other people. Even minimal isolation, such as staying indoors and home from school, can be difficult for children to accept and can cause them to feel alone and contaminated.

A more figurative sense of uncleanness, but a no less real one, can result when a child is physically disfigured or impaired by illness or injury. Children who are disfigured by ugly burn scars, who limp or stagger with cerebral palsy, who were born with a missing limb or who lost a limb later in life, who have lost their hair due to chemotherapy, etc., may find themselves to be the objects of ridicule or fear on the part of their peers and even on the part of adults. Sick children may encounter other people who fear catching a disorder that is not truly communicable or who are simply revolted by what they see.

Experiencing rejection and isolation, on a small scale or large, is included in the experience of most children who are ill enough to be hospitalized.

Within a religious perspective, elements of our biblical tradition can reinforce feelings of isolation and uncleanness on the part of the sick. In the literature of the Old Testament, we find references to the exclusion of the sick from the rest of the faith community:

> A man infected with leprosy must wear his clothing torn and his hair disordered; he must shield his upper lip and cry, "Unclean, unclean." As long as the disease lasts he must be unclean; and therefore he must live apart: he must live outside the camp. (Leviticus 13:45–46)[2]

Such an exclusion is not merely to live apart; it constitutes a radical separation from the community of faith and its worship of God, for uncleanness was ancient Israel's primitive experience of that which was displeasing to God. It should not be surprising to find, therefore, some association among illness, uncleanness, and sin:

> Yahweh, do not punish me in your rage,
> or reprove me in the heat of anger.
> Your arrows have pierced deep,
> Your hand has pressed down on me;
> no soundness in my flesh now you are angry,
> no health in my bones, because of my sin.
>
> My guilt is overwhelming me,
> it is too heavy a burden;
> my wounds stink and are festering,
> the result of my folly;
> bowed down, bent double, overcome,
> I go mourning all the day. (Psalm 38:1–6)

These passages are quoted here not because they are considered to be a religious ethic to be imitated, but because (1) they demonstrate that in religious thinking illness, uncleanness, and personal sin *may* be associated; (2) they reflect the lived experience of people who felt

---

[2]Biblical quotations in this chapter are taken from *The Jerusalem Bible* (Garden City: Doubleday, 1966).

the need to isolate those who were sick from the rest of the community so as to avoid the spread of infection.

Reflecting upon the experience of serious illness, we can see that the change of environment, the loss of control and power, the experience of pain, the anxiety over the future, and the feeling of uncleanness or contamination can produce in the patient a profound crisis of identity. In a real sense, the patient has lost his former self, or at least part of it. Patients may become new people with a new place and role in society. They may experience alienation and existential ambiguity as they live through the time of crisis. Children who are sick are by no means exempted from these problems; at times they may feel the alienation and loss of self even more profoundly than adults.

Ministry to the Sick

It is precisely here that the chaplain may be able to intervene quite effectively. If the patient's relationships with family and society have been disrupted, so has his relationship with God. Our horizontal relationships, i.e., those with other people, and our vertical relationship, i.e., our relationship with God, together form a system by which we as individuals experience and relate to that which is other than ourselves. The two dimensions, the horizontal and the vertical, necessarily interact with one another. Each informs the other, each influences the other, and to consider either in isolation is to fragment the human experience. In a time of sickness or injury, the chaplain intervenes to help the patient relate the horizontal to the vertical, and to help him or her to make sense of the experience taking place on each of the two axes. The chaplain may be able to help the patient to experience the disruption of illness or injury not as a curse, but as (1) the opportunity to place a new and radical trust in God, and (2) the opportunity to participate in a new way in the passion and resurrection of Christ.

The chaplain may be present to the patient's family in much the same way. They, too, experience the change of environment, the loss of control and power, the pain, the anxiety over the future, and the feelings of uncleanness. They, too, share the patient's distress, even if they experience it in somewhat different ways. They, too, find their normal horizontal and vertical relationships disrupted. They, too, need help in integrating the horizontal and the vertical.

The ministry to the sick has a threefold basis in the New Testament. First, there was Jesus' presence to the sick people whom he met. Unlike so many others of his time, Jesus was not afraid to touch the lepers, the unclean ones of society. The stories of his healings are among the oldest in the gospel materials. If we know anything about Jesus of Nazareth, we know that he was present to the sick in a powerful and loving way. His healings were signs of God's love for his people and promises of the kingdom which is to come.

Jesus sent forth disciples to proclaim that love and to announce that coming kingdom. This sending forth is the second New Testament basis for ministry to the sick. The disciples of Jesus continued his loving presence to the sick, and the gospels record that they, too, were able to effect cures.

A third New Testament basis for ministry to the sick is found in the Epistle of James. Addressing his audience, the writer of this epistle urges: "If one of you is ill, he should send for the elders of the church, and they must anoint him with oil in the name of the Lord and pray over him. The prayer of faith will save the sick man and the Lord will raise him up again; and if he has committed any sins, he will be forgiven." (James 5:14–5) Here, as well as in the gospels, the presence of certain members of the religious community to the sick is linked to the forgiveness of sin; the healing mentioned is healing of both flesh and spirit, and is once more a powerful sign of God's loving presence and a promise of the reign of God which is to come.

As a religious leader called by his faith community to serve others in the name of Jesus, the minister or chaplain becomes a powerful presence to those who suffer sickness or injury. Like Jesus, he is not afraid to join the sick, to walk with them a little way on their life's journey, to reach out in love and to touch. Ministers, empowered with the healing love of Christ, barge through the barriers of uncleanness which surround the sick. Their ministry requires that they reach out and touch, just as Jesus touched the lepers of his own day. They must be ready to smell the vomitus, the diarrhea; they must be ready to look at the disfigurement of burns or violence; they must push the wheelchair, grasp the malformed hand, and wipe off the blood and spittle. Ministry to the sick is intense for any human being, and it is intensely human: the minister will experience at close range the flesh's greatest glories as well as its worst corruptions.

Ministers who understand themselves to be serving others in the name of Christ will not be alone in their confrontations with human suffering, for Christ himself is present as patient and chaplain meet.

The presence of the minister is one that is sacramental: the minister becomes an outward sign, instituted by Christ, to give grace.

Ministers to the sick are outward signs precisely because they are *there,* in the flesh, tangibly present to the sick. The image of "reaching out to others" is all too often taken as a mere metaphor; the minister to the sick should understand this literally. There is simply no substitute for real, fleshly contact as one human being attempts to comfort another. This is especially the case with children. Chaplains, wherever possible, should offer their touch to children they meet in the hospital. The offer will not always be accepted, and a patient's desire not to be touched must be respected, but most of the time the chaplain's touch will be deeply appreciated. Quietly holding and patting a child's hand often communicates so much more than any words ever could. Touch is reassuring, touch is comforting, touch is affirming; it connotes protection, concern, and good will; touch is loving.

We have seen above how ministry to the sick was instituted by Christ and continued by his church. Jesus was present to the sick and suffering during his own earthly ministry, and he has called his followers to do likewise. More specifically, through the apostles, he has empowered them to act in his name, even with his authority. When Christian ministers work with the sick, they are obeying a command of Christ and continuing his work on earth.

Finally, we can say that the minister's presence to the sick is a presence that confers grace. The grace of God is, in a word, presence. And because this presence is God's, it is powerful, and never empty. God's powerful presence is first of all loving. Out of that love, God has created, so that we exist as his beloved creatures whom God has seen fit to call good and to provide for. And finally, in our weakness, be it physical or spiritual, God's presence is healing and forgiving. In this sense, God is not with us unless he is loving, creating, providing, healing, forgiving; and, indeed, he is always with us.

But God's presence to human beings does not take place in a vacuum, or in some unearthly realm of ideal forms. God meets us where we are, in the flesh, in the physical world. Indeed, God loved the world so much that his eternal Word was made flesh and lived among us. In Jesus of Nazareth, God's impulse to be present to us took a radical form: he became enfleshed, one like us in all things but sin. Jesus of Nazareth is God's grace, focused into one person, fully human.

As followers of Christ called forth by the church to serve, ministers who care for the sick continue the work of Christ. They continue to bring God's loving and healing presence to those in need. They are not God's grace, as Jesus was and is, but they mediate that grace, they deliver it. And thus they are not only signs of God's loving and healing presence to the sick, but they actually help to bring that presence about. Ministers who enter the hospital room are not alone: Christ enters with them. They are sacraments because they mediate his healing love, and that is the precise locus of their power.

The minister's intervention must not take the form of theological reflections or pious reassurances; still less should it become an attempt to deny the reality of the human suffering. Well meant, but unhelpful comments include:

—We all suffer, but it is God's way of testing us.

—Don't worry about your cancer. God is with you.

—Our pain is only an illusion, the devil's attempt to get us down. Keep on thinking positively, and praise God!

Rather, the chaplain's first step is to share in the patient's horizontal experience. Afterward, and *only* afterward, will he be able to help the patient to integrate the vertical experience. Chaplains must walk with patients through their experience of suffering. They may invite patients to allow this by encouraging them to tell their stories. As patients relate the story of suffering, chaplains may relate with empathy to them. They may accept a real share in the suffering, and become part of the patients' lives. Only after this sharing on the horizontal axis can chaplains effectively help patients in their vertical relationships with God.

As the chaplain begins to look at the patient's vertical relationship during the time of hospitalization, he must begin with an assessment of the patient's belief system and faith. To be avoided is the use of a list of questions which might make the patient feel as though he were taking an examination or filling out a questionnaire. But in conversation with the patient, the chaplain should be alert for the following information:

- What are the patient's basic religious beliefs? For example, is the patient a member of an identifiable religious group or church? It should be remembered that membership in a group does not necessarily determine a person's true beliefs.
- Does the patient belong to a specific religious community, congregation, or parish? If so, are there religious leaders there who are important to the patient?
- What is the patient's basic concept of God? Is God viewed as parent, punisher, savior, healer, or something else?

- How has the current hospitalization affected the patient's attitude toward God? Is the patient angry at God, afraid of God? Does the patient trust in God's good will and love?
- Does the patient feel close to God? Does the patient pray? Has this changed recently?
- If the patient faces death in the hospital, what is his concept of death and afterlife? How does he view his relationship with God in the face of death?
- Are there religious persons, rituals, or other religious activities which are important to the patient and which would be supportive during the hospitalization (e.g., receiving Holy Communion, praying with a minister, watching religious programs on television, reading the Bible, being visited by church leaders)?
- How does the patient conceive of the chaplain? Does the patient regard chaplains as ministers, as holy people, or perhaps as people who do not share his faith and are even unbelievers? What activities of the chaplain vis-à-vis the patient would be experienced as helpful and supportive?

At times patients speak freely and spontaneously about religious matters. At other times, the chaplain must seek such information. Particularly with children, obtaining information about religious beliefs and attitudes may take some time, often more than one visit. The chaplain may find that the best clues about a child's religious beliefs come during times of shared prayer, when the content of the child's prayer may be revealing.

Working with some knowledge about the patient's religious beliefs, the chaplain should bolster the faith which he finds on the part of the patient. When patients articulate belief in a God who is loving, merciful, and healing, chaplains can affirm and support this belief, using means which are compatible with the patients' religious traditions. For example, a prayer asking for healing, a story about Jesus healing a sick person, or sacraments such as Holy Communion or the anointing of the sick may be helpful to patients. The chaplain may talk about aspects of his own faith which agree with that of the patient's. The two may be able to share their spiritual journeys with one another, and to find in that sharing support, comfort, and inspiration.

There will be times when patients hold religious beliefs which are painful, which make the burden of illness even more onerous, and which militate against attempts to restore personal unity and integrity in a time of suffering. For example, a patient may believe that all illness is punishment from God; cancer becomes not only the occasion for physical suffering, but in addition causes severe feelings of guilt and unworthiness. Or a patient may be afraid of dying and going to hell; the struggle against death becomes even more desperate, the occasion for great fear and bitterness. In situations like these, chaplains may be of help by inviting the patients to consider alternative religious attitudes. Here again, they must avoid lecturing or moralizing, but may propose to patients alternative ways of thinking about life, death, and God, and invite them to accept more integrating religious beliefs.

From a Christian perspective, illness and suffering are not to be considered good in themselves. Indeed, we are called to be good stewards of our health and to avoid illness and injury wherever possible. Neither should suffering be considered as necessarily the result of sin (although it can be; consider the case of the person who, ignoring all warnings, smokes heavily for a period of decades, only to develop serious respiratory ailments). Suffering, rather, is part of the evil which is present in the world, and which at one time or another afflicts us all.

For Christians, times of suffering can become occasions for placing a new and radical trust in God. Even in the midst of suffering, one can know that God is near. People who are ill often experience God's presence in new and unique ways. It is precisely for this reason that the sick person assumes an important role in the faith community: sickness can become the opportunity to share new-found faith and inspiration with other believers, to the edification of all.

Secondly, Christians may experience personal suffering as an opportunity to participate in the paschal mystery of Christ. For the person who experiences illness merely as punishment or fate, there is no salvation in suffering. But there is another way, and it has its roots in our call to be members of Christ's body. Through membership in the church, and through Holy Communion, people become part of the body of Christ. Their identity with Christ is a radical one, which touches their inmost being. Identity with Christ occurs in many modes, and one of these is identity with the Christ who suffered for the world. Through the experience of suffering, Christians may participate in the paschal mystery of Christ, which has made the world whole and has united us with God the Father. The redemptive suffering of Christ gives new meaning to our own human suffering. Through our suffering, we are configured to Christ and we take part in the mystery of human redemption. Seen in this light, our suffering takes on a whole new dimension and character: it is not useless, it is not guilt-producing; still less does it become the occasion for despair. Rather, it may become the opportunity for a new and deeper union with Christ.

Chaplains may help those who suffer to integrate the reality of human finitude and suffering with the compassionate figure of Christ, the Servant of the whole world who redeemed it through his suffering. When this happens, illness is no longer the catastrophe which hurls the sufferer into an abyss of personal disintegration. Rather, it becomes the opportunity for a deeper integration of the realities of human existence, an existence marked by its glories and its sufferings. The reality of human finitude can be integrated by the sufferer in positive ways; this reality does not have to be a curse.

For Christians, faith is not in miracles of physical healing, but in the Redeemer who saves. We live in a world in which there are many evils. There is some relation among sin, sickness, and death. But causal lines should not be drawn. We should not assume that *because* we have sinned, illness will strike; nor should we view it as punishment for sin, either our own or that of others. In the same way, the prospect of death should not cause feelings of guilt. The presence of these evils simply reflects the reality of the human constitution. If there is a connection to be made among sin, sickness, and death, it is this: sin is the reason why sickness and death are the occasions of despair. It is our sin which prevents us from accepting our finitude. It is our sin which prevents us from understanding suffering and death as times of redemption, greater personal integrity, and greater unity with God.

Part of our Christian heritage includes stories of Jesus healing sick people. What are described in the gospels are miracles of physical healing. These healings do not occur in a vacuum: they are related to faith, and they are signs of the kingdom which is brought in the person of Jesus. The gospel writers repeatedly draw a relationship between physical healing and the faith of the sick person. At times, it is stated that faith has made the healing possible:

> Now there was a woman suffering from a haemorrhage for twelve years, whom no one had been able to cure. She came up behind him and touched the fringe of his cloak; and the haemorrhage stopped at that instant. Jesus said, 'Who touched me?' When they all denied that they had, Peter and his companions said, 'Master, it is the crowds round you, pushing.' But Jesus said, 'Somebody touched me. I felt that power had gone out from me.' Seeing herself discov-

ered, the woman came forward trembling, and falling at his feet explained in front of all the people why she had touched him and how she had been cured at that very moment. 'My daughter,' he said 'your faith has restored you to health; go in peace.' (Luke 8:43–48)

Indeed, faith is even presented as a *sine qua non* for healing:

Going from that district, [Jesus] went to his home town and his disciples accompanied him. With the coming of the sabbath he began teaching in the synagogue and most of them were astonished when they heard him. They said, 'Where did the man get all this? What is this wisdom that has been granted him, and these miracles that are worked through him? This is the carpenter, surely, the son of Mary, the brother of James and Joseph and Jude and Simon? His sisters, too, are they not here with us?' And they would not accept him. And Jesus said to them, 'A prophet is only despised in his own country, among his own relations and in his own house'; and he could work no miracle there, though he cured a few sick people by laying his hands on them. He was amazed at their lack of faith. He made a tour round the villages, teaching. (Mark 6:1–6)

Such stories can leave sick Christians believing that the progress of their illness is due to their own lack of faith. They remember such words of Jesus as, "Ask, and it will be given to you; search, and you will find; knock, and the door will be opened to you" (Matthew 7:7), or, "I tell you solemnly, if your faith were the size of a mustard seed you could say to this mountain, 'Move from here to there,' and it would move; nothing would be impossible for you." (Matthew 17:20) From this they conclude that because physical healing has not taken place, they must be lacking in faith or guilty of some sin that prevents their being cured. They have argued themselves into a corner, where they quickly fall prey to feelings of guilt, unworthiness, and despair.

Christians who fall into this trap do so because of two basic misunderstandings. First, they confuse the idea that *only those who have faith may be cured,* with *all who do have faith shall be cured.* Second, they misunderstand in a basic way the purpose of the healings of Jesus. Certainly we may infer that Jesus healed people because he felt compassion for them. But there is more than that. The healings functioned as signs that the kingdom of God was breaking into the world in the person of Jesus of Nazareth. They startled the witnesses into a new awareness of the presence of God's power there and then, and they functioned as promises of the kingdom which was "near at hand." The healings proclaim the coming kingdom; they should not be understood as proclaiming that all sickness should be healed.

In hospital ministry, there will be times when miraculous physical healing appears to have taken place. This can be easily integrated into our Christian faith, for such healings are clear signs of God's providential love and of God's power to change people's lives. These healings should be occasions for great rejoicing and should inspire believers to a deeper faith. And yet, they must be regarded as exceptional. We all must die, and when we do, it must not be understood to have occurred because of personal sin or lack of faith. Such an understanding sets up impossible expectations for the believer who is struggling to live a life in accordance with the call of Jesus and creates a situation where almost inevitably the one who suffers is driven to feelings of guilt and despair.

Conclusion

Those who suffer illness frequently find it to be not only a time of physical suffering, but also a time of personal disintegration, alienation from others, and a weakening or destruction of their religious faith. It is precisely as religious figures that chaplains can effectively address these problems and help patients to cope better with illness. By inviting patients to share their experience of suffering, ministers can join them briefly on their life journeys, becoming, in effect, a facet of patients' horizontal relationships. Then, ministers may help patients relate their horizontal relationships to their relationship with God. They can be of help in aiding patients to integrate the experience of suffering and the awareness of personal finitude into their understandings of themselves, their relationships with others, and their religious faith. It is possible for the experience of illness to become an opportunity both to trust God in new ways and to participate in the paschal mystery of Christ. When this happens, the patient's nourishing relationships are fostered and faith in God is bolstered.

RECOMMENDED READING

Bowman, L. *The Importance of Being Sick: A Christian Reflection.* Wilmington: 1976.

Kinast, Robert L. *When a Person Dies: Pastoral Theology in Death Experiences*. New York: Crossroad, 1984.

Knauber, Adolf. *Pastoral Theology of the Anointing of the Sick*. Collegeville: Liturgical Press, 1973.

Nouwen, Henri J.M. *The Wounded Healer*. Garden City: Doubleday, 1972.

Power, David N. "Let the Sick Man Call" in *The Heythrop Journal* 19 (1978) pp. 256–70.

Rutherford, Richard. *The Death of a Christian: The Rite of Funerals*. New York: Pueblo, 1980.

Index

Anointing of the sick, 36, 142, 183, 186

Baptism, 36, 37, 59, 142

Chart notes, 52–57, 65, 83
Child life workers, 48
Communion, 36, 37, 38–39, 186, 187
Compensation (as a defense), 107–109, 115, 116
Confidentiality, 32–33, 56
Confirmation, 36, 37
Confrontation, 105, 113, 115, 167
Consultation, 22, 23, 61, 62, 114, 116, 167
Controlling, 82, 100–102, 116
Corazzini, John G., 173–74
Crisis in development, 5

Death, 145–64; children's conceptions of, 145–51
Decathexis, 162
Defenses, 12, 82, 93, 95–116
Demonic possession, 61
Denial, 97–98, 116, 127, 151, 152, 162, 167, 169
Depression, 62, 170
Developmental stages, 1–24; au-tonomy versus doubt, 7–8, 15–16; generativity versus stagnation, 13–14; identity versus role confusion, 11–13, 21–23; industry versus inferiority, 10–11, 20–21; initiative versus guilt, 8–10, 16–20; integrity versus despair, 14; intimacy versus isolation, 13; trust versus mistrust, 6–7, 14–15
Displacement, 109, 116
Dolls, 80, 81, 103
Dramatic play, 18–19, 102–103, 109
Drawings, 63, 64–65
Dreaming, 170
Dying, stages of, 151–64; acceptance, 161–163; anger, 155–158; bargaining, 158–59; denial, 154–55; depression, 160–61

Ego, 3–5, 23, 96
Egocentric thinking, 17, 146
Erikson, Erik H., 1–14, 23, 141

Faith, 183, 185, 186, 188, 189, 190
Fantasies, 81, 180

Fatal illness, 145–64; children's awareness of, 146–51
Flight, 98–99, 114, 116
Friend, chaplain as, 26–28
Funeral, 26, 39–40

Games, 89–91, 93
God, 17, 18, 28, 35, 41, 117–29, 132, 134, 136–39, 141–44, 156, 157, 158, 159, 182–187, 189, 190
Grace, 184
Grief, delayed, 173; inhibited, 173; prolonged, 173
Grief therapy, 172, 174
Grieving process, 27, 162, 164–74
Guilt, 69, 70, 122, 157, 159

Head nurse, 48, 63, 64, 65, 66, 67
Holidays, religious, 70
Humor, 106–107

Identification, 82, 102–103, 190, 115, 116
Intellectualization, 82, 103–105, 114, 115, 116
Isolation, medical, 75, 176
Isolation, personal, 181

Jesus Christ, 26, 182–90

Kavanagh, Aidan, 140
Kübler-Ross, Elisabeth, 151–53, 159, 160

Labcoats, 73–74
Liaison, chaplain as, 31–34, 115
Link to institutional churches, chaplain as, 36–40

Magical thinking, 17, 37, 81, 126, 146

Meditation, 117, 129–39
Miraculous healing, 34–35, 188, 190
Moral dilemma, 41–43
Mourning, 40

Needle play, 103
Nouwen, Henri J. M., 129–32
Numbness, 167
Nurse, nurses, 35, 45, 50, 51–52, 70, 73, 75, 78, 84, 85, 92, 98, 101, 102, 109, 111, 125

Panic, 168
Paschal mystery, 187, 190
Phenomenology of illness, 176–82
Pining, 169–70
Play as a technique, 89–91, 103
Playladies, 48
Prayer, 25, 34, 35, 86, 117–44, 183, 186
Priest, 38, 58, 73, 142
Primary care nurse, 30, 48, 49
Projection, 110, 116
Punishment, 17–19

Rationalization, 105–106, 116
Reactive depression, 160
Referral, 173, 174
Regression, 99–100, 114, 115, 116
Repression, 111–112, 116
Ritual, 36, 40, 117, 140–44
Rounds, 67

Sacrament, 26, 36, 39, 58, 185
Scapegoat, 66
Sedatives, 168
Separation anxiety, 14–15, 179
Sitting on bed, 76–77

Stage thinking, limitations of, 163–64
Story telling, 18
Suicidal thoughts, 171
Support systems, 82–84, 93
Suppression, 112
Surrogate parent, chaplain as, 28–31
Symbolic religious figure, chaplain as, 34–36

Terminal illness—see Fatal illness

Time orientation, 86–88, 93
Titles, professional, 74
Touch, 184
Toys, medical, 80
Tranquilizers, 168
Transplant, 21–23, 58

Uncleanness, 180–82
Unit coordinator, 65, 66, 67, 68, 92

Waechter, Eugenia H., 147–51, 152